The Politics of Efficiency

Martin J. Schiesl

THE POLITICS OF EFFICIENCY

MUNICIPAL ADMINISTRATION AND

REFORM IN AMERICA

1800-1920

UNIVERSITY OF CALIFORNIA PRESS

Berkeley   *Los Angeles*   *London*

University of California Press
Berkeley and Los Angeles, California
University of California Press, Ltd.
London, England
Copyright © 1977 by
The Regents of the University of California
ISBN 0-520-03067-2
Library of Congress Catalog Card Number: 75-17285
Printed in the United States of America

1 2 3 4 5 6 7 8 9 0

To Sharon

Contents

Acknowledgments

I am especially indebted to Professor Clifton K. Yearley, who suggested that I study the history of urban governmental efficiency in the late nineteenth and early twentieth centuries. He has been a sympathetic and discerning critic since I began the research and wrote a dissertation on this topic. Professor John F. Naylor of the State University of New York at Buffalo likewise read the manuscript and offered valuable suggestions. Professor Daniel D. Sager of California State University at Los Angeles provided helpful insights along the way.

I want to thank the staffs of the Buffalo and Erie County Public Library, the Columbia University Library, the Franklin D. Roosevelt Library, the Lockwood Memorial Library of the State University of New York at Buffalo, the New York Public Library, the Henry E. Huntington Library, and the libraries of the Stevens Institute of Technology, Stanford University, California State University at Los Angeles, and the University of California at Los Angeles for assisting me in my research beyond the call of duty.

Finally, for her loving confidence, gentle prodding, and infinite understanding, I offer my most heartfelt gratitude to my wife, Sharon.

Introduction

American city governments in the mid-nineteenth century, judged by standards of cost and service, were democratic and congenial to the people of a community-oriented society. Municipal regulations for the protection of life and property, together with cooperation for public improvements through taxes and private contributions, had fostered a strong sense of community among urban populations. This self-sufficiency of local government began to decline, however, under the impact of industrialization and immigration. By the 1880s reform spokesmen of the middle classes in the large cities were railing at the sluggish response of public officials to new problems of social adjustment and control. They searched for means of political reform which would preserve older social values and provide better ways of maintaining order and discipline in municipal affairs.

The reform movement and the deterioration of city administration were partly the consequence of rapid urban growth in an environment where government had a limited role. In the years from 1850 to 1890 the development of new methods of municipal transportation made it possible for cities to spread beyond their earlier boundaries, thus permitting high- and middle-income groups to live some distance from where they worked. Established neighborhoods eroded, downtown areas became divided into sections for the performance of specific functions, and suburban communities emerged beyond the central city.[1] To officials living through this transformation, the whole process was bewildering. Governmental systems that had been adequate for earlier communities were strained beyond their capacity to provide urban dwellers with adequate services and efficient administration.[2] There were few ready programs to meet pressing problems and contrive some order out of the uncontrolled expansion. Thus, the need in each city for some coordinating institution became more apparent.

This need was met to some extent by the political parties. During the 1860s and 1870s existing "machines" within the parties had centralized bits of power scattered among the numerous precincts and wards of cities. By the eighties these organizations were attempting to tighten their grip on urban administration. In the process, it was the responsibility of the "boss" to keep the machine operating effectively and make sure that political power remained in its hands. While their methods of mobilizing the organization differed little from those used by mid-nineteenth-century predecessors, the bosses wielded a new authority derived mainly from the increasing size and scope of municipal government. In some instances they were elected or appointed officials, but more often they exercised outside control over public servants tied to the organization by bonds of loyalty and patronage. The survival of the machines depended upon the bosses' continuing ability to distribute public posts and social services to various groups in urban society.

It was this function of the boss as an "invisible" governor behind the constitutional structure of city government that aroused the wrath of political reformers in the late nineteenth century. Like other middle-class groups who interpreted democracy in terms of property rights and assumed that government should be in the hands of well-educated and "respectable" people, they were frightened by the growing social and political influence of immigrants and workers. They therefore denounced the party system which permitted these lower-class people to acquire such power. In this period both population increases and economic expansion owed much to the arrivals of successive waves of immigrants from European countries. Grateful for the boss's favors and services, these citizens usually voted the straight party ticket and accepted the corruption evident in the machine system as a distasteful, though natural, part of city politics. Feeding on the anxieties of the newer residential neighborhoods, reformers saw this entrenchment of bossism as the collapse of legitimate and responsible government. They demanded drastic modifications in established forms of political expression.

Such dissatisfaction led to an emphasis on governmental efficiency, which tended to be defined as the promotion of economic growth and development. In this context, it meant cheaper production and greater profit. "Although there are a number of ways in which economic growth may be served," political scientist Oliver P. Williams writes, "producer-oriented political activity often expresses itself negatively; that is, nothing should be done which might hinder the community's growth."[3] For the reformers, this policy meant more economy and regularity in the management of municipal finance. They believed that the growing expense of civic management was directly proportional to the degree of dishonesty and waste in machine administrations. By providing responsible officials with more efficient methods of control, they hoped to establish and maintain honest and economical government.

In promoting this program, the reformers were not mainly motivated by status anxieties as defined by George E. Mowry[4] and Richard Hofstadter.[5] True, there was a degree of concern among the older gentry over alleged threats to inherited values and prestige. But most of the younger patricians found in political reform an avenue to upper-class respectability and prominence. More importantly, the dedication of reformers, as Robert H. Wiebe has shown, stemmed from the "inherent dynamics" of their occupations rather than from class connections.[6] Differences existed, however. To older elements of the middle class in the eighties, efficiency was essentially a medium through which local government would be purified by the replacement of "bad" officials with "good" ones. Those who concerned themselves with the machinery of government felt that such a view was all too simple. For them, the character of two or three leading officials was of minor importance when set against the complexities of municipal management. The road to efficiency lay in the direction of new techniques of administrative control. By 1900 urban political reform was under the leadership of these progressive "structural" reformers. In addition to campaigning for honest government, the structuralists sought the total reorganization of city administration and eventual creation of a new bureaucratic system.[7]

This movement for governmental efficiency turned on three key concepts: nonpartisanship, the strong executive, and the separation of politics from administration. These themes suggested the need for more competent people in appointive office and the establishment of an area of policy making where there would be no political conflict. In this setting, government meant a nonpartisan or "businesslike" management of municipal affairs. The reformers believed that there existed an interest that pertained to the entire city and would always prevail over competing, private interest. Public policy, therefore, mainly involved technical problems and only those with formal training could manage the business of the city. These civil servants would be responsible to the office of the chief executive in which authority over administrative personnel would be centralized. Thus, this model left little room for debate over questions of party policy in municipal administration. To elements of the middle class and their reformist spokesmen proposing the model, public policy was not the result of thorough discussion by various interest groups. Rather, it was achieved by a totally different system of making public decisions.

In pressing for this sort of efficiency, political reformers introduced arrangements that facilitated the movement of efficiency-minded representatives of the middle and upper classes into centers of power in city government. Finding themselves in competition with the party bosses, these officials welcomed the proposals of "nonpolitical" elites because the implementation of such proposals ultimately meant an increase in their influence over subordinate employees and the centralization of authority within their respective departments and offices. To be sure, there would be some disagreement between them and reform elites outside government as to the purpose and scope of administrative efficiency. Furthermore, some party leaders integrated political reform principles into their programs and worked for competent civic management. But most administrators and structural progressives outside public office shared the aversion to the boss system and the conviction that nonpartisan experts were the best directors of municipal affairs. The end in view for them was the removal of as many areas of formal decision-making as possible from the currents of machine politics.

The pursuit of this goal raised serious questions about the efficacy of mass democracy in an urban-industrial society. Confronted with charges that their philosophy of government was undemocratic, the structuralists repeatedly retorted that efficiency meant a modernization of urban democracy rather than the destruction of popular government. In a time of far-reaching and rapid change, such a perspective, at least in theory, was directly related to the welfare and security of the urban masses. The political progressives were trying to replace the spasmodic welfare programs of the parties with a modern system of public services for all urban dwellers. Governmental efficiency, however, involved also a significant redistribution of political power in American cities. To the structural reformers it meant equal access to formal power for middle- and upper-class groups whom they felt were not being represented by machine government. But they overlooked the crucial issue of whether there could be equality in the exercise of power once these people were occupying key positions in municipal administration.

Chapter I

A NEW CONCEPTION OF POLITICS

Possibly because I was disorderly myself, I wanted
order. And I hated waste. That I had been taught to
esteem a cardinal sin, and American cities, I was told,
were wasteful because they were ruled by politicians,
whose only interest was in jobs.

Frederic C. Howe
The Confessions of a Reformer (1925)

To reform-minded members of the middle class who had a deep
and abiding respect for a political system that facilitated
economic advancement and usually protected the wealth and
position of its most "valuable" citizens, it appeared that popular
government had broken out of the stable framework in which
smaller communities had contained it. Now, to their eyes, mass
democracy ran reckless through the large cities and threatened
not only private property but also all the authority of local institutions. In 1878 the prominent patrician historian Francis
Parkman declared that the "diseases of the body politic" were
"gathered to a head in cities" and it was there that the need of at-
tacking them was "most urgent." For him, the source of the disease lay in a system of "indiscriminate suffrage" which elevated
an "ignorant proletariat" to positions of power.[1] In much the
same vein, Thomas Cooley, a supreme court judge in Michigan
and widely known authority on taxation, informed a Johns
Hopkins University audience in 1879 that elections did not indicate the "public judgment," and that those who wanted
responsible government were aware of the "danger that at some
time the better class of citizens" would "find themselves wholly
powerless."[2] Four years later John A. Kasson, a former congressman and later member of the Pendleton committee that
would devise civil service regulations for the federal government,

6

pleaded for the expulsion of the "ruinous principle ... which gives to a mere majority of irresponsible numbers the right of control over the municipality."[3]

In line with this resentment of mass democracy, spokesmen for the middle classes focused upon party government as the medium through which demolition of established institutions was being accomplished. A few conceded that this expansion of the political system was in part a consequence of the swift growth of cities since the Civil War, and that the unprecedented rise in public expenditures was a result of efforts to meet the needs of various groups in urban society. But most reformers shared the view that, as one authority on local politics put it, party government was the source of the "adulation of power and man-worship, the spirit of intrigue, suspicion and calumny ... and the insolence of place."[4] In 1875 the Tilden commission, formed in response to the Tweed Ring exposures in New York, spoke bluntly: "We place at the head of the list of evils under which our municipal administration labors, the fact that so large a number of important offices have come to be filled by men possessing little, if any, fitness for the important duties they are called upon to discharge."[5]

Other reformers agreed. In his *Critical Review of American Politics*, published in 1881, Charles Reemelin, former member of the Ohio legislature and then occupant of various commission posts, spoke of party governments which "eat out the substance of the people, leave them without good authorities, and conduct our public affairs to ruin and disgrace." Rather than being "free municipalities with vigorous administrative authorities," American cities, he argued, were subject to "mercenaries that rob society by levying taxes, taking blackmail, and heaping up public debts for posterity to pay."[6] Similarly, a Democratic party group in Buffalo, New York, heard a reformer declare in 1886 that the "injection of political virus" into municipal government had "poisoned the system."[7] Two years later James Bryce, an astute foreign observer of American politics, described the situation as follows:

As party machinery is in great cities most easily perverted, so the temptation to pervert it is there strongest, because the prizes are great. The offices are well paid, the patronage is large, the opportunities for jobs, commissions and contracts, pickings, and even stealings, are enormous.

Hence it is well worth the while of unscrupulous men to gain control of the machinery by which these prizes may be won.[8]

Such conditions had moved reformers to challenge the legitimacy of mass politics in municipal affairs. Simon Sterne, a reform lawyer and member of the Tilden commission, argued in 1877 that the "principle of universal manhood suffrage" only applied to "a very limited degree" in municipal administration because the city was "not a government, but a corporative administration of property interests in which property should have the leading voice."[9] In the same vein, Francis Parkman saw the notion of "inalienable rights" as an "outrage to justice . . . when it hands over great municipal corporations . . . to the keeping of greedy and irresponsible crowds."[10] E.L. Godkin, founder-editor of *The Nation,* one of the country's most influential organs of political criticism, pointed to unrestricted suffrage as the main source of misgovernment in major cities. "The reason why majority government succeeds so well . . . in small municipalities . . . and does not succeed in large cities," wrote Godkin in 1884, "is that all, or nearly all, voters are direct taxpayers, and thus feel local politics to be part of their private and personal affairs." He blamed the alleged indifference of nonpropertied classes to public expenditures for the rising costs of local government and recommended that they be prevented from voting on important civic measures.[11]

From this standpoint, political reform appeared to be a matter of running municipal government along the lines of the business corporation. One reformer described local administration in 1886 as "merely a business agency" which would be "most successful and efficient" when managed by people selected on the amount of "special adaptation to work."[12] In the same year George M. Browne, a noted Boston mugwump and educator, contended that city government should be a "business corporation" and added that its organization involved "no principle of suffrage or question of franchise."[13] Andrew D. White, former member of the New York Senate Committee on Cities and president of Cornell University, charged that cities were being governed under an "evil theory" that held that a city was a "political body." Instead the city, he felt, was a corporation, and "party political names and duties" were "utterly out of place there."[14]

These views suggested the need for a new strategy in municipal politics. Despite their distrust of railroad companies and concern over the expansion of industrial enterprises, elements of the middle class had come to see the corporation as a model for political reform. In their eyes it was an institution in which participants were seeking to maximize the attainment of goals with the most "efficient" use of available resources. Governmental reorganization, therefore, appeared to be a task of integrating business standards into the processes of administration.[15] A present-day political scientist, Fred W. Riggs, provides the following insight into such a program of reform: "In general . . . the administrative bureau is a counterpart of the formal economic market. Both are utilitarian, rational, maximizing institutions for making choices in a situation where means are scarce. . . . American market society seeks to apply in the administrative sphere the same basic values that apply in the market."[16] This viewpoint would often have relevance to the strategies adopted by reformers in pursuing governmental efficiency. Indeed, the ideology of political reform presumed this interrelationship of capitalist values and administrative methods.

Beyond the economic orientation of municipal reform, there was an attack on the fiscal consequences of party government. Simon Sterne charged that the parties had through the manipulation of suffrage organized a "communistic system" that led to the "confiscation of a large portion of wealth accumulated in our cities."[17] Another close observer of city politics complained about the "unremitting desire of the politicians to gather masses of votes" and the "placemen who furnish them to prey upon the city treasury."[18] In this indictment of party politics the issue in municipal finance was not simply the level of spending; rather, the reformers were more concerned about the groups from whom party leaders were extracting the revenues to sustain their organization. They saw local government as a logical extension of propertied interests in urban society. "Non-taxpayers, and payers of a poll-tax only," wrote John A. Kasson, "have no civil interest which demands equality of representative force in the municipality. . . . We here find a sound principle which would justify a limitation of municipal suffrage to property-owners and to the payers of taxes, who are affected by the liabilities to be created and the expenditures within the municipal jurisdiction."[19] Expressing the same thought but with a different emphasis, reformer Frank P. Crandon declared that a city was a "joint-stock affair in which the taxpayers are the stockholders" and that "to them substantially should the management of its business be committed."[20] Similarly, the prominent mugwump and biographer James Parton charged in 1887 that "men who have nothing impose the taxes" and held that the remedy for this situation was a government filled "only with city taxpayers" equipped to carry out the public business with "intelligence and economy."[21]

Complementing this corporate view of the city was the sharp distinction drawn by reformers between party and "patriotic" government. To them there had been an era when men were selected for office because they were dedicated statesmen rather than mere custodians of political organizations. In 1884 E.L. Godkin expected to see a time when politics would return to the "management of public affairs as distinguished from the working of the nominating machinery."[22] Five years later Moorfield Storey, a prominent Boston lawyer and member of the prestigious Massachusetts Reform Club, noted that it was an "evil day for a nation when its best men . . . cease to take an interest in its government." In his opinion, public questions and decisions required "cool and deliberate reflection" and only men of high intelligence and social standing could meet such standards.[23]

In a manner typical of most urban political reformers, Godkin and Storey glossed over the fact that politicians in the "good old days" often employed the ruse of disclaiming personal ambition when running for public office. By the late nineteenth century the pattern had not changed. Indeed, one could argue that the mugwumps made a fetish of the practice. Still, it was true that there was a noticeable absence of the "best men" from local government. "The people of means in all great cities," wrote the young Theodore Roosevelt in 1885, "have . . . shamefully neglected their personal duties and they have been contemptuously disregarded by the professional politicians in consequence."[24] Overlooking the fact that public employment in Europe had been traditionally in the hands of the upper classes and was not really confronted as yet with the pressures of mass democracy, James Bryce wrote that the "proportion of men of intellectual and social eminence" in office was smaller in America than in the "free countries of Europe." This situation, he felt, would not change until municipal posts were cleared of the "dirt heaps" put there by party professionals.[25]

Such conditions left the reform-minded members of the middle class in a painful situation. To what methods would they turn for political expression if they stayed out of established institutions? For many years most of them had recognized the need for parties in municipal government. Before a New York audience in 1881, George William Curtis, the distinguished editor of *Harper's Weekly*, declared that "organization is the lens that draws the fiery rays of conviction and enthusiasm to a focus and enables them to bury a way through all obstacles."[26] A few years later the "organization" was catering to the whims of the "dangerous classes" in urban society, responsible for the "plunder" of public treasuries, and destroying the last traces of "public spirit" in local government.[27]

Determined to regain influence in municipal politics, the reformers moved in two complementary directions. One was in large measure a rather conventional situation of the "outs" attempting to replace the "ins." But the strategy of political reform went much deeper than mere exchange of personnel. It also promised a basic reorganization of city administration. "The coming reform, to be effectual," wrote George Browne, "must be deep, radical, institutional; it must change the basis of municipal governments, and convert them into their proper form and function of business corporations."[28] Andrew D. White maintained that the parties should "have nothing to do with cities," and that those who brought "political considerations into municipal management [were] to be opposed."[29]

From this perspective, the task of reform was to purge local government of party politics and transform it into an institution run according to the social values of the middle classes. But there were some complications. Traditional channels of patrician leadership were breaking down under the impact of accelerating urbanization and rapid industrialization. During the seventies, urban society considered family position to be essential in appraising the standing of one's contemporaries. But the growing concentration of industrial wealth in large cities was blurring the lines of status between older and newer middle-class families.

Further, a more complex and specialized economy required higher levels of occupational professionalism. In this environment two cosmopolitan "elites" simultaneously interacted and competed for power and prestige: one comprised descendants of the older mercantile and landholding upper middle class; the other included younger professional men who were acquiring a new middle-class consciousness through loyalties drawn from their occupations. This interaction, as recently shown by one historian, was an "evolutionary, assimilative and conservative process" which encompassed attendance at select colleges, membership in metropolitan clubs, and the listing of one's family in the Social Register.[10] Pulling both groups into a reform coalition was a common aversion to urban democracy as expressed in party government. Governmental efficiency thus became a mutual objective and important area of cooperation among the older gentry and younger mugwumps.

Confident that there were alternatives to party government, the reformers focused on the notion of executive responsibility in municipal administration. To the Tilden commission the remedy for the "evils" of local government lay in the direction of separating "the exercise of executive or legislative discretionary power." Executive power would reside in the mayor, who would have powers of appointment and removal. The mayor, in turn, would hold the heads of departments "rigidly responsible for an efficient discharge of their duties." On the other hand, control of fiscal machinery would rest in an elective board of finance, since the commission felt that putting the control of the city treasury into the hands of one man, "with liberty to use it to keep himself in place, would be suicidal."[31] In the same vein, Thomas Cooley contended that there ought to be a "public sentiment" which required that an executive select officials "irrespective of party." But this influence, he noted, would not insure responsibility in urban government. Equally important was the need for more "unity in the executive," and this meant developing a system which made "officers and boards" directly responsible to the mayor. To William M. Ivins, city chamberlain of New York City and later counsel of the Fassett committee of the New York Senate which would investigate local governments in the early nineties, the "medley of functions and duties" had left the mayor's office a kind of "political junkshop." In this setting one would find "all kinds of administrative odds and ends in a condition of "decay or desuetude." One road out of this sad state of affairs lay in the concentration of responsibility and the "simplification of public issues." For Ivins this meant giving the mayor powers of removal as well as appointments.[32]

In conjunction with these proposals for a stronger executive, there was the more important effort to undermine and, it was hoped, drive out partisanship from municipal office. To the reformers it would not do simply to elect a good, strong mayor. This method, they felt, was only a temporary expedient which left the partisan system of municipal administration untouched. "There is no more just reason why the control of the public works of a great city should be lodged in the hands of a democrat or a republican," said the Tilden commission, "than there is why an adherent of one or the other of the great parties should be made the superintendent of a business corporation."[33] Another reformer likewise called for a "radical and perpetual divorce between partisan politics and the management of municipal affairs." John Fiske, professor of history at Washington University and popular lecturer on American government, similarly wrote in 1890 that electing a city official because he was a member of a party was "about as sensible as to elect him because he believes in homeopathy or has a taste for chrysanthemums."[34]

Ironically, it was the Republican party of New York which harbored one of the most ardent advocates of nonpartisanship in government. Elected in 1882 to the New York Assembly at the age of twenty-four, Theodore Roosevelt, a recent graduate of Harvard University, was upset by the "deplorable lack of interest in the political questions of the day among respectable, well-educated men—young men especially." Consequently, he sent invitations to nearly twenty New Yorkers to organize the City Reform Club.[35] At the first meeting, in October of that same year, they drew up a constitution which would set the tone for political reform in New York for the next twenty years:

We, citizens of New York, believing that national party lines should not divide us in the management of local political affairs and that it is of paramount interest to us all to whatever party we belong, to have local self government conducted by honest and capable men. . . . By aiding to the election of local office, without regard to party, of citizens of high personal character and known capacity, who will administer their offices on business principles as opposed to party methods.[36]

Confronted with the problem of organization, Roosevelt

decided that membership in the club should be restricted to those not holding public office. Being a member of the state legislature and having decided to run for another term, he withdrew from the club. The members resolved that "no member of any political organization shall be eligible who has bound himself to the unqualified support of candidate of said organization."[37] Composed of native-American business and professional men,[38] the club pointed its principles in the direction of giving political preponderance to what E.L. Godkin described as the "more intelligent class of voters" in the city. This perspective became clear when Roosevelt brought these themes to bear upon questions of reform in New York City. Focusing on the mayoralty contest of 1884, he charged that the public lived under the "rule of an aristocracy composed of the worst instead of the best element," and that this group was "kept in power by the plunder they [had] wrung . . . from the honest taxpayer." While conceding that no person was "more heartily a Republican" than himself, he felt that national issues had no place in the municipal arena. Rather, it was a "simple question of the servants of the city conducting the business of the city according to the rules of common honesty and common efficiency."[39]

Writing on the same theme in 1886, Roosevelt was more forceful in his dissatisfaction with political partisanship. After three years in the legislature, he was willing to admit that the complexities of government necessitated the existence of professional parties. But political realities were not license for the professional politicians to treat the city as some feudal fiefdom. To Roosevelt the parties were to be governed for the "benefit of the city," and not the city for the "benefit of parties." Like Thomas Cooley, he felt that it was not enough to have in office a man of "high purpose and character." More important was the hope that public officials should be "free from political entanglement with the beneficiaries of the present abuses."[40]

Behind these persuasive arguments lay a disturbing ambivalence in Roosevelt's position that mirrored the dilemma of municipal reformers. With one hand Roosevelt held to practical politics, but at the same time he stretched to grasp the armor of nonpartisanship. One explanation of this inconsistency lay in the realities of New York politics. Confronted with the powerful Tammany organization, Roosevelt was seeking to give his party an alternative set of proposals which he hoped would undermine public support for the machine, and, in the process, enhance the legitimacy and popularity of the Republican party in the city. But his strategy went beyond the nagging exigencies of practical politics. While resentful of party hacks, Roosevelt was confident that reform-minded politicians could maneuver the parties into supporting programs designed to eliminate machine corruption and promote efficiency in municipal government. If, on the other hand, responsible individuals found their parties deviating from "common rules of efficiency," Roosevelt was suggesting that they could repudiate the party's program and perhaps the organization itself.

Few respectable politicos, however, were prepared to jump on the bandwagon of nonpartisanship. In 1886 Kansas senator John Ingalls declared that "political parties, energetic, vigorous, and well-defined," were "indispensable to the success of free popular governments." Senator William Evarts of New York similarly informed his congressional colleagues in 1891 that "Party ties and party duties are the only mode in which free institutions are carried on in representative government."[41] More importantly, ambitious reformers inside the parties sought to reduce the power of the "bosses" and secure control of the decision-making centers in the organizations. Others adhered to an independent position and felt a moral responsibility to cleanse the political soul of the city.[42] As a result of these diverse motivations, a responsible and economical government seemed to be an acceptable compromise among reformers between the "politics" of party leaders and their own "business" view of local government. Even Andrew D. White, who, as we have seen, opted for no-party government, conceded that a "wise and statesmanlike view would dictate a compromise between the political idea and the corporate idea."[43]

The young Woodrow Wilson agreed. Graduating from the College of New Jersey in Princeton in 1879 and receiving a doctorate in history and political science from Johns Hopkins University in 1886, he quickly became a widely respected authority on political reforms on all levels of government. Driven by what Richard Hofstadter has described as a "deliberate and reasoned philosophy of politics,"[44] Wilson shared the groping of reformers for a new and coherent synthesis of old and new in city politics. "It is too late in this age of cities to dwell upon the importance of the subject of municipal organization," declared Wilson in 1888. "It looms so big in every quarter that there are not a few ... reforming people among us who regard it as the only subject worthy of present consideration. It almost seems as if city government, instead of national government, were to be the field of experiment and revolution for the future."[45] Seeking to change the forms and methods of civic management, Wilson seized upon efficiency as the key to political reform. In his *Congressional Government* published in 1885, he argued that "efficiency is the only just foundation for confidence in a public officer under republican institutions no less than under monarchs." It represented "power and the strict accountability for its use" in which there would be a "consciousness of being in an official station so conspicuous" that "no breach of trust" could go "undiscovered or unpunished."[46]

From this standpoint, political reform was essentially a question of structural controls. In what is generally considered a major departure in American political theory, Wilson outlined in 1887 a separation between legislative and administrative functions in government.[47] Convinced that the democratic system could not yet carry the "enormous burdens of administration" that were required in an industrial society, he proposed the creation of a bureaucratic realm in which a "competent body" of administrators would carry out a "detailed and systematic execution of public law."[48] At the same time, policy formation would remain in the hands of the legislative branch. Wilson wrote: "Administrative questions are not political questions. Although politics sets the tasks for administration, it should not be suffered to manipulate its offices."[49]

This formula left little room for the vicissitudes of party government. In contrast to the interaction of party and public roles in municipal affairs, Wilson recommended a system in which the cleavage was sharp, the roles assigned were limited, and, as a consequence, there would be a minimum of overlap between policy formation and policy execution. Such arrangements could result in an elitist order free from both party influence and the ballot box.

Moreover, while emphasizing the need for more administrative power in local affairs, the reformers were relegating the legislative process to the ashcan of municipal politics. In this period the state legislatures, dominated by rural elements, controlled politically important aspects of city government. They reserved the power to grant public utility franchises, appointed commissions to take control of police, health, and other patronage-laden municipal functions, and often removed various local powers from a city if it fell under control of a party not in a majority in the legislature. The reformers objected to such interference and demanded greater "home rule" for the cities.[50] More importantly, they were convinced that the council system was a demoralizing and disruptive force in municipal government. James Parton described the aldermen of New York City as "little but a gang of thieves" who, as a body, had "done scarcely anything but steal." Less rhetorically, Simon Patten, the prominent professor of political economy at the University of Pennsylvania, argued that legislative bodies reflected the "views and sentiments of the less progressive instead of the more progressive part of the public."[51] Boston's Gamaliel Bradford put the point more directly: "Government by legislature is, in the long run, impossible. It means corruption, inefficiency, quarreling, the dominance of private interest over public interest, in a word, anarchy."[52]

The reformers welcomed any scheme that promised a realistic alternative to this system. Brooklyn, New York, furnished one plan. Seeking to strip the city's aldermen of their power over mayoral appointments, Frederick Schroeder, former mayor of the city and member of the state senate, introduced a bill in 1881 to reorganize Brooklyn's government. After some debate over the proposal, the legislature approved the bill and it went into effect in January 1882. Under the new charter the comptroller and auditor would be popularly elected, but all other executive officers would be appointed solely by the mayor without confirmation by the board of aldermen. All departments would be administered by a single commissioner who would be responsible to the mayor and would serve a two-year term. Commissioners could be suspended at any time, but their removal from office required the confirmation of the state's supreme court. In addition the mayor, by refusing to sign necessary warrants and vouchers, could block expenditures of public funds of which he did not approve.[53]

Having brought one large city close to the reformist ideal of nonpartisanship, the charter was greeted with considerable enthusiasm. Shortly before it went into effect, the *New York Herald* wondered why New York City did not have a chief executive with "veto power and direct responsibility adequate to the management of the city affairs."[54] Gamaliel Bradford saw Brooklyn as one of the few cities with the "frightful audacity" to permit mayoral appointments without legislative confirmation.[55] "This Brooklyn system has great merits," wrote John Fiske. "It ensures unity of administration, it encourages promptness and economy, it locates and defines responsibility, and it is so simple that everybody can understand it. The people, having but few officers to elect, are more likely to know something about them."[56]

To Seth Low, a young Columbia University graduate and descendant of a wealthy mercantile family, the new charter meant the driving of political partisanship from municipal office. Elected to the mayoralty of Brooklyn as a compromise candidate of the local Republican organization in 1881, he sought to govern the city along the lines of businesslike efficiency. His appointments reflected merit rather than political persuasion. In addition, he held meetings in his office with various appointees. While hardly imaginative in administrative terms, the meetings were intended to convert the city's government from independent departments into an "organization working in complete harmony and singleness of aim." Low saw them as a means by which he could acquire an "insight into efficiency of the departments and also "bring the power and influence of his office to bear" on various officials in the government.[57]

Drawing upon his experience as mayor of Brooklyn from 1882 to 1885, Low emerged as a leading advocate of efficiency in municipal government. According to him, there had been a time in American municipal history when authority was diffused and as a result political control had slipped from the executive's hands into those of the legislature. So long as cities remained only villages or small towns, with few services to perform, this system worked reasonably well; but as towns underwent "phenomenal growth" and municipal functions became more complicated and expensive, it was almost impossible for the average resident to participate constructively in the affairs of his city. Meanwhile, local government, Low continued, evolved into a system where no officer "had the power to do much good" and a body of "bad men united for corrupt purposes" controlled the city in their own interest while avoiding responsibility for poor government.[58]

These views were not exactly an accurate description of the evolution of local government in the United States. Indeed, historians Carl Bridenbaugh and Richard C. Wade present considerable evidence indicating that cities in the eighteenth and early nineteenth centuries were developing a variety of governmental measures to meet the problems of economic growth and physical dislocation. In these years many cities broadened the powers of local officials through the adoption of home-rule charters, developed small administrative bureaucracies, appointed a number of boards to deal with social and economic conditions, and permitted their councils to establish committees which gave continuous attention to persistent problems.[59] On the other hand, the machine system and the lack of any central power to coordinate urban development produced much complexity and confusion in government. Low was pointing to the need for fundamental changes in the organization of municipal administration.

Equally disturbing to Low was the influence of national parties in municipal politics. In contrast to some of his fellow reformers, he felt that the trouble with the major parties was that they were organized around national and state issues and in relation to local affairs were only "seeking to control the local offices." Like Roosevelt, he argued that the party leaders sacrificed the needs of the city to their organizations. "In their eyes the administration of the city should strengthen the party," wrote Low in 1888, "whatever else it may fail to do. Few managing politicians are able to see that a man serves his party best who serves his city best." But the parties were only one dimension of the weakness in urban government. Since authority was divided, he noted, it was difficult to fix the blame for corruption on the parties, while everyone in office could claim that he was not responsible for any abuses or incompetence uncovered by reformers. In short, corruption and inefficiency lay in the combination of divided responsibility and political patronage.[60]

To remedy these weaknesses, Low proposed the reorganization of municipal administration. "For the general inefficiency of their city governments in the past," said Low in 1889, "Americans need not blame universal suffrage, nor the other special conditions which affect them. The fault has been organic in the structure of the city government."[61] Echoing the sen-

timents of most municipal reformers, he agreed that the city was
not so much a political entity as it was a corporation "organized
to attend its own business." In this context municipal questions
did not involve the "liberties of people" or affect the "inherent
rights of citizenship." Since the city was essentially a corporate
entity, the mayor was in actuality the president of a "great corporation" and should have enough power to carry out various
municipal functions. Like Wilson, Low felt that "power, with
responsibility to a constituency which can readily call it to account, is not dangerous. It is the first requisite of efficient administration." This would include the right to appoint officials
without consent of city councils. In turn these officials, Low continued, would serve at the "mayor's pleasure" and be liable to
dismissal in case of dishonesty or incompetence. Thus, the mayor
was responsible for departments under him and when malfeasance was revealed, he would have the authority to remove the
particular abuses.[62]

   In promoting these views Low, unlike most of the older gentry, did not hold immigrants and workers responsible for
municipal misgovernment and rejected the argument that their
presence was the main obstacle in the path of political reform.
Rather, governmental corruption and inefficiency were rooted in
the structural weaknesses of city management which could be
remedied without undermining popular democracy. "The req-
uisites for efficient administration and popular control go hand in
hand," said Low, "and as our city governments hitherto have
gone without the first, so they have been obliged to go without
the second."[63] But this argument rested on the specious assumption that the citizenry would easily accept the concentration of
power in administration. Indeed, Low overlooked the possibility
that governmental efficiency could result in a system which
proposed to let the people rule, while in reality they would hardly rule at all. Furthermore, there was too much emphasis on
proper organization and not enough attention to basic social and
economic needs of the masses, which were being met to a considerable extent by the welfare system of the parties.[64] Low and
many of his young colleagues had not as yet realized that administrative efficiency had to be integrated into a more positive
program of governmental assistance if the public were to be
served adequately.

Such considerations were overshadowed by the fears of political reformers that mass democracy under the direction of municipal machines might open the way to rule by a "tyrannical" majority. In fact, once an impartial role had been devised for administrators, the reformers were quite willing to place authority in the hands of fewer people drawn mostly from the middle classes. "Why should not the business men of the city," asked Moorfield Storey in 1891, "irrespective of their political ... opinions form a municipal party for the simple purpose of electing competent municipal officers and keeping them in office as long as they do their work well?"[65] Boston's Charles Francis Adams, Jr., argued in a similar vein before a gathering of municipal reformers in Quincy, Massachusetts: "By the 'best men' of a municipality ... is meant those who are recognized and looked to as best and most successful in the ordinary walks of life: and it is to a reasonable share of the services of these that ... every municipality is entitled as of right."[66]

Behind these appeals lay a recurrent tension in urban reform which most students of political mugwumpery have overlooked. Partly interested in structural changes in the party system to weaken the power of the bosses over local government, many of the younger mugwumps in the eighties sought mainly to limit the scope and greed of machines so that there would be more responsible administration. In practice, this viewpoint resulted in a movement for "regulated partisanship" through which the main aim of reform was not simply to defeat individual politicians but more to abolish the inducements that attracted partisan incompetents to municipal politics. Other genteel activists adopted a more "radical" position. Convinced that the large cities had lost sight of the principles of competent public service and were laboring under a marked decline in moral standards, they sought the ultimate destruction of political parties. This campaign enlisted support from most of the gentry and a number of younger reformers who found it difficult to shed some of the pristine morality of their older comrades.

Still, nonpartisanship was seen by all political reformers as the principle challenge to the "bosses" in the polling booths, while the reorganization of administration was expected to deprive them of the means of rewarding the party faithful. In the process there would be the gradual movement into public employment of what *The Nation* called "the highest expert ability" to replace political appointees in municipal office.[67] Few reformers spoke with greater influence on this aspect of political reform than Charles W. Eliot, president of Harvard University, and Albert Shaw, redoubtable editor of the *American Review of Reviews* and widely respected student of comparative local government. For Eliot, it would not do to restrict the suffrage when democratic government was shown to be "favorable to religious, social and industrial progress." But the "antiquated methods" of municipal administration and "insecure tenure" of departmental heads, he wrote in 1891, were responsible for the "greater part of municipal evils" which were bringing "discredit on free institutions." The solution to this problem lay in the creation of a realm in municipal government where there would be administrators with special skills and a special ethic. European municipalities, Eliot argued, provided evidence of both properties. He spoke of European cities in which departments and bureaus were managed by men of the "highest intelligence" who term of service depended on "good behavior and efficiency."[68] In the same vein, Albert Shaw, after investigating urban government in England, France, and Germany, reported that the reliance upon "administrative expertise would seem to rest so palpably at the bottom of all that is encouraging and inspiring in the recent progress of municipal life in Europe that a discussion from any more restricted point of view would be useless." He stressed the ability of German municipal officials to continually meet the social and economic needs of their communities with an extensive program of well-administered services.[69]

Granted that some European cities had developed better techniques of public administration, most American reformers overlooked the crucial fact that Europeans in the late nineteenth century were not dealing with the problem of "invisible" government in the hands of party organizations as well as with legal institutions of government. Furthermore, many cities, particularly in England and France, were also experiencing the dislocations of industrialization and a gradual breakdown in traditional methods and institutions of social control.[70] In any case, the response of the political reformers to European cities reveals more about them than about the European municipality: it illustrated the value of expertise in urban public life. "For the cure of the evils which now attend democratic government in cities," wrote Eliot, "it is of utmost consequence that the methods of municipal service ... be assimilated to the methods of the corporate services."[71]

Determined to translate this notion of public service into a new system of decision making, the political reformers retained their faith in democracy, but with considerable apprehension as to what lay ahead. Few subscribed to Francis Parkman's morbid view of popular democracy. With a firmer grasp on the realities of municipal politics, most reformers realized that any serious effort to discredit the principles of popular government in a culture long accustomed to the democratic process could invite intense, if not violent, resistance from the urban masses. But they were experiencing an intellectual and emotional disorientation which brought them to the edges of despair as they considered the possibility of urban political life degenerating into social barbarism. Writing to a close friend in 1884, Charles Eliot Norton, the distinguished scholar and editor of the *North American Review*, spoke to the issue: "I have as strong a conviction as you that 'democracy' will work; but it may work ignobly, ignorantly, brutally ... at least it does not look as if the better elements of social life, of human nature, were growing and flourishing in proportion to the baser."[72] E.L. Godkin similarly charged that the responsibility for misgovernment did not lie on the shoulders of "ignorant foreigners" but rested "very distinctly on the intelligent and well-to-do natives." In local politics the "enemies of the social order" and the politicians did not split on issues of public policy, while partisan interests generated conflict among the "respectable" classes over national issues and they remained divided in urban affairs. The remedy for this situation, Godkin wrote, lay in unity under the banner of efficient government, whereby the reformers could press for the administration of the city like a business corporation "in complete independence of party."[73]

Precisely how these goals would be achieved was a bothersome issue in most reform quarters. It was inconceivable that the powerful machines could be thrust from the municipal arena. Moreover, no party leader was prepared to see his organization slip into the hands of people who saw the city as a corporation in which elements of the middle classes were the board of directors. Recent studies of the party system in the late nineteenth century reveal a relentless effort of the Democratic and Republican organizations to become the majority party by developing a more issue-oriented program which could attract support from all social classes.[74] This situation makes the political thinking of the reformers seem quite unrealistic. But their corporate view of government implied a profound shift in theory and practice in municipal politics. Unquestionably, the older gentry sounded increasingly irrelevant in their calls for political purity and disinterested service to a society fragmented by ethnic and class conflicts. Unlike their colleagues, though, the younger middle-class reformers were not longing for an earlier time when men were more loyal to their communities, but were seeking to understand and resolve the social problems of urban-industrial life. They realized that the cities demanded continual attention and scrutiny. Yet both groups, by opting for no "politics" in city administration, were promoting a program that jeopardized the existence of the only institutions capable of responding to groups at all levels of the social structure. For reformers municipal administration was to be a frictionless realm in which the mayor was the indispensable leader. Behind him would stand a corps of intelligence officers ready to run local government according to the tenets of efficient management and cost accounting.[75]

This system represented a possible alternative to party government in American cities. True, there would be a recurrent ambivalence in political mugwumpery as to whether the "character" of officials or administrative organization was the best measure of order and discipline in the city. But the successes of reform would result less from the lessening of class tensions and more from the necessity of adjusting the machinery of government to the pace and requirements of a new industrial age. The reformers were pinpointing the roots of social discontents in the execution of public policy and defining the yardsticks of performance against which the bosses could be measured more accurately. Apart from being avenues to wealth and power for various individuals, the party machines were rooted in a set of arrangements that guaranteed access to social and economic influence for various groups in urban society. In becoming partisans of nonpartisanship, the efficiency-minded reformers were challenging the legitimacy of this political order and proposing a new system designed to mitigate the painful effects of rapid growth and if possible to serve the needs and wants of all urban dwellers.

Chapter II

PATRONAGE AND POWER

It may seem strange that a people so eminently practical as the Americans acquiesced in a system which perverts public office from its proper function of serving the public, destroys the prospect of that skill which comes with experience, and gives nobody the least security that he will gain a higher post, or even retain the one he holds, by displaying the highest efficiency.

James Bryce
The American Commonwealth (1888)

Determined to reorganize the lines of administrative authority in local government, political reformers seized upon civil service reform as the panacea for the ills in municipal politics. For them party patronage was the root and source of corruption and incompetence in urban public affairs. In 1877 one authority on city government charged that in the spoils system were "some of the worst vices of both democratic and despotic governments."[1] Seth Low branded spoils in 1882 as the "foe which has converted the machinery of government all over our land into a formidable engine for personal party ends." He added: "Not the good of the people ... but the wish of some irresponsible magnate controls the administration, where the incumbent owes his place to influence born of patronage."[2] In the same vein, Herbert Welsh, publisher of Philadelphia's reformist *City and State*, spoke of the "innumerable corrupting influences" and the "injury which the spoils system inflicts upon the government of our great cities."[3]

Municipal service was not so corrupt as these observations suggested. Indeed, a few prominent reformers, while resentful of the machine-created bureaucracies in local government, conceded that there was some responsibility in public life. "Speaking generally," wrote James Bryce, "the smaller cities are not ring-ridden. . . . The administration is fairly good; the taxpayers are not robbed."[4] Albert Stickney, a New York lawyer, pointed out that the "large majority" of politicos in office were trying to "give us as honest and efficient administration . . . as they can un-der existing circumstances."[5] Reviewing his experiences as a member of the New York legislature, Matthew P. Breen felt that it was "illogical and unfair" to draw sweeping conclusions about local government because of occasional "scandals" arising from the spoils system.[6] One authority on the reform of the federal civil service provides a perspective which equally applies to city administration: "[The] government could not have functioned at all if corruption and incompetence were as universal as reformers alleged. Nevertheless, professionalism was almost nonexistent in the civil service and politics permeated it to the core."[7]

Consistent with the view that government should be run on "business principles," it was this presence of "politics" in ap-pointive offices which brought municipal reformers together in a common effort to reorganize public employment. To be sure, many of them interpreted civil service reform mainly as a moral crusade. In this context, it meant rescuing the democratic process from political corruption and restoring "Christian character" to local government.[8]

But moral outrage does not explain the strategy of civil service reform. Convinced that city administration required talented as well as honest people, political reformers were seeking to replace spoils with new standards and more effective means of control. In the process they hoped to loosen the grip of party bosses over offices in local government. Speaking before the Social Science Association in 1882 on the government of Philadelphia, John C. Bullitt, a reform lawyer, contended that the source of most "evils" in the present administration was not to be found in per-sonal dishonesty, but rather in the "inherent defects" of the system. The direction of reform lay in a reorganization of municipal government that would insure the administration of the city upon "business principles."[9] While convinced that "by and large" the cities in America were "generally well governed," William M. Ivins warned in 1887 that the "chief danger" to local government lay in "the ever-growing army of public servants." This meant that the civil service "must be taken out of politics" and "all appointments determined solely by competency."[10] Woodrow Wilson likewise saw civil service reform as a "prelude to further administrative reform." By making public employment nonpartisan, it would establish the sanctity of municipal office as a "public trust" and thus make local administration more "businesslike."[11]

From this perspective, civil service reform became a question of governmental efficiency. To some extent, the movement can be seen as the effort of a "displaced group" of reformers seeking revenge on the politicians of this decade who thwarted their efforts to recapture seats of power in local government.[12] But, as a group, civil service reformers in urban society argued, as we have said, from a strong philosophical position as well. For them a system based on merit instead of political persuasion would presumably attract well-educated people to public service and result in a more efficient administration of municipal government.

Few men in the 1880s were more forceful than Dorman B. Eaton in advocating civil service reform. Recently, one historian has noted that the leading newspapers in this period so associated him with this aspect of municipal reform that it was often called the "Eatonian" system. After receiving a law degree from Harvard, Eaton, who came from an old New England family, joined a law firm in New York City in 1850 and soon became one of the city's most prominent lawyers. During the next two decades he was a member of various reform associations which sought better municipal services and continually denounced the political machines in New York. By 1880 he had come to the conclusion that the key to reform lay not simply in "throwing the rascals out," but more in reorganizing the administrative lines of public employment.[13]

Like most political reformers, Eaton saw the problem as essentially involving suffrage and the parallel increase of party influence through the application of spoils politics to public office. In considering the issue of suffrage, however, he felt that any restriction on voting would discredit reform by "going against the tide of progress in every liberal country." Moreover, it was not simply enough to elect honest officials. In most cases this strategy did not affect the partisanship in municipal government. Drawing a distinction between policy issues and municipal services, Eaton argued that the former was the responsibility of the parties, while the latter should be in the hands of nonpartisan administrators.[14]

From this standpoint, administrative reform became a question of tenure on merit rather than rotation. While conceding that party politics was "both useful and inevitable," Eaton hastened to point out that the bulk of governmental work was carried on by "administrative and ministerial" personnel and that the "political opinions of such subordinates" should not be the criteria for selection or retention of officials.[15] In local government, he complained, tenure of office was rooted in a "pernicious monopoly" of officeholding in the hands of party managers and "jobbers in politics." Eaton invited reform-minded officials to counter this system by introducing "rigid examinations" and insisting that higher offices be filled by "competitive promotions from lower positions." They would then be "suppressing a partisan intermeddling" and giving "respectability and efficiency" to municipal government.[16]

Equally important for Eaton was the belief that such a system would attract "able and self-reliant men" to municipal office. In the past, he felt, these people were reluctant to seek positions of public employment because party leaders usually passed over them and distributed offices to those who had done their bidding during campaigns.[17] Such conditions would be rare in a merit system. "Civil service rules, competitive examinations, or any other," Eaton told the Pendleton committee in 1882, "are not ends in themselves. . . . Their purpose is to bring into the public service those persons, and those alone, who are fit to serve the government in the particular department, the particular bureau, and the particular office to which the examinations relate."[18]

Eaton's expectations overlooked an important fact. By the late nineteenth century some of the "fittest" men in society already were holding positions in municipal government. Indeed, some city administrations included many respectable persons who, like their counterparts in the federal government, interpreted the merit system as a threat to their power and dismissed the new reform as the scheme of the "outs" irate at being denied a share of the patronage.[19] Yet, apparently ignorant of this response or perhaps choosing to see it as an uncomfortable aberration in municipal politics, the reformers pressed for the competitive system. Before the same congressional committee, Silas W. Burt, naval officer of the New York Custom House and later head of the New York Civil Service Commission, argued that competitive requirements were not new but rather were replacing a "competition of influence" with a system which gave the citizen an "equal chance to serve his country and the service the largest range of selection." Confronted with the charge that the system might spawn a privileged class of officials, he retorted that the present system encompassed a "favored class of politicians" who controlled patronage on all levels of government. In much the same vein, Everett P. Wheeler, a reform lawyer from New York, vigorously defended the merit system before the Pendleton committee. To him it reflected the "American idea" that there should not be any "favored classes." While it was futile to expect to see all men "equal in capacity," it was possible to make them "equal in civil rights and in legal opportunities." George William Curtis told the committee that the system was essentially democratic. In contrast to an "absolutely oligarchic" system, the public service under a merit system would require no "blood right or privilege." Curtis asserted: "A system which opens to free competition, upon perfectly equal terms, of all the persons who desire to enter the public service, seems to me as far removed from aristocracy as any purely popular, honorable, fair, equal system can be."[20]

Behind these arguments lay a conception of the civil service which students of mugwump reform have overlooked or simply dismissed as pure rhetoric. Granted that the mugwumps, like Wheeler and Curtis, were assuming that some men were more capable than others for public office, they were also suggesting that the spoils system was not so "democratic" as party professionals in the late nineteenth century were quick to assert. While the party leaders or "bosses" were ultimately responsible to the rank and file, they exercised considerable power over them because of their control of patronage. In return for their endorsement and support in an election, they usually extracted promises from the candidate that the "machine" would distribute the jobs and favors that he would control after election. Given this concession, the boss was able to use this stock of patronage to "bribe" these officials when necessary to follow his views in matters of public policy and appointments. True, there were factors, particularly the desire to maximize votes, which were dysfunctional to the control of patronage. But it was quite difficult for members of the party in public office to check the influence of the boss over policy and lines of administrative control. Thus, patronage became a means whereby the bosses could induce officials to surrender to them part or in some cases all of their legally vested powers.[21]

In this context, it was extremely difficult for municipal administrators to be more responsive to changing social and political conditions. True, spoils did function as a medium through which formal power was continually distributed among representatives of various groups in urban society. But the rapid and largely uncontrolled growth of cities was putting considerable strains upon local governments. During the eighties, for example, New York's population grew from 2.0 to about 3.5 million, Chicago's increased from a half million to more than a million, and Detroit, Cleveland, and Milwaukee doubled in size. The population increase owed much to arrivals of successive waves of immigrants from various European countries.[22] Such concentration of foreign-born people complicated the strained ability of local governments to provide all urban dwellers with adequate services. Everett P. Wheeler described the situation:

A city should be well lighted, and its streets clean and well paved. . . . We ought to be able to walk our streets at any time, night or day, with safety; and our property and our houses should be safe from fire and from violence. These are the objects of a municipal government. They have no possible connection with party politics . . . and yet . . . the headship of Departments has been sought, not by professional men whose experience and training qualify them to discharge its duties, but by active political leaders. That is not the fault of the leaders. The fault is in the system.[23]

Most municipal reformers agreed. They saw in party patronage the relentless pressure on city employees to supplement their official work with outside political activity. In lieu of spoils politics, there should be an "openness of procedure and publicity of method" by which the requirements of appointive offices would be determined by the "character and capacity of each successful competitor."[24] This criterion, however, reflected middle-class social values and could result in a system of public employment as partisan and static as government dominated by the spoilsmen. But civil service reform also implied a new functional expression of service in which performance was less a question of the traditional obsession with party loyalty and more a consideration of the public obligations of non-elective officials. The political reformers were seeking to replace the restrictive influence of spoils on administration with regulations designed to expand the capacity for more adjustment and responsiveness in municipal government.

Confident that this goal could be achieved by severing the lines of interest that extended into the government from the Tammany organization, reformers in New York had established an association in 1877 to promote the merit system. After nearly two years of dissension between reformers demanding the destruction of the spoils system and those wanting to curb the excesses of political patronage, the organization fell apart. Feeling that New York could be the place to launch a national organization, George William Curtis and others revived the agency and in 1880 it reemerged as the New York Civil Service Reform Association. This association, unlike the parent body, was under the control of businessmen and professionals who felt that civil service reform should be based on a careful investigation of municipal administration coupled with a realistic assessment of the reform's probable effectiveness.[25]

To the New York association, which included among its members such noted political reformers as Dorman B. Eaton, E.L. Godkin, Everett P. Wheeler, and Theodore Roosevelt, the objective of reform was to "establish a system of appointment, promotion and removal" based upon the principle that entrance into public office should be determined by "proved fitness." In seeking implementation of this principle, there would be a "demand" for the introduction of competitive examinations in relation to "subordinate executive offices." Equally important was the process of removal from office. According to the association, the only basis for dismissal was dishonesty, negligence, or inefficiency and not the usual charge of "refusal to render party service."[26] Similar convictions led other reformers to form civil service organizations. By early 1881 associations modeled on the one in New York had emerged in Boston, Cincinnati, Milwaukee, and Philadelphia and were being organized in Buffalo, New Orleans, St. Louis, and Baltimore. In the same year representatives of these associations met in Newport, Rhode Island, and organized the National Civil Service Reform League. Composed mainly of delegates from the New York association, the league's executive committee issued a statement which called for the enforcement of civil service reform on all levels of government.[27]

In conjunction with the campaign for the merit system in the federal government, New York reformers pushed equally hard for the system in municipal government. Elections in their home state provided the opportunity to secure public endorsement for their program. During the campaigns of 1882, the association sent out letters to various candidates for state and local office. In a letter to Allen Campbell, the Republican candidate for mayor of New York City, the association assumed a cautious approach: "In your judgment should either the political opinions or party affiliations be made a test for appointments to municipal offices, or, on the other hand, should superior capacity for performing duties of the office be made the criteria for the appointments and the employment under city government?" Campbell's response was encouraging: "Municipal affairs should ... be conducted without regard to party politics, and on business principles. ... It seems to me that a city officer would be faithless to his Trust if in the appointment ... he did not make selections on the ground of merit, efficiency and character."[28] Few reformers could have said it better. Indeed, this endorsement of civil service reform by a "politician" indicated that the key to political reform, as men like Low and Godkin continually pointed out, lay in an alliance with those executives committed to a lasting reorganization of public employment.

Like their counterparts in other cities, the New York reformers were not asking for something that was beyond a reasonable request. True, they expected to receive more than would ultimately be given them. But their suggestions left open the possibility that some politicians would come to see merit regulations more in terms of governmental efficiency than as a foolish effort to revolutionize political morality in urban life. "When we can lay before the public the evidence to prove that municipal government is inefficient and corrupt," proclaimed the *Civil Service Record* in 1883, "and at the same time offer a satisfactory plan for making it better, public opinion may be safely relied upon to do the rest."[29]

But in the perspective of political reform "the public" was usually confined to middle-class society. There was little hope that civil service reform would draw support from the urban masses. Since the mid-nineteenth century, spoils had facilitated the shift in authority from patricians to party professionals who were more representative of the multiple interests in growing cities. In the process, people from the lower orders who would have been barred from public employment because of educational, ethnic, or social disqualifications were introduced into the lower levels of city administration under the cover of party patronage. By the eighties spoils politics provided many workers and immigrants a measure of economic security and social status.[30] Insensitive to this situation and convinced that the lower classes were incapable of handling administrative responsibilities, the reformers could not allow for differing degrees of competence among appointive officials and pressed for standards in accordance with middle-class notions of efficiency.

True to its long tradition in behalf of political reform, New York became the first state to require civil service regulations in public employment. Drafted by the New York Civil Service Reform Association, a bill on civil service reform went to the Assembly in April 1883. Dorman Eaton and other members of the association urged its immediate enactment, and after considerable debate the bill became law the following month. In line with the Pendleton Act, which had introduced civil service regulations into the federal government, the New York law established an independent commission with the authority to supervise civil service rules and employ examiners to administer competitive examinations. Moreover, it removed classified employees from the direct control of party professionals by prohibiting campaign assessments and removals from office for political reasons. Finally, it provided mayors with authority to introduce civil service regulations into their governments.[31]

Given the fact that cities were not compelled to adopt civil service rules, reformers were somewhat disappointed by the law. But most felt that it was a good start in the right direction.

George William Curtis informed a gathering of the National League in 1884 that the New York law was a "prodigious achievement" in political reform.[32] Developments in New York City, Brooklyn, and Buffalo confirmed Curtis's optimism. Pressured by local reformers, Mayor Franklin Edson of New York, an anti-Tammany Democrat, in August 1884 issued rules for admission into the public service. These rules brought all departments under the state law except those officers who entered public employment under the authority of the Board of Education and those who had "personal custody of public moneys or public securities." In the same month Seth Low went beyond the provision of the law regarding cities and brought the police, fire, health, and law departments under civil service regulations. Later that year Mayor Jonathan Scoville of Buffalo introduced the competitive system for appointments into major departments.[33]

Similar developments were taking place in Massachusetts. In July 1883 the Massachusetts Reform Club, an organization of prominent Boston mugwumps, appointed a committee to formulate a program for civil service reform. After some months of consultation with the reform leaders in New York, the club drafted a bill which went to the legislature and became law in June 1884. Modeled on the New York law, it provided for a supervisory commission and a merit system and prohibited political assessments on those in the public service. In addition, the law brought the selection of laborers in Boston under civil service regulations.[34] For Henry Lambert, president of the Newton, Massachusetts, Civil Service Reform Association, this provision was most significant: "It is seen clearly that no reform which aimed to free the administration of cities from political influence, could be complete while the class of laborers, so numerous, so dependent, and, consequently so liable to be influenced by political schemes was left beyond its reach."[35]

These laws illustrated the tone of civil service reform. Recognizing the improbability of modernizing public employment with a few sweeps of the broom, the political reformers were advancing a program which would be the basis for more administrative reorganization in later years. At their 1884 convention, the National League welcomed the "admirable beginning of a reform which shall yet become effective in every city . . . and give to them economy instead of wastefulness, and efficiency instead of partisan and incompetent administration." Everett Wheeler, a member of the league's executive committee, informed a gathering of New York's Constitution Club that under the new rules offices were no longer to be "prizes" of political activity or the "rewards" of personal friendship. Provided that he was of "good moral character," any citizen was eligible for tests given by the board of examiners. These tests, he continued, would be "strictly practical" or else they would "fail of their true principle and purpose." In some instances the examinations would not be considered an absolute indicator of ability. According to Wheeler, there might be some "local condition" or "temporary excitement" which would hinder the candidate's performance. In such situations the examiners would rely on an eligible list from which they would fill vacancies in office. Moreover, departmental heads could select subordinates from this list. There would be another opportunity for those who for one reason or another were not selected for a particular position. Wheeler, however, did not expect to see the new system eliminate spoils entirely. With the powerful influence of parties in municipal politics, it was enough to expect that the new reform would curb the excesses of the spoilsmanship and thus promote greater "efficiency" in municipal government. Brooklyn's civil service commission reported in 1884 that the "humiliating sense of personal favor and demoralizing weight of political obligation" were being gradually replaced with "superior intelligence and efficiency." On the other hand, the commission saw a reluctance of some "intelligent men" to seek office because of a "lingering and traditional belief" that political considerations had "some sort of weight" with the examiners.[16]

Confronted with this "traditional belief," the political reformers remained firmly committed to nonpartisanship. Civil service reform was an integral stage in their effort to reorganize the lines of authority in municipal government. From a theoretical standpoint, it pointed the way to a government run by professional administrators. But the reformers' temperamental preference for gradualism was resulting in a modified view of the merit system: it could only apply to appointive offices. Furthermore, there was little desire for civil service positions. In the fear of being stifled by the requirements of nonpartisanship imposed on appointive employees, reformers chose to be sponsors of the new system rather than tools of it. "The Civil Service Reform movement was one from above downwards," recalled Theodore Roosevelt in his autobiography, "and the men who took the lead in it were not men who ... possessed a very profound sympathy with or understanding of the ways of thought and life of their average fellow-citizen. They were not men [who] desired to be letter-carriers, clerks, or policemen. . . . Having no temptation themselves in this direction, they were eagerly anxious to prevent other people getting such appointments as a reward for political services."[37]

Civil service reform thus involved mainly the question of tenure. George William Curtis pointed out that the notion of rotation was defended on the grounds that there was no "vested right" in office and that in public office there was a tendency toward mere routine, resulting in a kind of "dry rot of official vigor and efficiency." But both arguments, he felt, disappeared in a system where the "power of removal" was restricted and the "remedy for inefficiency" would be on the "responsible head of office." Albert Shaw similarly commented that public employees should have "intelligence enough" to understand that guarantees of long tenure were a "sine qua non" of city administration.[38] The National League spoke more bluntly. While "fully recognizing that the absolute power of removal must be vested in the appointing power," the league held that the "system of making removals upon secret charges ... without opportunity for explanation or denial" was "inquisitorial in its character, unjust in its results, and like the spoils system itself, repugnant to the spirit of American institutions."[39]

Apart from the rhetoric, these arguments suggested the thrust of urban political reform. In one sense it was an effort to insulate public office from the spoils system. More importantly, it involved an attempt to create an efficient bureaucracy in city government. For both objectives civil service became the laboratory in which reformers could translate their vision of nonpartisan civic management into political reality. But there still remained some disagreement as to what was their main purpose. For the older gentry who had been snubbed by the politicos and "embraced a devil theory respecting their enemies,"[40] merit rules promised the removal of the bosses' chief means of power and the eventual destruction of the party system. This goal was unrealistic to many of the younger patricians who recognized that the party organizations provided local governments with a measure of discipline and regularity. They hoped that better administrative structure would keep machine incompetents out of appointive offices and attract honest, educated men to government work. Both groups, however, agreed that a merit system represented a step in the right direction.

But there was little evidence to indicate a decline in spoils. In a report on conditions in New York City, the municipal supervisory board of commissioners noted that "no obstacle to the successful working" of civil service rules was so serious as the belief among appointing officers and candidates that competition was "not really intended to sift the candidates" and not designed to "give the office to the best men."[41] Political reformers, on the other hand, overlooked the possibility that some bosses could readily adjust to the new system. In Milwaukee, for example, the Trade Union Assembly in 1882 put forward Democratic candidates for major offices on a platform promising, among other things, the removal of the fire and police departments from spoils politics. Realizing that patronage would be useless if they were defeated by the Republican party, the Democrats endorsed the platform and won the election. Two years later, labor's civil service plank had been adopted by the Republicans and their mayoral candidate's endorsement of the merit system helped him defeat the Democratic candidate by a sizable majority.[42] The Milwaukee Civil Service Reform Association did not expect that local Republican leaders would pressure the Republican legislature into implementing this commitment to the merit system. To their surprise the city's Republican boss, Henry C. Payne, campaigned for the passage of a civil service law. In his perceptive analysis of Wisconsin mugwumpery, David P. Thelen writes that Payne's "order of priorities differed from that of earlier Wisconsin bosses who had placed their entire emphasis on patronage. Payne's sympathies were closer to those of the state's increasingly powerful quasi-public corporations.... His major goal was to win elections so that he could make policies sympathetic to this corporation, and he did not hesitate to sacrifice patronage employees to that end." This policy resulted in the passage of a civil service law in 1885 that brought Milwaukee's fire and police departments under the control of a nonpartisan civil service commission with authority to administer competitive examinations for appointments and promotions.[43]

But most party bosses seldom encountered campaigns by organized labor for economy and competence in local government. The merit system, as has been pointed out, constituted a formidable threat to the political and social status of urban workers. More importantly, civil service reform struck at the very foundations of political parties. Confronted with the number and frequency of elections, the expansion of party organization across the nation, and the efforts to enlarge party machinery in urban areas, the bosses could not afford to see their assessments of political appointees disappear in the gradual reduction of the supply of offices. "To be sure, had parties been financed voluntarily or through the legal assignment of tax moneys, spoils might have been localized and restricted earlier and more rapidly," C.K. Yearley writes. "However, conditions which might have allowed this did not exist in the United States nor could anyone reasonably foresee them. The threats to parties produced by civil service reformers and by public resistance to the adequate expansion of the fiscal basis of each level of government, therefore, struck at the stoutest underpinnings of the American party system."[44]

Given these conditions, it appears that in promoting the merit system the reformers were tilting at windmills. But under the new plan the bosses found it increasingly difficult to maintain effective control of appointive offices. Civil servants would no longer be required to protect their jobs by contributions to the machine. They could identify more with a city department and accept its standards of performance. In the process, the government could provide urban dwellers with better service. Thelen relates this Milwaukee experience, which was matched in other reformed cities: "After 1885 the nonpartisan Board of Fire and Police Commissioners, basing its appointments and promotions on competitive and practical examinations, filled an important institutional need as it transformed the police and fire departments into competent and modern bodies that could provide effective protection for the burgeoning metropolis."[45]

Few outside reformers, however, had a comprehensive conception of what efficiency implied for the development of municipal management. It was a mechanism through which they could stop the flow of public revenue to the parties and secure more economical government, but there was little talk of what efficient administration meant in terms of prescribing relationships among various components of city government. Still, it is incorrect to argue, as do two authorities on American public administration, that efficiency as a concept was seldom seen in the late nineteenth century as an important aspect of a reformed civil service system.[46] Reformers such as Eaton and Wheeler and also the National League saw civil service reform as the means to promote administrative efficiency. "Once admit that it is proper to turn out an efficient Republican clerk in order to replace him by an efficient Democratic clerk, or vice versa," wrote Theodore Roosevelt in 1890, "and the inevitable next step is to consider solely Republicanism or Democracy, and not efficiency, in making the appointment." Another reformer asserted that it was "useless to hope for economy and efficiency in city government until civil-service reform principles [were] applied to all its departments."[47]

This commitment to efficiency in public service was in keeping with the distrust of party government. Recognizing the fact that the structural roots of this system lay in political patronage, the reformers continued to focus on civil service reform as the key to an alternative system of government. Speaking before the Civil Service Reform Congress in 1893, Seth Low complained about the fact that many municipal officials paid less attention to questions of efficiency and more to the demands of the boss. He pointed out that the "immediate source" of the boss's lay in the control of nominations for public office. In order to maintain this position, the boss had developed extensive control over the distribution of offices. For Low this situation created a "powerful motive" for civil service reform. In a government under civil service rules, it would become virtually impossible for a party leader outside public office to "manipulate the patronage of the city to increase his own power." But this was not enough to insure a high level of efficiency in the conduct of municipal administration. Low envisioned the emergence of a class of administrative technicians in local government. To improve the quality of civil service, he invited reformers to insist upon "fitness" for appointment, work for permanency of tenure during efficient performance, and demand that promotion be based on the "ground of merit." In the process there would be a separation of politics from administration, and city government would be removed from the "larger game of party strife."[48]

To municipal reformers who assumed that there could be a divorce of politics from administration, such neutrality for public servants would be a logical consequence. But how could this system be responsive to a citizenry which expressed its wishes through the machinery of elections and political parties? In seeking to resolve this problem, they continually fell back on the argument that the merit system was more democratic than spoilsmanship. For Roosevelt, standards which permitted all men to enter public office provided they were "worthy to enter it" was "in its very essence democratic."[49] In the same vein, one student of municipal government felt that officials whose promotion depended upon "proficiency, character and patriotism" would be in closer "touch with people." Franklin MacVeagh, a reform lawyer from Chicago, asserted that the "most significant political change" since the Civil War was the "popular perception of the democratic essence of the merit system and the oligarchic essence of the spoils system." This perception provided "a basis for unlimited political reform."[50]

There is little reason to doubt the sincerity of these arguments. In his recent study of American public administration, political scientist Frederick C. Mosher argues that in these years "civil service reform accepted the principles of egalitarianism" which would guarantee "widespread access to public office among the citizenry." Furthermore, the stimulus to the movement did not derive from an attempt to shift control of public employment from "one class to another" as was the case in several European countries in the late nineteenth century.[51] But this viewpoint overlooks the recurrent ambiguity in civil service reform. In one breath reformers were lauding the merit system for its democratic features, while at the same time they assumed that most urban dwellers were incapable of governing themselves.

Confronted with this ambiguity, the historian might conclude that it was rooted in a halfhearted effort to delude the public on the real objectives of civil service reform. In the context of mugwumpery there is some validity in this interpretation. But as to those reformers who were coming into positions of influence at this time such a conclusion misses the complexity and intent of their plan. True, political activists such as Seth Low, Theodore Roosevelt, and Woodrow Wilson agreed with the older gentry that honest, efficient service required government by an elite class of men like themselves. In contrast, however, they also felt that merit regulations would promote administration more responsive to the needs of all urban residents. Civil service reform thus meant the modernization rather than the destruction of popular democracy. Furthermore, they did not really see the new reform as a device to exclude the lower classes from public employment. But could this be avoided under a new system based on merit rules? "Although the reformers disavowed any intention of cutting lower-class men out of government service," writes one recent historian, "the examination system would probably do just that. . . . A reformed civil service would not necessarily serve the people as a whole. Instead, it might become the pawn of the educated class, a small and nonrepresentative portion of the nation's population."[52]

Confident that the merit system was compatible with the democratic process, political reformers focused on the lack of efficiency in city administration. In 1892 Frank P. Prichard, a scholarly lawyer, charged that the "ordinary administrative machinery" of local government was becoming inadequate and in its place there had to be a "more scientific construction and a more systematic operation." Convinced that it was wrong to assume that all problems of municipal administration resulted from dishonest officials and equally erroneous to assume that any honest person of "ordinary business capacity" could manage a department or office, he urged reformers to deliver themselves from "occasional spasms of public morality" and develop reforms which would secure "uniform efficiency" in all departments. Similarly, Charles A. Wilby, a young lawyer and leader of the civil service movement in Cincinnati, told the National League: "Without a reformation in the methods of filling the . . . non-elective offices . . . no thorough and permanent advance can be made toward the goal of good city government."[53]

Most urban taxpayers agreed. For them, the worst abuse in party government was the rising tax burden that professional politicians had foisted onto the shoulders of municipal property

holders. Wrote one student of local government in 1892: "I can
... understand that the average city councilman is strongly in
favor of having . . . more taxpayers' money to spend no matter for
what. It all adds up to his influence, his opportunities of finding
or creating places for his friends. . . . But I do not understand why
a taxpaying citizen who sees around him municipal extravagance,
bad management, and fraud should take such a view."[54] Seeking
to alter this situation, reform spokesmen of the middle classes
focused upon insulating public finance from spoils politics. In
1892 a group of business and professional men in New York
organized the City Club to "promote . . . honesty and efficiency
in the administration of city affairs," and their counterparts in
Philadelphia established the Municipal League to "see that our
municipal government be conducted upon non-partisan and
strictly business principles."[55] The following year representatives
of business and professional organizations in Milwaukee formed
its Municipal League and sought to persuade the Wisconsin
legislature to pass a law which would extend civil service
regulations beyond the fire and police departments to include
every appointive post in the government. Without the lure of
spoils, the league reasoned, fewer jobs would be created by future
administrations to reward the party faithful and officials could
thus manage the affairs of the city in a more businesslike manner
that included a reduction in taxes.[56]

In pressing for passage and then for enforcement of civil service regulations, these civic groups encountered stiff resistance
from party professionals who charged that their only goal was to
secure tax relief for urban property owners. This criticism was
not very accurate. True, a number of upper-class members of
reform organizations were required to pay the city's largest tax
bills. But many of them were also profiting from underassess-
ment of property due to "collusion" with officials.[57] Moreover,
criticism of the merit system ignored the obvious appeal of a
reformed public service to the middle classes who wanted both
tax relief and competent government. In January 1894 a
"National Conference for Good City Government," which included delegates from 21 cities in 13 states, listened to veteran
reformers record such "evils" of local government as national
political partisanship, dominance of corporations in municipal
affairs, and the spoils system.[58] Most persuasive was the speech of

Carl Schurz on civil service reform. After a distinguished career in national politics, he had moved on to become a prominent political reformer in New York. By the time he appeared before the conference, he had become a leader in the movement for the merit system as president of the National League.[59]

Choosing to ignore the uncomfortable fact that he had reached national office in 1877 through the spoils system, Schurz charged that party bosses were attempting to entrench themselves against the "better element" by increasing their control of patronage. Given the fact that patronage encompassed mostly positions of public employment, the politicians would attempt to expand the number of offices "regardless of the public interest." In order to prevent this development, there should be an effort to bring all clerical employees and laborers under a system of competitive examinations. At the same time, promotion should be based on examinations together with an inquiry to determine the "practical efficiency and executive ability" of particular candidates. Under these conditions, Schurz continued, the public service would depend more on professional competence and less on political persuasion. These standards would apply to higher as well as subordinate positions in public employment. Schurz urged that mayors confine their selection of departmental heads to "professional men of good standing." With civil service regulations stripping the chiefs of departments of patronage, there would be less inducement to select for these positions men who would use their offices for political ends. To Schurz the "widest possible application" of civil service reform was not only a desirable but an "indispensable complement of all other reforms." In the end there would not only be improvement in "efficiency and economy," but the means for "feeding and organizing the mercenary element" would gradually disappear.[60]

Armed with these imperatives, political reformers in Milwaukee pushed hard for the extension of the merit system in the city government. In March 1894 newly elected members to the common council conveniently forgot their endorsement of the new reform and refused to pass the resolution needed to direct the state legislature to approve the extension of civil service regulations beyond the fire and police departments. Charging that the aldermen were "drunk with the wine of partisan politics and infatuated with the doubtful glories of machine tyranny," the

Milwaukee Municipal League sent delegations to the legislature to lobby for the civil service bill and sponsored a petition drive among all social classes in the city. In winning considerable support for its bill the league secured the assistance of Henry C. Payne, who, as was the case in 1885, saw civil service reform as a means of maintaining his control of Republican machine in the city and the state. Not prepared to run the risk of undermining popular support of the machine by sanctioning the excesses of spoils, and anxious to tighten his control over the council by having his corporations provide jobs for the party faithful, Payne signed one of the civil service petitions and instructed Senator William H. Austin, a close associate in the top echelons of the Republican machine in Milwaukee, to press for the passage of the league's bill. In July 1895 public employment in Milwaukee came under a civil service law which removed the power of appointment from the city council and placed it in the hands of a "City Service Commission" with authority to administer competitive examinations to applicants.[61]

Considerably impressed with the success of political reform in Milwaukee, the Chicago Civil Service Reform League pushed hard for the merit system in its city. The league sought to make it "unprofitable" for partisan incompetents to hold appointive office. Furthermore, civil service reform appeared to be a relatively inexpensive way of expanding municipal services to meet the needs of the city's growing population. Accordingly, the Reform League, aided by the Chicago Civic Federation, drafted a bill which went to the state legislature and became law in 1895. Chicago received an option concerning the act's full provisions. Influenced by the vigorous campaign of reformers for merit regulations, the voters approved the creation of the Chicago Civil Service Commission, which was empowered to classify offices under merit rules, select candidates for appointive posts by competitive examination, and remove civil service employees for incompetence. Similar reform campaigns led to the adoption of the merit system in other cities. By the middle nineties the electorates of Philadelphia, Toledo, New Orleans, and Seattle had approved charter amendments which established civil service regulations in their governments.[62]

This sequence of victories showed that political reform could stand the test of the polls. But formidable challenges to the enforcement of civil service regulations lay ahead. Speaking in 1896 before the National Municipal League, an organization of prominent middle- and upper-class reformers founded in 1895 by a committee from the Conference for Good City Government, George Burnham, Jr., president of the Philadelphia Municipal League, declared: "As might . . . be expected, the spoilsmen are taking alarm and the political organizations . . . are passing resolutions condemning the civil service reform movement."[63] Toledo's reform mayor, Samuel M. "Golden Rule" Jones, spoke more perceptively: "I am satisfied that the desire of the politicians to set aside the civil service is not entirely a venal one; to a great extent it is inspired by love and the real wish to do something to make places for . . . men who find it impossible to get a foothold upon the earth in our present competitive struggle."[64] Most party bosses would not have said it differently.

This struggle over civil service reform was rooted in what Samuel P. Hays has observed as a competition for power between two systems of public decision-making in urban society. One system, rooted in the relatively compact physical structure of the central city, involved extensive participation of disparate groups in local public affairs through the ward representation of partisan government. The other, growing out of the integrative economic and political activity of cosmopolitan business and professional groups committed to city-wide programs of efficient and economical management, meant a gradual centralization of government in which decisions would flow from fewer and narrower centers outward toward the rest of the body politic.[65] Those who supported the former would look with apprehension upon the loss of power that administrative centralization implied, and those who advanced the latter would continue to look with contempt upon the alleged inefficiency of government directed by political bosses.

Chapter III

STRENGTHENING THE EXECUTIVE

> In any other business, occupation, or enterprise but
> that of city government, a man who should ...
> declare that nothing would induce him ... to put a
> Democrat or a Republican in a place for which he
> was eminently fit, would be treated as a lunatic and
> confined in an insane retreat by sorrowing friends.
>
> "What a Mayor Should Be"
> *Nation* (October 11, 1894)

Underlying the movement for the merit system were the
recurrent fears of political reformers that the expansion of mass
democracy threatened the moral foundations of public affairs.
Because popular government was supported by an increasing
population of foreign-born workers, respectable people shrank
from assuming their share of civic responsibility and thereby
provided opportunities for unscrupulous politicians to hold the
balance of power in a city. Holding this opinion, the reformers
hoped to ease the way for more men of "good" character in the
ranks of the middle classes to gain greater access to municipal
office. At the same time, they also sought to inject what one
authority on urban politics describes as "capitalist realism" into
the administrative tissues of local government. In this context the
enemies appeared as wasteful expenditures, confusion of responsibility, and incompetent administration. To overcome these conditions, they called for continuous programs of governmental
efficiency.[1]

Both expressions of municipal reform were mutually reinforcing and there was seldom a clear demarcation between them.
In practice, political reformers leaned more heavily on the notion

of efficiency. For them it was not just a question of regulating the administrative output of local government. They wanted to be sure that the bosses would not be in a position to undermine their proposals. In attempting to translate efficiency into a set of procedural innovations, the reformers knew that if they were to be successful their organizations had to be as efficient as the machine and that designs to reorganize municipal government had to be complemented by practical schemes to gain and keep political power. Such conditions produced the search for controls which would centralize authority in the executive branch of local government.

In this setting municipal reform became a problem of alternative strategies. To some business-minded mayors of the late nineteenth century, reform meant the political arrangements which would keep them and their supporters in power. For example, Chicago elected as its mayor in 1879 Carter H. Harrison, a wealthy real-estate broker and former Democratic member of Congress who promised to "consult the interests of the party and the public in everything" and declared: "I shall not remove a man without putting a better man in his place, and I believe I can find good Democrats."[2] Ruled by Republican mayors from 1863 to 1878, residents of Chicago waited with intense curiosity the mayor's selections for various departments.[3] Harrison was careful to appoint only competent Democrats to important positions, and he left a number of experienced and capable Republican employees in office. One Republican newspaper, the *Chicago Daily News*, conceded that his partisan appointments took administrative ability into consideration rather than simple political allegiance.[4]

This policy was undermining the party's traditional conception of patronage. For Harrison, the indiscriminate use of spoils represented an "element of weakness and not of strength to a self-seeking man." In appointing a number of the "poorest" Democrats to various offices, the mayor reasoned that efficient government, as one student of his administrations pointed out, "would be worth more to him in the long run than a government of politicians for politicians."[5] Viewing the government from a more pragmatic perspective, the leaders of the Democratic organization objected to this interpretation of patronage. Harrison informed a gathering of New York reformers in 1881:

"[The"] bitterest of all partisan complaints made to me since I have held office has been that men I appointed have been no good for the party."[6]

More distressing to the politicos was the effort to infuse a large dose of businesslike efficiency into the area of public expenditures. Attempting to place the city on a firm financial basis, Harrison struck at the main artery of political assessments: the salaries of municipal officials. Toward the end of his first administration, he ordered the heads of departments to reduce the salaries of their employees. Matthew Benner, Democratic head of the fire department, felt that his department was already underpaid and refused to administer the salary reductions. Harrison then removed him from office. Many Democrats, fearing the possible consequences for political patronage, denounced the mayor for his action. Support for these dissidents came from reform Republicans who felt that Benner was a capable and responsible official. Mindful of the coming election, Harrison quickly appointed a qualified Democrat to the position.[7]

Benner's removal mirrored the thrust of fiscal efficiency in the period from 1881 to 1885. Receptive to complaints from middle-class taxpayers about "waste" and growing expenditures in the government, Harrison expanded his program of fiscal retrenchment. Behind this drive for economy in government was the effort to gain support from the influential taxpayers who voted Republican. One opposition newspaper noted in 1885 that the mayor's fiscal program was "not open to censure." By this time Harrison had lowered the salaries of various officials, introduced economies into various departments, and dismissed those employees "not absolutely necessary."[8]

Harrison's reelection in 1885 was partly the consequence of fiscal efficiency combined with the integration of merit into the city's public service. He had translated administrative reform into political assets. His drive for economy in public finance attracted the support of the middle classes of both parties. By retaining capable Republicans in office and appointing responsible Democrats, the mayor presented the electorate with administrations they could endorse, thus continuing him and his party in power during this period. Harrison asserted later: "I gave Chicago good government, and thereby won the support, not only of my own party, but of thousands of the best elements of the opposing party."⁹

Equally effective in his effort to provide efficient city government was Seth Low. As mayor of Brooklyn from 1882 to 1885 Low adopted a different strategy. Placed between the hammer of the reform Republicans and the anvil of the regular Democrats, he moved carefully in his appointments. "I made up my mind at the beginning," recalled Low, "that it would be impossible for me to cope with self-seeking politicians by underground methods. . . . I was frank and straightforward with all applicants for office, never encouraging any man to entertain a hope where I knew [that] there was no basis for it."¹⁰ In line with the reformist plea for "respectability" in public employment, all of the appointees were drawn from wealthy and socially prominent families in the area. While many of them were affiliated with the major parties, few practiced politics as a profession. On the other hand, none of the appointees had much technical expertise, but as one Brooklyn reformer later observed, "Inferior men were made to do superior work. There arose a sort of respect for the government of the city, first in the city itself, and then far beyond its borders."¹¹

Expecting to reap a harvest of patronage under Low's administration, Republicans were soon disappointed. Low appointed Ripley Ropes, a former alderman and supervisor, to the presidency of the board of city works. During his years in the Brooklyn legislature Ropes had vigorously opposed the spoils system. Before he was in office a month, he dismissed some thirty employees, among whom were several Republicans. The commissioners of the fire and police departments also removed political appointees. Shortly after entering office, the fire commissioner abolished political conclaves in engine houses and replaced the "pernicious habit of applying to persons outside the department . . . for privileges" with regulations requiring that "all applications for . . . any privilege whatever . . . be forwarded to . . . headquarters through the proper officers." Upon finding the police force a rich pasture for spoils politics, the police commissioner demanded that men in his department be appointed and promoted "for reasons which actuate business men in the management of their private affairs." By the time of his retire-

ment in 1884 there was little evidence of partisanship in the
department; further, his tenure brought a needed increase of
competent personnel in congested areas of the city.[12]

Complementing these reforms was the expansion of the merit
system. We have seen that the state legislature of New York had
passed a law which authorized mayors to prescribe civil service
regulations for their cities. By 1884 most appointments and
promotions in the fire, police, health, sanitation, and law
departments were based on competitive examinations and
meritorious service. In the process there was a notable increase in
administrative efficiency and improvement in the quality of
public services.[13] "The humiliating sense of personal favor and
the demoralizing weight of political obligations," declared the
city's civil service commission in December 1884, "have at least
begun to abate.[The] persons selected under the civil service examinations have been ... of an intelligence and efficiency
superior to the average prevailing since the service of the city
became as numerous and as varied as it now is."[14]

No less important to Mayor Low than the introduction of
nonpartisanship into city government was his commitment to
fiscal reform. During the previous machine administration, many
upper-class property holders in Brooklyn had become delinquent
in payment of city taxes and others had persuaded sympathetic
officials to under-assess their property. Low saw this arrearage
problem as the main impediment to placing the city's financial
affairs on a sound basis. With the passage in 1883 of the Evarts
bill, which authorized the city to sell at public auction the
property of those who were not paying their taxes, he vigorously
enforced the new law and at the same time pressed for the full
assessment of property. By 1884 arrearage had been reduced
from $14 million to $6 million and more than $11 million in
back taxes had been collected. In addition, property assessments
increased by $36 million and the tax rate went from $2.33 per
$100 of assessed valuation in 1881 to $2.59 in 1883. This
program, of course, encountered much protest from Brooklyn's
property holders. They expected reform government to be
relatively inexpensive. Low, in response, reduced the city debt by
$7 million and persuaded the board of estimate to increase ap-
propriations for services reaching mainly middle- and upper-class
sections of the city.[15]

Apart from these developments, Low did little else in the area of social reform. True, he had shifted the tax burden from small to large property owners. Moreover, municipal departments were in a better position to extend a wider range of services to the entire community. But questions such as regulation of public utilities, tenement house reforms, and assistance to workers were not seen by the mayor to be as important as the extension of the merit system and rationalization of public finance. Like Harrison, he naively assumed that the remedy for most urban problems lay in the abolition of partisan incompetence and in the reorganization of city administration along the lines of economy and efficiency. Low, however, had brought his city closer than any other American municipality to a realizing of the reformist ideal of responsible government. As news of his accomplishments spread to other cities, political reformers seized upon charter revision as the key to efficient management. Edward M. Shepard, a prominent lawyer from Brooklyn, wrote later that "municipal reformers the country over used to delight us by sending for its [charter] text as if one enactment . . . of the legislature of New York were full of political healing."[16]

Subjected to intense pressure from reformers, the city council of Boston appointed a commission in 1884 to investigate the government, consisting of the chairman of the board of aldermen, the president of the common council, and three citizens selected by the mayor.[17] After a thorough study of government in Boston and other cities, the commission submitted a report which emphasized the need to reorganize the lines of authority within the government. Pointing to evidence of incompetence and irresponsibility in particular departments, the commission proposed the immediate separation of legislative and executive powers so that the people could "fix the responsibility for inefficiency" in these departments. One source of inefficiency lay in the exercise of executive functions by the common council and board of aldermen. To remedy this problem the commission recommended that the mayor be given absolute powers of appointment and removal. Seeing the multiplicity of departments as the other source of inefficiency, the commission proposed a drastic reduction in the number of departments to eliminate "political influence."[18]

Objecting to the "arbitrary exercise of power" by the city's legislature, the commission recommended the establishment of an executive council composed of a limited number of elective officials. Opposed to any changes in the structure of the legislature, many members of the city council refused to accept the other proposals of the commission. To overcome this opposition, the reformers organized a bipartisan citizen's association which adopted the principal recommendations of the commission. Drafted by the association, an amended charter for Boston went to the state legislature in 1885 and became law the same year. The two branches of the city council kept their original form but without executive powers. The revised charter provided the mayor with powers to appoint and remove city officials, subject to confirmation by the board of aldermen. Moreover, the mayor could veto separate items in an ordinance involving fiscal appropriation.[19]

Emulating their counterparts in Boston, reformers in Philadelphia seized upon charter reform as the panacea for inefficiency in municipal government. Political conditions in the Quaker City provided a more dramatic context. Organized in 1880, the Committee of 100, a reform organization composed mainly of businessmen, advocated a public service based upon "character and ability." Seeking to undermine the infamous Gas Ring in Philadelphia, the committee supported an alliance between the "independents" of both parties for political hegemony in the city. The elections of 1881 and 1883 witnessed the entrance of independents into important positions in the government.[20] Dependent upon the sustained support of the reformers, these officials were sympathetic to proposals designed to weaken the Republican machine in the city. William C. Bullitt, a distinguished lawyer and congressman from Philadelphia, introduced a bill concerning reorganization of the city's government into the state legislature in 1883. Sensing a threat to their political influence in Philadelphia, the machine politicians in the Republican party persuaded their counterparts in the legislature to smother the bill. The following year witnessed a struggle between James McManes and Senator Matthew Quay for control of the Republican machine in Philadelphia. Capitalizing upon this schism in the machine's hierarchy, supporters of the Bullitt bill secured its enactment into law in June 1885.[21]

Stipulating that the mayor be held responsible for the "good order and efficient government of the city," the new charter provided that the mayor with the consent of the council could appoint persons to the directorships of the departments of public works, public safety and charities, and correction. By written orders giving his reasons, the mayor could remove from office the heads of these departments. Each head of a department would send an annual report to the mayor containing a record of all the official duties of the department, while the mayor could appoint a commission of three men at any time to examine the affairs of the department. Moreover, all appointments and promotions by the mayor and departmental heads would be made in accordance with rules providing for open and competitive examinations.[22] To Edward P. Allinson, a noted reform lawyer from Philadelphia, and Boies Penrose, also a lawyer and later a powerful figure in the Republican party as member of the Pennsylvania legislature and then the United States Senate, the new charter represented both a challenge and opportunity for political reformers in urban affairs:

It is not to be expected ... that the new charter presents a perfect system.... Much of its immediate success will depend on ... the character and good faith of the men who are first called upon to administer its provisions. It is believed, however, that neither individuals nor the machine can wholly prevent its good aim nor break down the barriers which are raised up against corruption and incompetence of the past—that, with the act of 1885, a point has been made in the interest of good government not alone for Philadelphia but for all the great cities in America.[23]

Inspired by political developments in eastern cities, reformers in Los Angeles sought to restructure the lines of authority in their government. They organized a "Board of Freeholders" and drafted a new charter in 1885 designed to weaken the position of political machines in the city. The board proposed to weaken the council by enlarging the mayor's powers of appointment and removal, place official departments under nonpartisan commissions, and eliminate wards by reducing the numbers of legislators and electing them at large. Arguing that a stronger executive and a smaller legislature might create an "omnipotent machine," the party bosses and councilmen vigorously opposed

the charter. The voters, less dissatisfied with public management
than the reformers, rejected the document. The Board of
Freeholders then drafted a second charter that "stressed efficiency, avoided nonpartisanship, endorsed the common council . . .
and otherwise so respected present realities that it secured electoral approval in 1888."[24]

The context of charter reform in cities like Boston,
Philadelphia and Los Angeles mirrored the emerging struggle
among three political groups in municipal affairs. First, interpreting governmental efficiency primarily in terms of personal
advancement, the anti-machine or independent politicians would
be slow to accept and then reluctant to continue reorganization
of municipal government. Second, imprisoned by their vision of
an administrative state, the "structural" reformers were seeking
to take the "politics" out of politics in local government. Third,
relying on complementary techniques of coercion and cooperation, the bosses were moving their organizations into a strategic
position between the reformers and the independents. The focal
point in all these different perspectives was the mayor's office.
Indeed, the pace, direction, and effectiveness of these political
forces depended greatly on the temperament, philosophy, and
organizational skill of the city's chief executive.

For example, elected to the mayoralty of New York in 1886,
Abram S. Hewitt, former ironmaster and Democratic congressman from 1878 to 1886, would attempt to fulfill the vision
of the reformers by demonstrating the merit of stern executive
direction.[25] In his eyes, the citizenry had permitted the
"ignorance" of the community to be organized for city government. With an "insatiable passion for efficiency" and recently
described as the "classic example of the businessman in politics,"
Hewitt sought to end the diffusion of administrative responsibility and make all appointive officials accountable for their actions.[26]
The New York charter, however, did not provide the mayor with
extensive powers. His authority over departmental chiefs was
limited. In most cases, they had a tenure outlasting the mayor's
term of office. Moreover, he could make removals only for
serious offenses and then only after public hearings. After being
appointed by the mayor, the heads of departments were responsible for subordinate appointments and policy which, in turn,
weakened the executive functions of the mayor.[27]

Faced with these limitations on his power, Hewitt moved cautiously in implementing administrative reform. When he took office, the health department was a victim of inefficiency and corruption. In the summer of 1886 Mayor William R. Grace had removed the head of the department; but, for political reasons, Governor David Hill failed to confirm the removal. Adopting a vigorous defense of Grace's action, Hewitt was able to persuade the governor to acquiesce in the removal. To the chagrin of the politicians, he appointed an experienced engineer to head the department. The new official notified medical employees: "Where private interests conflict with public service the alternatives presented are resignation or removal for neglect of duty."[28]

Confronted with charges of inefficiency and corruption in the bureau of elections, Hewitt attempted to remove the head of the bureau, John O'Brien, a Republican district leader. After the election of 1886, the Republican party had investigated O'Brien's activities in the department and denounced him for "improper practices." Aware that O'Brien's three-year term expired in August 1887, Hewitt issued an order bringing this office under civil service regulations. O'Brien argued that the elective officials were exempt from merit rules and refused to take the competitive examination. The day his term expired, the civil service board conducted an examination and the three top names were sent to the police commission. Ignoring the three candidates, the commission retained O'Brien in his position. "They have failed to obey the law," lamented Hewitt, "and there is no power which can compel them to obedience."[29]

Finding it difficult, if not impossible, to remove political hacks from office, the mayor exhibited a degree of independence in his appointments. Committed to principles of nonpartisanship, Hewitt steered a perilous course between the Tammany organization and the local Republican party. While endeavoring to consider the interests of the city without regard to political divisions, the mayor hastened to add that it would not be to the "disadvantage of a Democrat that he has been recommended by the organization whose nominee the mayor was in the late election." Having evidence of petty graft in the dock department, Hewitt let the Tammany commissioner go when his term expired in May 1887, and appointed Charles Marshall, a businessman and member of the County Democracy, in his place. The same month, he named three other County Democrats and one Independent Democrat to important commissionerships. Ignoring the pleas of the County Democracy, Hewitt renominated Richard Croker, an influential boss and later leader of the Tammany machine, for fire commissioner in place of Edward Smith, an outgoing County Democrat.[30]

Reviewing his appointments in 1887, *The Nation* observed that the mayor was trying with "great sagacity and pluck" to give the city local government conducted upon "sound principles." Attempting to reconcile administrative efficiency with practical politics, Hewitt confined his appointments mainly to capable members of the County Democracy. Though logical in terms of principle, this policy was deficient in political strategy. When Hewitt entered office, Tammany had expected a plentiful helping of jobs. Having been left out in the cold, the organization, knowing that the incoming mayor would have the appointment of several commissioners and heads of departments, abandoned Hewitt and nominated Sheriff Hugh Grant for mayor.[31] The Republican leadership, irate in the meantime over receiving little patronage, greeted the mayor's candidacy in 1888 with vigorous opposition. Of the twenty-five heads of the city departments, only three were Republicans. The party endorsed Joel Erhardt, a reform lawyer, for mayor. Along with Tammany's opposition, the Republicans insured the defeat of Hewitt in 1888. Grant won the election and thus would enjoy more power than any of his predecessors since the days of the Tweed Ring.[32] Measured by its political effectiveness rather than by its admirable goals, reform in New York had failed. In the face of entrenched opposition from Tammany and the growing resentment of reform-minded Republicans, Hewitt was unable to forge a political alliance which would have continued him and the regular Democrats in office.

Viewed in perspective, however, Hewitt's mayoralty showed the thrust of political reform in large cities in the late 1880s. As far south as New Orleans, reformers directed their energies toward reorganizing administrative authority in municipal government. Here in the Crescent City the administration of Joseph A. Shakspeare, a popular businessman, attacked political partisanship in the police and fire departments. In 1888 the state legislature passed an act which placed the police in New Orleans under a supervisory board, required all patrolmen to pass certain tests, and prohibited them from taking part in politics. Mayor Shakspeare, however, ignored the new board and proceeded to reorganize police authority himself. He selected as chief David C. Hennessey, one of the most capable and dedicated officers the city had ever known. Adherents of the board act appealed to the courts, and the city authorities were directed to abide by its terms. In their reorganization of the police department, the commissioners compelled all officers to undergo physical examinations and civil service tests.[33] "The fact that the mayor seriously believed himself a better guardian of police efficiency and morals than a board," writes one recent student of New Orleans politics and reform in the late nineteenth century, "did not impress many prominent businessmen. Boards of civil service were coming into vogue at both the national and state levels, and Shakspeare was struggling against a rising tide of public opinion in favor of such boards."[34]

Contrary to his objection to the police board, the mayor sought to take city firemen out of politics by establishing a paid department under the supervision of a board. Since 1885 there had been contractual agreements between the city and the Fireman's Charitable Association for volunteer service. By 1890 many partisan incompetents belonged to the 19 volunteer companies of the association and had support in politics by other firemen. With the government in the hands of reformers, the politicos in the volunteer companies failed to thwart Shakspeare's drive for a full-time, professional department. In 1891 the government purchased the companies. Shortly after the transfer, the city council passed an ordinance which established a board of fire commissioners with authority over the policies and personnel of the fire department. Moreover, members of the board would be appointed by the mayor.[35]

Bending its efforts toward divorcing local government from partisan politics, Shakspeare's administration reflected the conscious response to the movement for governmental efficiency in American cities. Addressing the city council of Minneapolis in 1893, P.B. Winston, the outgoing Democratic mayor, observed: "I had one promise to make—a strictly business administration in which the city should be regarded, not as a political body, but as a corporation whose affairs are to be managed on business principles and in a business way." For the new mayor of Minneapolis, William Eustis, a reform Republican, efficiency would be the central theme of his administration. In a letter to Albert Shaw, Eustis captured the pace and tone of municipal reform: "The administration starts off very quietly. Changes will come slowly and only as they seem necessary for efficiency and the better government of the city."[36] Reviewing the progress of administrative reform in large cities, the *Review of Reviews* singled out Detroit as one city in which one could observe competence in most municipal departments.[37]

Such notoriety merits a closer look. In the fall of 1889 two members of Detroit's city council were indicted for bribery. Charging that another Democratic administration meant further corruption and increasing extravagance in public expenditures, the Michigan Club, an organization of prominent business and professional men, searched for a suitable candidate to run for mayor on the Republican ticket. To the dismay of the club, a number of prospects declined the nomination, but finally Hazen S. Pingree, a wealthy shoe manufacturer and former president of the club, was pressed into accepting the nomination. Appearing on a carefully selected ticket of candidates from various ethnic groups, he directed his campaign at these groups and their votes gave him a sizable majority in the election.[38]

In line with the idea that the city should be treated as a business corporation, Pingree initially directed his reforms at the paving and sewage problems. Failing to equip themselves to handle modern road surfacing, and preferring to hire low-priced unskilled labor, a group of contractors had let the streets of the city fall into wretched condition. Although the contractors lacked the skills and equipment to do modern paving, their collusion with the Democratic machine was sufficient to overcome their technological deficiencies. Determined to undermine this collusion, Pingree persuaded the council in 1890 to adopt street paving specifications which included concrete foundations and hard-road surfaces for the city's major arteries. By 1893 the council had accepted the mayor's further proposals that road bids would be a routine part of the city's future paving policies. Uncovering similar conditions in the administration of the city's sewage system, Pingree requested an engineering investigation of the system which revealed that many recently completed mains and lines were decaying and crumbling. Although part of the blame lay with faulty craftsmanship, the mayor charged that the problem had its source in the collusion between Democratic councilmen and the city's cement supplier. While the Democratic commissioner of public works was trying to defend his purchase of inferior supplies, Pingree in 1892 appointed two business-minded Republican commissioners who quickly brought an end to previous policies. The new board of public works dropped the cement company from its list of suppliers, established rigid specifications for purchasing, and solicited bidders from outside the city.[39]

Complementing these reform developments was the infusion of economy into the government. In 1890 Pingree was presented with a request from municipal clerks for overtime pay to prepare the city's tax lists. With the clerks only working a six-hour day, the mayor saw no need for additional compensation and vetoed the proposal. He refused to approve a pay raise for election inspectors, on the grounds that their unsatisfactory work did not warrant an increase in salary. At the same time he fought against the continual proliferation of city jobs and employees. He rejected measures to increase the number of attendants on the Belle Isle Bridge and worked to reduce the number of city hall janitors who were political appointees. In addition, he pressured various officials into providing more efficient service and directed all employees to perform a full day's work.[40]

This crusade for efficiency was in line with the reform administrations of most large cities. From 1890 to 1892 Mayor Pingree had directed the force of his administration to driving out corruption and irresponsibility, regulating public expenditures, and bringing more rationality into Detroit's government. However, the mayor did not share the view of other political reformers that extensive social and economic reform could not be considered until partisanship had been eradicated and local government reorganized along business lines. He firmly believed that municipal misgovernment could be corrected by replacing the constant collusion between big business and city administration with a political order designed to guarantee equal economic opportunity and social justice for all groups in the city. In the years from 1893 to 1897 Pingree forced down the rates of gas, telephone, and streetcar companies, established a municipal light plant, and reformed the city's tax structure. He also constructed more schools, parks, and recreation areas and introduced a program of work relief for the poor and laboring classes.[41]

In moving toward social reform, the mayor alienated many of the upper-class elements and businessmen who had sponsored his nomination and supported his projects for governmental efficiency. Faced with this defection and forced to rely on the lower classes for power, Pingree worked to establish a political organization loyal to him and his policies. By an assiduous courting of the ethnic vote, the Democratic machine had captured a large share of the votes of groups such as the Polish- and German-Americans. Determined to pierce this "ethnic nerve" of the Democratic party, Pingree continually nominated men from these groups for various positions in the government. The machine saw a threat to its control of patronage and usually opposed the nominations. Enraged at this opposition to the mayor's candidates, the Poles and Germans marshaled considerable support for Pingree. Fearing the possible defection of their ethnic constituencies, some Democratic councilmen were induced to approve the appointments. In the process Pingree assimilated these Democrats into a bloc on the council which approved further nominations.[42] Meanwhile the mayor campaigned for those politicos who were committed to both efficiency and public welfare. Relying upon his patronage and political influence, Pingree secured the election of many Republicans to the city council. Here lay the political base of his administrations. These Republicans joined the anti-machine Democrats in a coalition which supported the drive for social justice and kept Pingree and his party in power.[43] By 1897, his last year as mayor, Pingree had emerged as a strong executive. He had advanced positive programs and centralized political power in the office of the mayor.

Paralleling these reform developments in Detroit was the program of Mayor Nathan Matthews of Boston. In the city elections of 1888 anti-Catholic agitation had contributed decisively to the defeat of Mayor Hugh O'Brien, an Irish Democrat. Searching for a respectable Protestant Democrat who could appeal to both Yankee reformers and party regulars, Patrick Maguire, head of the Irish machine in Boston, settled upon

Matthews, a prominent lawyer and organizer of the Young Men's Democratic Clubs. To the surprise of his patrician acquaintances, Matthews gladly accepted the nomination and, directing his campaign in 1890 at all segments of Boston society, carried 20 of the city's 25 wards, including upper-class Republican districts.[44]

Consistent with the preoccupation of charter framers in the eighties with administrative centralization, Matthews pressed for more executive control of public expenditures. He resisted continual efforts by the legislature and the board of aldermen to "pork barrel" with city appropriations and inflate the operating costs of the government. Inheriting a fiscal system which lacked complete and accurate data concerning the city's costs and revenues, the mayor introduced a system of accounting which systematized its financial records. Drawing upon information secured from this system, he infused standards of economy into particular departments. He also reduced the city's debt and tightened up on tax collections.[45]

Although Matthews saw economy as the key to efficient administration, he rejected the reformist notion that the city was mainly a physical plant to be managed like a corporation. In his eyes, the city's rapid growth necessitated an expansion and improvement of municipal services. "While the modern city is technically a corporation," wrote Matthews, "its constitution, machinery and objects are wholly different from those of private companies. It is not controlled by a limited number of stockholders casting their votes proportionate to their holdings, but by a great number of people, each with a single vote, most of whom have no direct property interest in it. . . . Its object is not to make a pecuniary profit for its members, but to provide for their safety, health and comfort, their education and pleasure . . . and generally do things that no business corporation was ever chartered to accomplish."[46] The mayor allocated $20 million for sewers and improvements connected with the problem of drainage. In addition, nearly $40 million was set aside for street widening and new street cleaning services, and some $20 million was spent for the construction of a metropolitan water works. Matthews also forced down the costs of utility rates and increased appropriations for police, education, parks, and public works departments.[47]

Toward the end of Matthews's mayoralty reformers in Boston
were conceding that higher offices were filled with nonpartisan
officials as capable and responsible as any in the past. More
gratifying to the Republican party was the mayor's decision to
retain competent Republicans in office. When Matthews took
office there were among the heads of departments twenty-seven
Republicans. Of these, eighteen were either reappointed or
transferred to some other department.[48] The reformers, however,
were critical of the appointments to lower offices. In this situation the mayor was adjusting reform to political reality. "While
resisting the special aggrandizing projects of aldermanic cliques,"
Geoffrey Blodgett writes, "Matthews recognized his obligations
to the Irish organization. Irish infiltration through the lower
realms of city offices . . . continued in the 1890's."[49]

Beneath this practice of bipartisanship lay the structural roots
of Matthew's administrations. By retaining Republicans in key
positions he was able to attract the support of the professional
politicians within the party; his appointment of Irish Democrats
to lower offices gained for him the support of the organization;
his program of fiscal and administrative efficiency appealed to the
reform elements in both parties. Together, these factors provided
the electoral base from which Matthews secured sizable majorities in the elections from 1891 to 1894. In effect, he used his
office to demonstrate the feasibility of socially responsive government under vigorous executive direction.

The administrations of Pingree and Matthews mirrored the
political philosophy and strategy of reform-minded mayors in the
late nineteenth century. Placed between the entrenched position
of the machine and the aspirations of self-conscious independents, they were attempting to harness efficiency to the
wagon of practical politics and provide more imaginative
leadership. Here lay the importance of patronage. It was the key
factor which shaped the power structure of reform administrations. Defined in terms of nonpartisanship, patronage
meant the entrance into municipal office of upper-middle-class
persons who feared the decentralized pluralism of machine
government and sought to centralize control within administrative agencies. Expressed in terms of practical politics, it
meant concessions to party professionals who accepted the social

heterogeneity of the city and provided various ethnic groups representation in local government. These conflicting notions of responsibility revealed the ambivalence of structural reform in urban public affairs.

New York City exemplified this situation. Investigating the government in 1894, the Lexow committee of the New York State Senate revealed political and police protection of commercialized vice in the administration of Tammany Mayor Hugh Grant. Against this background, reformers and politicians opposed to Tammany began to coalesce into a movement to defeat the Democratic machine in the election of 1894. In seeking to cloak their movement with respectability and thus mask the more important issue of political power in the city, representatives of Good Government Clubs, State Democracy, County Democracy, and the Republican county organization conveniently agreed in September of the same year that a "nonpartisan" slate was the "surest way" to defeat Tammany Hall. It followed that the mayoralty candidate should be one whose past record would insure an "absolutely nonpartisan administration" if elected. Meeting the same month, a group of prominent businessmen, including such men as Cornelius Vanderbilt, J.P. Morgan, and Gustav Schwab, called for an administration which would conduct the city's government "solely in the interests of efficiency and economy."[50]

Out of these conferences emerged an organization of independent business and professional men dubbed the Committee of Seventy. The committee held two large conferences which brought together representatives from the Republican party and delegates from various anti-Tammany organizations.[51] At the second conference, the committee presented a list of candidates, headed by William L. Strong for mayor. Addressing a letter of acceptance to the committee in October, Strong, a wealthy merchant and banker, declared that if elected he would administer the affairs of New York City in the "interests of good government" and "make all appointments without regard to party lines." Faced with this coalition of organizations committed to a "nonpartisan" government, Tammany selected for mayor first Nathan Straus, a dry goods merchant and Democrat of good reputation. Distrustful of his sponsors, Straus withdrew from the race, and Tammany substituted Hugh Grant. Identified with the Lexow exposures, Grant had little chance to win. William Strong conducted a vigorous campaign in which he denounced the Tammany organization for inefficiency and corruption and promised more competent and equitable administration of municipal services. He won the election by a wide margin.[52]

Beginning with his reorganization of the police department, the new mayor worked to give the city a government based on "business principles." Passed by the state legislature in 1895, the Power of Removal Act authorized the mayor to remove department heads from their positions within six months if he considered their work unsatisfactory. Inheriting a police department allegedly beset with incompetence and spoilsmanship,[53] Strong removed two Republicans and a Tammany man from the police board. In their place he appointed two reform Republicans (one of them Theodore Roosevelt) and a regular Democrat. Eager to insulate the department from Tammany politicians, the new board established a board of civil service commissioners to examine candidates for positions in the department. More distressing to the local politicians was the board's practice of soliciting candidates from different parts of the nation. Subjecting the applicants to mental and physical examinations, the board appointed about 2,000 men in the period from 1895 to 1897. Moreover, merit rather than political persuasion became the basis for promotion in the department.[54] Theodore Roosevelt reported in 1897: "For the first time the police force has been administered without regard to politics and with an honest and resolute purpose to enforce the laws equitably.... The old system of blackmail and corruption has been almost entirely broken up."[55]

Equally impressive was the reorganization of the street cleaning department. Under the dynamic leadership of George E. Waring, an internationally recognized sanitary engineer and drainage expert, the department became the model for efficiency in Strong's administration. Attempting to sever the lines of interest that extended into the department from Tammany, Waring dismissed a number of men for "inefficiency" and replaced them with men who possessed technical backgrounds. In the belief that a thorough system of discipline could insulate the department from politics, he issued directives specifying departmental requirements and the penalties to be imposed for being remiss in various duties. Waring also assured his employees that promotions depended only on merit. They in turn accepted new standards of performance and provided better service.[56]

Similar developments occurred in other departments. The mayor chose Stevenson Constable, a professional architect, as head of the building department. Utilizing techniques of control similar to those practiced by Waring, Constable subjected the plans of builders and contractors to thorough examination before issuing the necessary permits. Strong appointed E.L. Godkin and Everett P. Wheeler to the city's civil service commission. The agency extended civil service regulations to workers, particularly those employed in the department of public works.[57] With the support of the mayor, the Public Education Association, an organization of upper-class business and professional people devoted to school improvement, uncovered poor management of the schools and advocated replacement of the ward boards of education with a centralized system run by expert administrators. Opposed to this plan were some party leaders, various school officials, and representatives of middle-class ethnic groups. The association, aided by other city-wide reform groups, persuaded Mayor Strong to sign a state enabling bill that removed powers to hire and supervise teachers from local committees and transferred these responsibilities to a central board with a staff of superintendents.[58] Meanwhile, reporter-reformer Jacob A. Riis pressured the board of health into vigorously enforcing tenement laws and abolishing the worst conditions of slum housing. Riis also used his influence with the mayor to promote school improvements and more parks and playgrounds in working-class areas.[59]

Strong's administration was clearly an attempt to provide New Yorkers with enlightened government and adequate services. In the interest of maintaining balance and continuity in the operations of the government, the mayor ignored his campaign slogans and practiced not nonpartisanship but bipartisanship in his appointments and removals. This policy, however, antagonized some of the elements that had figured in the fusion victory. Many prominent members of Good Government Clubs felt that Strong had sacrificed the principles of reform to win the support of party regulars, and therefore declined to take office under him. They circulated memorandums which charged that fusion was essentially an effort to strengthen the Republican state machine.[60] Party officials in the Republican organization charged the mayor with breaking preelection pledges by his removal of some Republicans from office. In selecting some people for their personal qualifications and others in repayment for political services, Strong had considerably weakened his administration.[61] In 1894 dissatisfaction with Tammany had been the main cohesive force behind the fusionists. In the election of 1897 basic antagonism between the regular Democrats and Republicans reappeared. Moving into the breach, Tammany nominated Robert Van Wyck for mayor. Viewing Seth Low, the candidate of the new Citizens' Union, as another Strong, the Republicans nominated for mayor Benjamin Tracy, a former brigadier general and law partner of the son of Thomas Platt, the Republican state boss. The election scattered enough votes to provide Tammany with a minority victory. On the shoals of patronage, the fusion ship had gone down.[62]

While bringing New York closer to the reformist ideal of non-partisan government, Strong's administration also illustrated the growing politicalization of the efficiency movement. There was little opportunity and still less desire for nonpartisanship as defined by the theorists. Finding their organizations in a subordinate position vis-à-vis other parties, some mayors viewed administrative reorganization primarily as the means to undermine the appeal and structure of the majority party. Others, reflecting a greater degree of independence in their policies, worked to create a cohesive corporate government of middle-class personnel that could be run along business lines, free from spoils politics. Exemplified in Pingree's regime in Detroit, reform developed into an executive machine which promoted social reform for lower-income groups as well as middle-class notions of governmental efficiency. Finally, the movement was becoming a medium of rebellion for anti-machine independents of major parties. Lincoln Steffens, a reform journalist and later a widely respected observer of municipal government, noted in 1894: "I should say that ... intelligent men, once strong partisans, are neither Republican nor Democratic. They are holding to a high standard and ... are going to be the determining force in our politics."[63] These reform-minded politicians were giving a stamp of legitimacy to the efficiency movement and helping to break up traditional lines of power in urban society. The achievement of responsible civic management thus moved on from the problem of getting more upright men to take part in city administration to the problem of how these men would best be able to govern effectively. The most arduous tasks for political reformers lay ahead.

Chapter IV

THE POLITICS OF
NONPARTISANSHIP

> To administer the affairs of a village of 1,000 in-
> habitants is a simple matter, requiring only ordinary
> intelligence; the government of a city of 100,000 is
> much more complicated; while that of a city of
> 1,000,000 or of 5,000,000 demands expert
> knowledge, ability, and character of the very highest
> order. Josiah Strong
> *The Twentieth Century City* (1898)

In the campaign for more governmental efficiency, municipal
reformers continually encountered resistance from the political
machines. Fragmented administrative structures encouraged the
flow of power into the hands of men outside the machinery of
local government. Consequently, the bosses developed, as has
been pointed out, extralegal forms of authority. Henry Jones
Ford, managing editor of the *Pittsburgh Chronicle-Telegraph*, later
professor of politics at Princeton University, described the boss
in 1898 as "a center of control outside of the partitions of
authority which public prejudice and traditional opinion insist
upon in the formal constitution of city government."[1] But
the reforms of "business" administrations had undermined
this system to some extent. Gradually, governmental efficiency
evolved into a new political order in which executive functions
were transferred back to city hall.

Few mayors were more committed to the centralization of
power than Josiah Quincy of Boston. In the years from 1884 to
1895 Quincy had become the "pre-eminent manager" of the

Democratic party in Massachusetts while serving in the legislature. He directed gubernatorial campaigns and, as assistant secretary of state in 1893, distributed offices to various people in the party. Expecting similar rewards in local politics, the Irish Democracy nominated him for mayor of Boston in the 1895 election, which he won by a considerable margin.[2] To the surprise of the machine, Quincy sponsored a vigorous program of political reform. Shortly after taking office he established the Merchants' Municipal Committee, a seven-man advisory board representing the influential business organizations of the city. In keeping with the resentment of the middle classes toward machine government, the committee, which included men who were "deeply interested in public affairs" but not politicians in the "commonly accepted sense of the term," charged that legislatures left the voters at the "mercy of the machines," and proposed a reorganization of the city council. Like most municipal legislatures, Boston's council contained two branches, a board of aldermen elected at large, and a common council elected from various wards. In the belief that political offices should be more "conspicuous," the committee drafted a bill which provided for a single-chambered council of 37 members, 25 to be elected annually, one from each ward, and 12 at large for two-year terms, six to be elected each year. But the electorate, as expected by party leaders, rejected the proposal even though it had been passed by the state legislature in 1896.[3]

Considerably influenced by this effort to reorganize the city's legislature, Quincy moved quickly in the direction of centralized administration. Council appropriations for public improvements ate into the city budget and forced the mayor to appeal constantly to the state legislature for permission to borrow above the city debt limit. To remedy this situation, Quincy established a board of apportionment with power to formulate a "scientific" distribution of the city budget and created a municipal bureau of statistics which would provide an accurate and comprehensive fiscal record of the city's various departments.[4] More important, there was the effort to infuse nonpartisanship into municipal departments. Feeling that the complexities of administration required the services of a "public spirited and successful class of people," Quincy established nonsalaried commissions which supervised the public services of the city.[5] One reformer observed

that members of these bodies showed "marked ability" and oc-
cupied the "highest standing in the community."[6] In this respect
public employment in Boston, as was the situation in many other
cities, was attracting representatives of the new middle classes
who assumed that their values were synonymous with the public
interest and hence saw themselves as elites attempting to restore
local government to its "proper" functions.

Besides looking for quality appointees, Quincy sought to
strike an equitable balance between the patronage claims of the
various organizations in the city. Here the relationship with the
Irish machine was the most important. The mayor created an extralegal body, composed of Irish district leaders, to divide the
patronage and manage the electioneering of the local party.
Dubbed the Board of Strategy, this organization tied the important Democratic bosses to Quincy's administration. This shrewd
use of patronage, however, conflicted with his drive for efficient
government, particularly in the area of municipal finances. Fearful that the board of apportionment would gradually control
fiscal allotments, aldermen and council members turned against
the mayor. Moving into the breach, Martin Lomasney, a powerful boss who had remained outside the Board of Strategy,
engineered the repeal of Quincy's plan for a "scientific" budget
system. Enraged over this setback, Quincy promptly removed
many Democrats from the city's payrolls. A group of rebellious
Democrats and Republicans launched an investigation of the
removals and obtained a vote of censure against him. Against this
background, the Democrats divided into various factions.
Deprived of the support of the Irish organization, Quincy did not
seek renomination in 1900. Capitalizing upon the schism in the
machine's hierarchy, a Republican businessman defeated Patrick
Collins, the most respected figure in the Irish Democracy, in the
mayoralty contest.[7]

Displaying more attention than Quincy to his sources of
power, Mayor Carter H. Harrison, Jr., a prominent businessman
and inheritor of a powerful name in municipal politics, worked to
build an organization that would resist the pressures of the
machines of both major parties in Chicago.[8] Elected mayor in
1897, the young Harrison sought a compromise between the
utopian strain in the efficiency movement and the demands of
practical politics. The mayoralty, he wrote afterward, "com-

manded the respect even of the most hardened gangster; men no longer approached me as in the olden days."[9] To his dismay, however, Harrison inherited a police department which was described by the *Outlook* as being "in the throes of a disgraceful political struggle." In 1895 the Republican mayor had taken advantage of the ninety-day period before the civil service law went into effect to remove thousands of Democrats from office and replace them with members of his own party.[10] Seeking to regain their posts, 700 policemen organized a powerful political lobby, the Star League, and contributed substantially to Harrison's election in 1897. Shortly after assuming office, the mayor appointed the league president as chief of police and promised reinstatement of the policemen. Encountering some resistance from the city's civil service commission, he dismissed two commissioners and replaced them with a prominent lawyer and a former mayor of Chicago. The commission amended its rules and restored the Star Leaguers to their former positions.[11]

In line with his attitude toward reinstatement of the policemen, Harrison looked upon other aspirants for public office as people "in actual need." Behind this generosity was the more important attempt to build a political coalition which would keep him in office. Promising to take care of the "most deserving of my unfortunate adherents," Harrison packed the administration with personal favorites. In some instances men were put on as temporary appointees and carried for as long as two years by simply renewing their appointments every two months. Job descriptions and titles of positions were altered in order to avoid the lists of those who had passed civil service examinations. Two prominent officials, the city clerk and the city collector, refused to notify the civil service commission of vacancies in their departments and personally appointed office personnel.[12]

By 1900 Harrison had fulfilled his political commitments. Then, seeking relief from the "hungry horde of intemperate office seekers," he changed his position as to the merit system. Behind this shift was an attempt to gain the support of reformers in both parties. At the expiration of one member's term, in a notable concession to reform sentiment, Harrison appointed John W. Ela to the civil service commission. Ela was a prominent reform lawyer and active member of the city's civil service reform association. Under his leadership, methods of testing were revised so as to lessen the suspicion of partiality. The commission increased the use of promotion examinations and, as an aid in determining fitness for promotions, introduced a system of efficiency records. Most important, the mayor reduced the number of provisional appointments. By 1905, Harrison's last year in municipal office, examinations were being held for every office in the classified service. William Kent, a reform lawyer in Chicago, informed Lincoln Steffens: "We erratic people have fought that thing [the merit system] through and it is here to stay."[13]

Faced with pressure from both the machine and the reformers, Harrison had reached into the ranks of both groups to build a "benevolent city hall organization" committed to competent administration.[14] Bending governmental efficiency to considerations of power, other municipal executives adopted a similar strategy. In a letter to editor Albert Shaw in 1900 one Baltimore reformer noted that his city's Democratic mayor was attracting considerable attention from "the students and friends of good municipal government."[15] Functioning under a new charter which provided the chief executive with limited powers, Mayor Thomas G. Hayes, a lawyer and former state senator, picked capable men from his own party to head various departments.[16] Inheriting a school system in a "deplorable condition of affairs," the mayor named Joseph Packard, president of the Baltimore Reform League, to the presidency of the board of school commissioners and selected qualified individuals for the other positions on the board. At the same time, the board appointed a superintendent of schools who launched a comprehensive reform of the entire system during the next administration.[17]

Consistent with these developments in public education, Hayes selected men for various posts on the grounds of fitness and capacity. His choices for city engineer, building inspector, water engineer, and health commissioner were experts with at least five years' experience in the practice of their respective professions. One local newspaper declared that "good and faithful service has become the standard of requirement that the community habitually and automatically exacts of its public officials." Attempting to undermine the influence of machine politics in the city government, the mayor was setting new standards of honesty and performance for appointive employees.

More important, Hayes's administration witnessed the emergence of bureaucratic partisanship. The inner core of Baltimore's government was composed of self-conscious civil servants hostile to the influence of machine stalwarts over policy execution.[18]

Seeing governmental efficiency in the context of power politics, the administrations of Harrison and Hayes mirrored the boldness and sagacity of reform in American cities. Eager to seize control of the centers of municipal power, the efficiency-minded mayors knew that if they were to be effective in office the administrations had to be as strong as the machines. This necessitated the building of coalitions loyal to them. In effect, political reform became to these men more a problem of effective strategies and less a preoccupation with programmatic purity. Other reformers, however, insisted upon strict adherence to the orthodoxy of nonpartisanship. They intensified their demand for governmental efficiency which would replace party government with a corporate body managed by political independents and professional administrators. Seeing the influence of parties in municipal legislatures as a "travesty of free government in our cities," Franklin MacVeagh urged that all executive power and authority be taken away from city councils.[19] Similarly, Dr. Leo S. Rowe, professor of government at the University of Pennsylvania and president of the Academy of Political Science, told a gathering of the National Municipal League in 1897 that "city problems" were primarily of an administrative rather than of a political character. Influenced by the "petty dickerings" of local interests, the popular vote could not insure "proper standards" or enforce responsibility in city government.[20]

Behind this growing dissatisfaction with representative politics was the recurrent assumption that public dishonesty and inefficiency resulted primarily from the structure rather than the theory of popular government. The remedy lay in a new expression of urban republicanism. The reformers indicted the notion of "centrifugal" democracy which assumed that politics meant the dispersion of power and municipal functions among the electorate. In the conviction that local government was being endangered by too widespread a distribution of power, they advanced a philosophy of "centripetal" democracy which rested on the belief that municipalities would be well governed if they were administered by nonpolitical bureaucrats.[21] This elitism had little to do with traditional expressions of superiority. True, some of the older mugwumps still saw themselves as an hereditary aristocracy upholding the moral foundations of urban public life. But most political progressives attacked mass democracy under the banner of efficiency. "Democracy is a principle with us not a mere form of government," wrote Woodrow Wilson in 1901. "What we have blundered at is its ... successful combination with efficiency and purity in governmental action."[22] In the minds of urban progressives, the city suffered not from too little but from the wrong kind of democracy. They felt that administrative experts were best prepared to cope with the complex problems of an urban-industrial society.

Probably no reformer spoke with greater authority on this view of democracy than Professor Frank J. Goodnow. Upon receiving a law degree from Columbia in 1882, Goodnow went to work in the offices of Judge John F. Dillon and the following year accepted an offer to fill a vacancy in Columbia's School of Political Science. By 1900 he had become a prominent figure in the development of advanced study of public administration and published three influential works on city government. Like Woodrow Wilson in 1887, he sought a solution to the problem of how to establish and maintain local government that was at once representative and efficient. "The problems that Goodnow faced were that not only were urban conditions apparently detrimental to the flourishing of democracy," writes one recent historian, "but also that principles of representative government and effective administration seemed mutually exclusive. His solution to the interlocking problems of adapting democracy to urban conditions, creating efficient municipal government, and reconciling democracy and the expert, lay in his famous distinction between politics and administration."[23]

Goodnow, unlike many of his fellow reformers, felt that the political party, publicly controlled, could contribute to administrative responsibility because it was a necessary device for expressing and executing community demands. Henry Jones Ford saw this notion as a "strange non sequitur" which ignored the "organic structure" of party organization.[24] On the other hand, Goodnow contended that popular democracy had been maintained in America at the sacrifice of efficiency. He proposed more rigid division of policy formulation and execution. Policy matters were in the area of legislation and politics. While there must be popular control over the execution of legislative programs, politics should not enter into the general realm of administration.[25] Goodnow described government management as having three main divisions. In the first, there was the enforcement of statutes which required precise action or simply punishments for violations of the law. In the second was the work of bureaus responsible for collecting data for state records, census returns, municipal statistics, and the like, which these agencies made available to the citizenry. Closely tied to this work was the technical administration of the third division, in which there was the planning, construction, and maintenance of various public works. In Goodnow's analysis, all these comprised "fields of semi-scientific, *quasi*-judicial and *quasi*-business or commercial activity" which had "little if any influence on the expression of the true state will." He argued that these functions of administration required "a force of government agents absolutely free from the influence of politics."[26]

This bureaucratic freedom was especially important in the cities. In contrast to federal and state governments, Goodnow argued, local governments faced few questions of policy and required the consistent administration of policies which usually remained unchanged for relatively long periods. Civil servants should thus be subject to control in their general conduct but not in their particular actions. Public employment would in that case become more attractive to qualified personnel. Like Dorman Eaton and George William Curtis, Goodnow believed it was necessary, once the main requirement of independence from politics had been met, to give permanent tenure to the "best class of clerical and ministerial officers" and also to officials in higher posts such as city engineer and corporation counsel. This would result in an increase in efficiency and the replacement of amateur employees with expert career officials. Such administration, he felt, could give force to various programs and remain responsible to the municipal legislature which dealt with matters of public policy.[27]

In keeping with the antipolitical bias of his fellow structuralists, Goodnow overlooked the fact that professional administrators also saw bureaucratic efficiency as the means to increase their status and power. To be sure, those entering local government under "business mayors" were repulsed by the coarse favor-trading of party politics, and they usually identified with the city as a whole. But if politics involved mainly the reorganization of authority in municipal administration, then these officials were clearly functioning in a political context. In practice, it seemed irrelevant whether one appointive official was more influenced by party affiliation and another more devoted to the ideals of his profession and office. Both types operated in a partisan apparatus which sought greater control over both the formulation and execution of public policy.

Lending powerful support to this development was the model program of the National Municipal League. In an effort to discover the "essential principles that must underlie successful municipal government," the league formed a committee in 1897 for the purpose of constructing a model system of administrative organization for American cities. Composed of five lawyers, two professors of political science, a journalist, and a retired industrialist, the committee investigated local government in the United States and Europe. After two years of extensive research on the patterns of decision making in various cities, it submitted a final report which consisted of five proposed constitutional amendments, eleven essays on particular issues in urban reform, and a draft for a municipal corporations act. The league published the report in 1900.[28]

Consistent with the ethos of governmental efficiency, the National Municipal League had moved away from the "descriptive" tone of mugwump reform to the growing "prescriptive" style of urban structural progressivism.[29] Its draft corporations act provided for a strong mayor system with a unicameral legislature selected at large for six-year terms. The mayor would appoint all department heads and fill subordinate posts with persons who had passed civil service examinations. He could investigate the management of any department or the conduct of any administrative official. Provided that he set forth his reasons in writing, the mayor had the power to remove public officials from office.[30] On the other hand, the league committee, fearful that the chief executive could bend his powers to political interests, put into the act civil service regulations designed to keep politics out of municipal administration. Each city would have a civil service commission of three or more members, appointed by the mayor. Such commissions were to classify positions, provide competitive examinations, prepare eligibility lists, and make probationary appointments. Restrictions on the power of removal protected the tenure of employees. Neither the mayor or department heads could remove or transfer employees because of "religious or political beliefs." Finally, all appointments were to be without fixed terms and subject to the "pleasure of the mayor."[31]

Searching for an institutional compromise between popular government and efficient management, the National Municipal League settled upon an administrative system that would insure executive power and at the same time provide adequate checks on this power. Viewed in a theoretical perspective, such a scheme appeared quite sound; enmeshed in the web of municipal politics, it revealed a serious problem. In one sense, centralized administration meant the perpetuation of the spoils system if the mayor was subservient to a particular party. But weakening the city's chief executive in a period of machine rule could render a subsequent reform mayor impotent. Faced with this situation, the structuralists persisted in their efforts to create an elite realm of officials who would resist the machine and continue to rationalize the functions and organization of administrative offices.

Developments in New York richly illustrated this trend in urban political reform. The years from 1897 to 1901 witnessed widespread corruption and incompetence in the administration of Robert Van Wyck, a Tammany mayor. Against this background, the Citizens' Union, an organization composed of leading businessmen, professional people, and political independents, hoped to secure the election of a reform mayor in 1901. Convinced that the defeat in 1897 was due to an uncompromising policy of nonpartisanship, the leadership of the Citizens' Union now sought an alliance with other anti-Tammany groups. The president of the organization observed that these political groups were "more or less efficient" and could assist it in the "pursuit of its ends." Meanwhile, Republican state boss Thomas C. Platt, anxious to undermine the power of the Democratic machine in the city, declared in January 1901 that his party was prepared to accept a nonpartisan candidate for the mayoralty. The following month the Republican county committee endorsed the proposal for a fusion campaign. Meeting in September, representatives from anti-Tammany organizations, including the Greater New York Democracy, Brooklyn Democracy, Citizens' Union, and Republican county committee, recommended Seth Low for the mayoralty. These organizations then assembled in separate conventions and endorsed the mayoral nominee of the fusion conference.[32] In the face of this opposition, Tammany leader Richard Croker dumped Van Wyck and nominated Edward M. Shepard, a long-time critic of Tammany who had a good reputation in reform circles, for mayor. Shepard accepted the nomination in the belief that he could resist the bosses and reform the party from within. In confining themselves to personal attacks on Low, the machine found little with which they could campaign. Capitalizing upon the familiar theme of Tammany's corruption, the fusion forces won the election.[33]

Consistent with his policies as mayor of Brooklyn, Low chose professional men from the Yankee upper class to supervise various departments. To head the board of health he named E.J. Lederle, a distinguished chemist, as commissioner. Similarly, Gustav Lindenthal, an engineer, was selected as commissioner of bridges. To head the newly established tenement house department, Low ignored political considerations and named Robert W. DeForest of the Charity Organization Society as commissioner. In other appointments there was an attempt to establish closer ties with ethnic minorities and social workers in the city. Low appointed large numbers of Italians, Jews, and Negroes to various administrative offices. James B. Reynolds, head resident of the University Settlement House, was named as the mayor's private secretary to keep open communication with social workers seeking to redress the grievances of the impoverished East Side. Similarly, Low chose Homer Folks, a nationally known authority in the field of public welfare and secretary of the State Charities Aid Association, to head the department of public charities.[34]

This recruitment of qualified personnel was matched by the effort to bring the government in line with fiscal equity and responsibility. Low was not pleased with the fact that a large number of wealthy property owners had persuaded the assessors appointed in the preceding Tammany administration to undervalue their holdings. Consequently the city's tax receipts were coming mainly from small property holders. Pointing to these conditions as the source of the city's financial difficulties, Low introduced a plan by which property was assessed at its true market value. The result was an increase in the value of the city's real estate which expanded the government's borrowing capacity. In the meantime the tax rate dropped as a result of the fact that the large property owners were now paying a more equitable share of the real estate taxes. Together, these developments reduced the annual increase in the funded debt and enabled the mayor to cut the city budget by $1.5 million with the removal of Tammany hacks from office.[35] "Economy and efficiency are the watchwords in all departments," observed the *Review of Reviews*. "Petty abuses are being lopped off, hundreds of supernumeraries are being dropped from the pay-rolls, and high standards of justice and intelligence, with true business-like energy, are ruling throughout the city as almost never before."[36]

From the standpoint of structural reform, this program of economy meant the eventual demise of machine rule in New York. Low, however, shared the view of settlement workers that the progressives could never hope to permanently end Tammany's domination of the government until they could distribute the kinds of services which would attract the lower classes away from the machine. In a city deprived of adequate welfare agencies, the machine continued to provide the immigrant masses and poor with various favors and vital social services. While aware of these ties that bound the masses to Tammany Hall, the political reformers had not lost sight of the exploitative nature of the relationship. In 1902 Albert Shaw told the National Municipal League that the appeals of Tammany for votes had "often been to poor men's prejudices and to ignorant men's fears," while the motives of all its leaders had been "spoils, offices, or purely personal and private advantages of some kind."[37] Lincoln Steffens, usually a sympathetic critic of machines, put the point more accurately:

Tammany leaders are usually the natural leaders of the people ... and they are originally good-natured, kindly men. . . . But they sell out their own people. They do give them coal and help them in their private troubles, but, as they grow rich and powerful, the kindness goes out of

their charity and they not only collect ... cash for their "goodness";
they not only ruin fathers and sons and cause the troubles they relieve;
they sacrifice the children in the schools; let the Health Department
neglect the tenements, and worst of all, plant vice in the neighborhood
and in the homes of the poor.[38]

Seeking to replace these deplorable arrangements with a
system designed to provide the best possible services, Low sponsored a broad program of social reform to meet the needs of the
lower classes and at the same time answer the plea of various
middle-class civic groups for more municipal improvements. In
this context, Melvin Holli's contention that Low "had nothing to
offer the voters but sterile, mechanical changes," is a gross distor-
tion of political progressivism in general and his administration in
particular.[39] True, he was preoccupied with considerations of
efficiency and thus imposed middle-class social values upon the
entire community. But Low and his administrative officers also
realized that a city experiencing rapid growth demanded more
socially responsive government. By 1903 the mayor had set aside
$74,000,000 for the expansion and renovation of city parks and
buildings, allocated almost $19,000,000 for rapid transit and
bridge construction, and spent nearly $15,000,000 for new
schools.[40] At the same time, the health, charities, and tenement
houses departments secured more appropriations and provided the city's underprivileged with better services. Staffed with a
corps of professional medical personnel which had replaced Tammany employees, the health department instituted an immuniza-
tion program in the public schools and enlarged existing facilities
for detecting and controlling contagious diseases. In the process
there was a decline in the general death rate from 20.00 per
1,000 in 1901 to 18.75 in 1902. The charities department
abolished abuses in city hospitals, orphan asylums, and old-age
homes and modernized their various services. Meanwhile, the
tenement house department vigorously enforced the 1901 New
York State tenement law which set minimum sanitary and structural standards. By 1903 the department had filed 55,055 notices
of violations that resulted in extensive plumbing repairs, removal
of trash from public halls and stairways, cleaning of cellars, and
construction of fire escapes.[41]

Unfortunately, this synthesis of administrative efficiency with social welfare was not enough to prevent the Tammany organization from regaining control of the city's government in the election of 1903. Low failed to establish intimacy with the entire citizenry and make the right impression on the public mind. His insistence on enforcing the law against Sunday drinking alienated many workers and immigrants. The main problem, however, was the diffusion of power to nonpartisan administrators, anti-machine politicians, and civic groups. Low, like Mayors Abram Hewitt and William Strong, failed to construct an equitable balance between the patronage claims of the various organizations supporting his fusion alliance. Together, the Republican party and the Citizens' Union had cast the greatest percentage of the fusion votes. A fair distribution of political patronage would have given both organizations the bulk of mayoral appointments. Of the top 31 offices filled by Low, 15 went to Republicans, 11 to independent Democrats and the remaining 5 to members of the Citizens' Union. Enraged over the dearth of patronage assigned to it, several members of the union greeted the mayor's policies with vigorous resentment. Adding their voice to the chorus of protest were Republicans who repeatedly demanded that the mayor give their party its fair share of patronage. By 1903 this opposition had developed into an anti-Low coalition. But, unable to agree on a Democratic nominee for mayor, the fusionists reluctantly renominated Low. In their effort to exploit this dissension within fusion, the Tammany organization nominated George B. McClellan, Jr., a former congressman and son of the Civil War general. Emphasizing the inability of Low's administration to resolve a number of social problems, the McClellan supporters achieved a decisive victory over the fusion forces in 1903.[42]

Other reform mayors emulated the strategy of men like Carter H. Harrison, Jr. and built stable organizations for themselves. In Cleveland, for example, Tom L. Johnson, a streetcar magnate and former Democratic congressman, was elected mayor in 1901 with the avowed goal of divorcing the city's government from the influence of irresponsible business interests and promoting extensive social reform.[43] Johnson saw efficient city management as the key to both political power and humanitarian administration. "In selecting my cabinet and in making other appointments," he recalled, "I looked about for men who would be efficient and when I found one in whom efficiency and a belief in the fundamental principles of democracy were combined I knew that here was the highest type of public officer possible to get."[44] Providing the arrangements for implementing these principles was the city's "federal plan" charter. It eliminated all of the old boards and consolidated executive power in the hands of the mayor, assisted by his appointed cabinet of six directors. Reaching into the ranks of the Democratic party, Johnson picked Charles P. Sahlen, a former city clerk and director of accounts to head the department of public works. To direct the department of charities and correction, he chose Dr. Harris R. Cooley, a respected figure in social service work. Two prominent attorneys, Harry Payer and Newton D. Baker, were chosen to direct the law department.[45]

At the same time capable Republicans were given major posts in the government. Johnson informed Lincoln Steffens: "While I would employ by preference Democrats ... we won't keep a man, no matter how much his political pull, if he is not competent and reliable." He selected Fred Kohler for police chief and placed William J. Springborn on the board of public service. Pursuing a systematic reorganization which included transfer and the "weeding out of incompetents," Kohler turned the police force into the most efficient and responsible department in the administration. Springborn modernized the street cleaning department and introduced efficiency into other departments. Representing the greatest degree of expertise in the administration was Edward W. Bemis, superintendent of the water works. Former prominent professor of political economy at the University of Chicago and later head of the department of municipal monopolies in New York City, Bemis introduced a system of statistics and efficiency records which required that professional stature rather than political influence be the criterion for employment in the department.[46]

In addition to these officials, the city witnessed a movement of educated young men into the lower levels of the government. Johnson wrote afterward: "As time went on our organization gathered to itself ... students of social problems known to the whole community as disinterested, high minded, clean-lived individuals."[47] With such personnel behind him the mayor pushed for the redistribution of economic power in the city and attempted to distribute the amenities of middle-class life to the masses. In the process he, like Mayor Pingree, alienated upper-class groups and was forced to make a deliberate bid for the votes of lower classes to implement social welfare projects. Frederic C. Howe, a reform councilman from 1901 to 1903 and later a prominent member of the Johnson organization, recalled the situation: "Before the expiration of the first two years of Mr. Johnson's mayoralty the city was divided into two camps. . . . On the one side were men of property and influence; on the other the politicians, immigrants, workers, and persons of small means."[48] The mayor fought for municipal ownership of utilities and forced down the street railway fares from five cents to three, brought cheap natural gas into Cleveland over the bitter opposition of the artificial gas firms, and shifted the burden of taxation from small property owners to the large corporations. There was also an expansion of public services. Johnson made garbage collection and street cleaning municipal responsibilities, forced down the cost of water rates, eliminated substandard tenement houses, and constructed recreation facilities and public baths.[49]

This impressive program mirrored the growing emphasis in executive centralization on the social implications of governmental efficiency. Indeed, it appeared that the combination of efficient management and recognition of public social needs made political reform itself unbeatable at the polls. "In none of the campaign literature of the opposition," recalled a respected Cleveland lawyer, "was there ever a charge of Mr. Johnson's being inefficient as a chief executive. . . . Coupled with this goes the fact that Cleveland citizens without doubt know more about the public business than the people of almost any city in the country."[50] James T. Young, professor of government at the University of Pennsylvania, wrote in 1903 that effective administration would not be achieved by just replacing the "rascals" with honest, reliable men; rather the road to permanent reform lay in the development of more "positive" programs of civic improvement. He pointed to the expansion of executive functions as the most striking evidence of this trend: "Our collective legislatures . . . have escaped almost completely from popular control and the people are therefore turning . . . toward the executive. . . . In so doing ... we have grasped the only agency for securing the adoption of those real economic and social benefits which are of such vital importance under present conditions."[51]

Developments in Jersey City, Philadelphia, Cincinnati, and Toledo confirmed Young's optimistic view of urban political reform. Capitalizing on dissension within Jersey City's Democratic party, Mark Fagan, former member of the local board of freeholders, secured the nomination of the Republican organization for the mayoralty in 1901. Fagan conducted a vigorous campaign in which he promised new and better services such as more schools, well-paved streets, a new municipal hospital, and more efficient police and fire protection. Shortly after his election, the new mayor found that the city did not have sufficient funds for the expansion of housing, education, and public health services. One lucrative source of additional revenues lay in the equal taxation of railroad-owned real estate. The railroad companies continually transferred their land purchases from the local tax levy to railroad property assessed by state tax authorities at lower rates. In the process, the city was being deprived of considerable revenue while individual home-owners paid an inordinate amount of taxes. Seeking to replace these arrangements with a more equitable tax system, Mayor Fagan required the listing of railroad properties in the record of municipal ratables so that the government could assess railroad corporations at full local rates. This fiscal reform brought about a more even distribution of the tax burden in which the property taxes of Jersey City's home owners dropped considerably. These middle- and upper-class residents provided heavy majorities for Fagan in the 1903 mayoralty election, and he defeated the regular Democratic candidate by a comfortable margin.[52]

Inspired by his reelection and the public support of tax reform, Mayor Fagan advocated equal taxation and regulation of public utility companies. His administration soon found that the city could neither tax nor regulate these corporations effectively. Fagan then proceeded to emulate the policy of Tom Johnson and recommended a three-cent trolley fare and municipalization of all public utilities. This program, however, brought the Mayor into conflict with the regular Republican organization, headed by Samuel Dickinson. Fagan accused Dickinson of obstructing passage of an equal taxation measure and insisting on a perpetual franchise for the Public Service Corporation, which exercised control over most of the state's gas, electric, and trolley companies. In the election of 1905 Fagan deserted the regular organization and presented himself in the mayoralty contest as a reform leader committed to the destruction of boss rule in Jersey City. He defeated his Democratic opponent by more than 3,500 votes despite the combined opposition of regular Democrats and Republicans. This victory led to the establishment of a "New Idea" party among Republican supporters of Mayor Fagan as an alternative to bossism and an instrument of progressive political reform.[53]

Similar concern with organization shaped politics and reform in Philadelphia. Elected to the mayoralty in 1903, John Weaver, a former district attorney and machine nominee, would not accept dictation from the Republican organization and seized upon the merit system as the key to executive power. Headed by a machine appointee, the civil service board was used, one reformer observed, "only to keep out those who were objectionable to the bosses."[54] Faced with this situation, the mayor removed the machine's man and picked Frank M. Riter, a reform lawyer, to head the board. Anxious to insulate public office from party influence, Riter suspended the eligible lists certified under the previous administration and prepared new ones. He also drafted a set of regulations which prohibited officeholders from engaging in politics. Clinton R. Woodruff, secretary of the National Municipal League and close observer of Philadelphia's government, reported that these measures were making the merit system a "real and vital force" in placing the city's service upon a "substantial basis of efficiency."[55]

Confronted with this effort to undermine spoils politics, the machine fell back on utility franchises to maintain its influence over the government. In return for generous franchises from the machine-ridden council, the city's gas interests supplied substantial funds to the Republican organization. An ordinance in February 1905 provided for a new lease to the United Gas Improvement Company by which the city would receive $25,000,000 for terminating the existing lease and extending the new one to 1930. Pointing out that the city would be accepting a compensation less than what it was entitled to while the price of gas for consumers would remain fixed, the Committee of Seven-

ty, an organization of business and professional men committed
to political reform, mounted a campaign against the ordinance.
The mayor shared this resentment and vetoed the measure.
However, his veto required the approval of a third of the council.
Weaver proceeded to remove two politicos, the directors of
public safety and public works, and replaced them with persons
ready to help him in the struggle with his former sponsors.
Realizing that the mayor could now control directly the
patronage of these departments, the council sustained the veto.
Shortly afterward several machine adherents in the government
were arrested for alleged corruption. Weaver quickly joined
forces with reformers in an election campaign which brought
about a complete defeat of the organization in November 1905.[56]

Capitalizing upon a wave of public resentment against the
Republican machine in Cincinnati, reform Democrats secured
the election of Edward H. Dempsey, a respected judge of the
city's superior court, in 1905. Dempsey sought to improve the
quality of municipal services by increasing expenditures, expanding agencies, and hiring trained personnel. Viewing the park
question from the standpoint of public efficiency, the mayor persuaded the board of public service to appoint a commission to
adopt a plan for a park system, and supported a large bond issue
to provide it with funds to hire an expert consultant. He likewise
provided the health department with a sizable increase in funds
with which it launched a campaign to clean up the milk supply.
Regarding tenements as the chief sources of disease in the city, he
introduced an ordinance which set up a commission to revise the
building code. Convinced that problems in the street repair and
cleaning departments were rooted in poor organization, the
mayor removed the supervision of repairs from the board of
public services, placed cleaning and repair in one department, and
selected the former president of an electrical manufacturing company to administer the agency.[57]

Equally determined to provide an alternative to boss rule was
Mayor Brand Whitlock of Toledo. Drawing on his experiences
as a prominent trial lawyer, he saw dishonesty and inefficiency in
office as the outgrowth of machine politics which permitted big
business to exercise a demoralizing influence upon city government. Six years before his election in 1905 his predecessor,
Samuel "Golden Rule" Jones, a manufacturer who disassociated

himself from party regulars and pursued an independent course of political and social reform, had contended: "There is little hope for improvement ... in the direction of scientific government in our municipalities until we shall first get the people freed from the baneful superstition of partisan politics."[58] Whitlock, however, was willing to meet the city's boss-ridden Republican party on its own ground. He and reform-minded politicians organized the Independent party, with delegates from every precinct and ward in the city. The organization placed before the electorate complete tickets of candidates selected for their honesty and efficiency. By 1907 it had gained control of the city council and other public offices. At the same time the mayor was consolidating power within the government. Reaching into the ranks of his own organization and the parties, he appointed qualified men to various administrative posts. Together, these arrangements enabled Whitlock to fight for municipal ownership of street railways and promote social welfare projects such as smoke control, careful inspection of meat shipped into the city, and penal reform.[59]

By using their power to advance efficiency and social reform, Whitlock, Dempsey, and Weaver provided additional evidence of the superiority of strong-mayor government for large cities. With its cumbersomeness and lack of administrative coordination and leadership, the weak-mayor plan made it quite difficult for voters in all areas of the city to tell with some accuracy what was going on inside the government and determine who was responsible for carrying out policy. The strong-mayor system, on the other hand, permitted greater coordination of departmental functions, metropolitan planning, and more public exposure for administrative authorities. In the process an "executive-centered" coalition was assuming the functional role of the machine in city management. But the growing dependence on appointive civil servants also placed the mayor at the center of intersecting lines of authority.[60] Further, it was unclear as to what were the main goals of executive centralization. The development of fiscal reform would produce conflicting views of governmental efficiency in urban progressivism.

Chapter V

FISCAL INSTRUMENTS OF EFFICIENCY

> The necessity of financial control over municipal
> receipts and expenditures has been demonstrated
> time and again in every municipality of any size in
> the country; and the question is not at this time
> whether control should exist, but how and by what
> authority should it be conferred, and in whom should
> it be vested.
>
> Albert F. Crosby
> "Financial Control Over Municipal Receipts and Expenditures"
> *Proceedings of the Columbus Conference for Good City Government*
> (1899)

Inspired by the growth of executive responsibility in local
government, the political reformers and their business-minded
cohorts in office focused upon budget reform as another means to
reorganize administrative authority in municipal affairs. Support
came from urban property holders who had become what one
political scientist has described as "pariah capitalists." Faced with
rising taxes that were taking away the value of the services being
supported by their monies, they turned to reformers for the
remedy to their problem. To those officials who answered to party bosses, the increasing taxes were an inevitable outgrowth of a
budget program enabling them to raise the salaries of political
appointees and increase the number of jobs in machine administrations. But urban taxpayers were confident that these
practices could be replaced by new standards and controls.[1] Thus,
they asked sympathetic officials to increase services and at the
same time to reduce expenditures by stopping payments to the
political machine.

Defined in the last decade of the nineteenth century as "a valuation of receipts and expenditures or a public balance sheet, and as a legislative act establishing and authorizing certain kinds and amounts of expenditures and taxation,"[2] the budget as a control mechanism had been developing since the 1830s and in significant form after the Civil War. By the nineties there were three basic forms of budgeting in American cities: the simple tax levy, the tax levy preceded by detailed estimates, and the tax levy accompanied by detailed appropriations. Particularly distressing to reformers was the first type. Under this procedure there was no formal process which set a limit to expenditures, either in the aggregate or by departments. Rather than being lodged in the executive, the apportioning of money to various departments was done by the city council in granting periodic contracts and permitting bills from month to month. Confined mainly to smaller cities, this system permitted occasional collusion between council members and interest groups, who interpreted municipal expenditures more in terms of economic advancement and less in terms of public considerations.[3]

The second type was the system of taxation based upon a detailed account of receipts and expenditures. Business-minded officials, usually on boards of finance and assessment and continually under pressure from middle-class groups to reduce taxes, submitted "projected budgets" to their city councils in which specific expenses were enumerated. Not legally bound to adhere to the items used in determining the tax rate, city councils, particularly those under the thumb of political machines, were reluctant to accept the proposed budgets and bent them to considerations far removed from the canons of efficiency and economy. Frederick R. Clow, a close student of municipal finance, reported that a "corrupt gang in control of the council can let the estimates distribute the funds wisely, at the time of year when the making of the budget attracts public attention . . . and later further their selfish ends by directing the funds to purposes not named in the estimates."[4]

Determined to avoid this situation, some cities required a provision for annual appropriations, thus fixing expenditures for the year. In Cleveland, for example, the council was instructed to make "detailed and specific appropriations for the several objects for which the city has to provide." Similarly, the budget for

1897/98 in Boston required "respective sums of money hereinafter appropriated for the several departments" and these were to be met out of the "current income of the year." In Denver, Omaha, and Minneapolis officials collected taxes and then allocated the revenues for particular expenses. Similar provisions were required by state law in Indiana, Illinois, and New York.[5]

While they differ in theory, there was seldom a sharp line of demarcation between these forms of budgeting, particularly in respect to the first and second types. One city would have no estimates beyond oral reports and discussions; another would permit particular officials or departments to use written estimates for their individual use; still another would require that departments submit detailed estimates of expected needs and expenses. The key point of separation lay in the scope and influence of the estimates. If an estimate encompassed all revenues and expenditures and was laid before the council as the criterion in determining the tax base, the budget clearly belonged to the second type; if either of these aspects were absent, it belonged to the first.

Between the second and third types of municipal budgeting, there was a clearer and more crucial distinction. Rather than being subject to legal restraints, the city councils, by accepting the morality of economy in government, were expected to adhere to specific estimates in distributing monthly appropriations. In practice all of the merits of a budget which provided annual appropriations would be realized, though the city might be operating under an informal budget of the second type. Subjected to continual alteration in city councils, however, a budget of the third type could be so little regarded in the actual distribution of money during the year as to be almost useless. In this light the budget could be the means whereby a legislature could shield the fiscal aspects of party government from reforms designed to undermine that sector.[6] "It was the uncontrolled and uncontrollable increase in the cost of government that finally jostled the public into an attitude of hostility to a system which was so fondly called the 'American system,'" recalled a prominent fiscal reformer. "This growing hostility to doing business in the dark, to 'boss rule,' to 'invisible government,' became the soil in which the 'budget idea' finally took root and grew."[7]

Moreover, in keeping with the emphasis upon administrative centralization, business-minded officials in local government joined the struggle to adjust legislative processes to the requirements of fiscal efficiency. Particularly influential in developing controls over public finance was the board of estimate and apportionment in New York City. Composed of the mayor, comptroller, president of the department of taxes and assessments, president of the board of aldermen, and corporation counsel, this administrative body set the tone for fiscal reorganization in municipal affairs. Responsible for making a provisional budget for the ensuing year, the board was distrustful of lump sum appropriations and required that department heads submit estimates which included the specific salaries of each employee and the specific purpose of each expenditure. Drawing upon this data, the board submitted a provisional estimate to the city council. Within fifteen days the board of aldermen would return the budget to the board of estimate, with a statement of their objections or rectifications. Following a brief period of hearings on the proposed appropriations, the board considered the suggestions of the board of aldermen and a majority vote would decide the final budget.[8]

Periodically the board of aldermen, as might be expected from its political composition, increased the appropriations of the provisional estimate. From 1873 to 1888 they added, on the average, about a half million dollars annually to the estimate. But, continually overruled by the board of estimate, they in time proposed fewer changes in the estimates. In the years from 1890 to 1898 the largest increase in the budget proposed by the council in any one year was considerably smaller in comparison with the earlier years. Responding to consistent pressure for economy in government, particularly from middle-class groups experiencing the brunt of taxation, the board of estimates ignored the proposed increases of the council and continued to reduce the level of public expenditures.[9] At the same time, the budget system in New York permitted the city council to exert some informal control over public spending. The Greater New York charter of 1898 transformed this informal control into formal power which permitted the council to alter the proposed budgets. Specifically, the council could decrease but not increase the amounts fixed by the board of estimate. If the mayor vetoed any reductions made by the council, a five-sixths vote in the legislature was necessary to override his veto. Most important, there was to be no reconsideration of the appropriations by the board of estimate after the council had acted upon them. Under these provisions of the charter, the council lost its advisory role and assumed direct responsibility for public expenditures.[10]

Influenced by New York's fiscal system, reformers in Baltimore introduced a new charter in 1898 which altered the structure of fiscal authority in the government. Previously the budget had been prepared and submitted to the city council by a joint committee of the council. The charter provided for a board of estimate composed of the mayor, city solicitor, comptroller, president of the board of aldermen, and city engineer. Required to prepare and submit to the council a "precise estimate of the necessary appropriations" for the next fiscal year, the board had to accept any reductions proposed by the council provided that it did not "divert any appropriation from the purpose for which it was originally designed." After revising the budget as submitted by the mayor, the city council in Cleveland was required to submit a tax ordinance to the board of tax commissioners for approval. In Detroit the budget needed the approval of a board of estimates, while in Columbus and Toledo a board of tax commissioners would approve the tax ordinance before it went into effect.[11]

Behind these boards of finance lay a crucial development in the efficiency movement. Larger cities were restricting the role of the council in executing fiscal policy and committing the administration to executive officers. Beyond granting approval of the budget, the councils had little to do with the procedures of fiscal administration. This system, in turn, was bringing the lines of fiscal authority in closer touch with municipal departments. At the center of this interaction stood the city comptroller. Devoted to financial efficiency, allegedly nonpartisan, he usually measured public expenditures according to the principles of cost accounting and efficient management. New York's comptroller, Bird S. Coler, in 1899 wrote: "The rights of the people of the city are always safer in the hands of a capable and conscientious Mayor and Comptroller endowed with ample power carrying with it full responsibility, than they could possibly be when left to the care of a multitude of irresponsible office holders, whose own personal and political interests must of necessity be confined to a district or a borough."[12] There were bureaus in Coler's office responsible for the collection of interest on bonds, collection of taxes, and formulation of assessments. Along with this jurisdiction was the right of the comptroller to prescribe the form of all claims against the city, require statements from banks holding municipal funds, and investigate the fiscal policies of various departments. Similarly, each department of Cleveland's government by 1907 was reporting to the comptroller all daily monies received and the deposition of them. Consequently, the comptroller was held accountable for all warrants drawn on the city's treasury and had the authority to prescribe the accounting methods of all departments, as well as the form in which their reports were made to his office.[13]

Other cities followed the same pattern. In Philadelphia the comptroller, as one student of city administration pointed out, had the "power to direct the fiscal policy of the city."[14] All bills against the city required the comptroller's approval before being allowed, even when they were sanctioned by the city's council. To keep a close check on the city's treasury, he inspected the bonds of the treasurer and required statements from banks indicating the amount of city money on deposit. In St. Paul and Omaha the treasurer was required to inform the comptroller daily of the amount on deposit in various banks. Similarly, the comptroller in St. Louis supervised public finances and was entitled to a seat in either branch of the city council with the right to speak but not to vote.[15]

In conjunction with the jurisdiction of various boards over public finance, the powers of the comptroller reflected the increasing influence of administrators over lines of fiscal authority. Most influential in this development was the campaign of the National Municipal League for uniform accounting in city government. The league insisted that a comptroller keep general accounts of money received and expended for the city by all officials and separate accounts of the purpose and payment of departmental appropriations. These recommendations soon became the basis of some significant reorganization of public finance. In Chicago, for example, the Merchants' Club, after closely investigating the collection and distribution of public monies, submitted a report to Mayor Harrison in 1900 on

various impediments to centralized administration such as dis-
crepancies between the accounts of departments and those of the
comptroller, inadequate auditing procedures, and no records of
departmental supplies and materials in the comptroller's office.
The mayor immediately authorized Charles W. Haskins, dean of
the New York University School of Commerce, Accounts and
Finance and also a respected public accountant, to install better
techniques of fiscal control in the government. Two years later
there was little trace of the old methods. The main features of the
new system were the centralization of accounting in the comptroller's office, monthly reports from all departments and approval of all contracts, and requisitions for supplies by the comptroller.[16] By 1903 Boston, Providence, and Baltimore had
adopted similar procedures in the practical application of the
league's program of uniform accounting.[17]

Most cities, however, were not reforming their fiscal systems.
There were no complete annual accounts of functional expenditures because different parts of the government had separate
finance procedures based on special taxes and funds. Furthermore, capital expenditures were seldom separated by departmental heads from operating costs in account totals. Fiscal officers,
therefore, had little notion of what the appropriate level of operation expenses on any particular function or service should be.[18]
"One of the first and most essential reforms in American cities is
an improvement in financial methods," wrote Richard T. Ely, the
prominent economist and tax authority at the University of
Wisconsin, in 1902. "Municipal accounting needs a thorough
overhauling, and a good budgetary system must be part and
parcel of every excellent municipal government."[19]

More disturbing to reformers was the susceptibility of fiscal
authority to considerations of party policy. "In spite of the great
power held by a minority, even of one, in the board of estimate,
the dominant party must at times use the budget as a political
engine," observed Edward Dana Durand, former legislative
librarian of New York, in 1898. "There are often strong party
differences among the departments, or between certain departments and the mayor; and the control of the appropriations can
hardly escape being occasionally employed to favor a political
friend or punish a political foe."[20] Partisan finance, however,
went beyond mere favoritism. Durand also noted that in New

York City the "outer form and the practical working of the financial system" had been "intimately dependent upon the conditions of the general municipal administration and of state and national politics."[21] This situation existed throughout Northern states and cities. During the 1870s and 1880s the widespread evasion of property taxes by upper-class elements and private corporations, the middle-class complaints about the inequities of the tax system, and the demands of growing urban populations for more services resulted in a general breakdown of public-revenue-gathering machinery in the North. Knowing that governments could not function without the parties, professional politicians had established an intricate network of political taxation and budget controls to support and maintain their organizations. This extralegal money machinery enabled them to meet the growing costs of elections, reward the rank and file with public offices, and provide rudimentary welfare services to the urban masses. By the late nineties city and state governments were dependent upon these needs and responsibilities of the political parties.[22]

Most reformers, however, overlooked this functional interrelationship of party and government finance. Politics in city financial operations only meant continuous waste and inefficiency. The remedy lay in the direction of more economical techniques of administrative management. On the other hand, fiscal efficiency did not necessarily mean economy at the sacrifice of social programs. The rapid concentration of people from rural areas and abroad in cities forced some political reformers to pay more attention to the need for additional public services which earlier urban populations had not required. Woodrow Wilson informed a Johns Hopkins audience in 1896: "The modern industrial city, with its wide social functions, must act in many things involving the heaviest expenditures, not for property owners, but for the working and economically dependent classes. . . . For my part, I do not believe that the persons who pay the largest taxes are the best judges of the needs of the city." In the same admonitory vein, New York's comptroller Coler argued in 1901 that the "better element" of citizens possessed "little or no general knowledge of the vast social, political, industrial, and economic conditions and problems involved in the regulation of all the affairs of a great city." Successful reform, concluded Coler, would be "a movement with a broad and liberal policy for building up, not a mere negative force to stop progress in order to show a smaller expense account."[23] In this light, the reorganization of fiscal authority was only an intermediate step toward the end of efficient government: to assure that the needs of urban residents were satisfied by the performance of essential municipal functions. These included, as defined by one authority on city finance, maintenance of the government, care of defective classes, public safety, and public convenience.[24]

But it was quite difficult, if not impossible, to determine the extent to which local government actually conformed to necessities arising from urban conditions without comparative statistics on public services. The U.S. Census Bureau proposed to prepare such material on an annual basis and bring city statistics under federal jurisdiction. In the years from 1870 to 1900 urban population had jumped from nearly 10 million to more than 30 million.[25] By 1903 the proportion of total population defined by the bureau as "urban" was more than 40 percent. While this did not necessitate the intrusion of the federal government into municipal reform, the fact that such a large percentage of the population was dependent upon local government to assure its general welfare justified the anxiety of the bureau over whether municipal functions were being efficiently and adequately carried out. The bureau was not ready to present material that would outline the importance of city living conditions for the organization of local administration. Instead, it sought to evaluate the performance of the services presented by reformers as the purpose of municipal government. The bureau defined the subject of its statistical series on cities of more than 30,000 population as "all corporations, organizations, commissions, boards, and other local public authorities through which the people of the city exercise any privilege of local self-government, or through which they enjoy the exclusive benefits of any municipal function."[26]

In adopting this perspective, the Census Bureau had to focus its attention on conditions experienced by all city populations and the general responsibilities of urban government. Consequently, the model of efficient, service-oriented government became the basis of the statistical program. The bureau's definition of governmental functions conformed to that employed in reform ideology: "Most of them [municipal functions] are essential to the existence and development of government and to the performance of the . . . duty of protecting life and property and of maintaining a high standard of social efficiency." As further defined by the bureau, these functions included general administration, public charities and correction, public highways and sanitation, and public education and recreation.[27] Few cities, however, had administrative sectors whose operations conformed to this classification derived from the theory of efficient government. The bureau moved quickly to establish federal authority over the determination and control of "official statistics of the cities." This program brought it into the front ranks of the efficiency movement and encouraged cities to reform their administrative structures.

The reports of the Census Bureau provided each city of more than 30,000 with a detailed explanation of its annual expenditures classfiied according to the five essential governmental functions. In those cities operating under the uniform accounting system designed by the National Municipal League, fiscal officers were already keeping accounts according to this classification. For them the federal statistics were an applicable source of comparative data on public expenditures of other cities. In trying to illustrate the relationship between urban populations and expenditures on functional service, the Census Bureau presented statistics in a comparative format in which cities were ranked by population size and grouped into classes of which per capita expenditures were estimated. These tables showed that larger per capita expenditure was required to perform services adequately as a city's population increased over time. With such information and convinced that cities spent too little, the bureau instructed local officials to accept the fact that the main requirement for better services was to raise the level of per capita expenses.[28]

More important to the Census Bureau was whether city governments were carrying out all of the five essential functions. In the reports of 1902 and 1903 there was considerable evidence indicating that some of the variation in per capita expenses was due to the need for more expenditures as population size increased. On the other hand, variations in expenditures among cities, the bureau noted, also arose from the extent to which municipal functions were being performed by state government agencies and private institutions. This information required cities to conform to the model of proper governmental responsibilities advocated by political progressives. It was clear to those cities lacking responsibility for essential municipal functions that their governments required basic administrative reorganization. LeGrand Powers, chief statistician of the bureau, informed the National Municipal League in 1908: "The census financial statistics provide the basis for making the experience of one city the test and measure of the economy, wastefulness, or the efficiency of the administration of our larger cities. . . . These statistics are now consulted more or less in the preparation of the budget in over one-half of our large cities."[29]

This model of functional responsibilities and expenditures represented an important contribution to the fiscal reordering of municipal administration. In focusing upon the need for more public services, the Census Bureau showed that growing costs were not necessarily a sign of corruption and partisan mismanagement. Per capita expenditures, however, were not sufficient to measure the efficiency with which governmental services were being distributed. Urban political progressives, along with their allies in the federal government, were more concerned with getting administrative officials to adopt a form of unit cost accounting developed by private businesses. Frederick A. Cleveland, professor of finance at New York University, pointed out that in most cities there was "no way in which the chief executive [could] inform himself accurately and regularly on questions of current business."[30] The Census Bureau outlined the remedy for this problem: "In private business . . . every factor of business administration is brought under accounting control by means of what the business world now knows as 'cost accounting.' It is by such methods that the leaders in modern private business have made accounts and accounting of supreme administrative assistance in avoiding bad and securing good financial results."[31]

Extremely influential in promoting the reform of municipal finance were activists in the rising professions of accounting, administration, and social work. In outlook and program they were close to the views and goals of the business and professional elites whom David B. Tyack calls the "administrative progressives" in urban educational reform. Impressed with the methods of integrative control and coordination of modern business, these educational reformers saw in the decentralization of school governance only political corruption, bureaucratic parochialism, and vestiges of an outmoded localism. They worked to replace these conditions with corporate systems of control in which decision making was centralized in the hands of professional school administrators.[32] Similar concerns motivated the structualists in fiscal reform. In the decentralized system of urban finance they uncovered corruptive partisanship, misallocation of public monies, and confusion of authority. They sought to eliminate these conditions through the introduction of the business system of accounting controls into city government. Receptive to this program were top-level officials seeking greater regulation of departmental appropriations and functions. The end in view for both groups was the bureaucratic rationalization of public expenditures and centralization of administrative decision-making on the metropolitan scale.

Most important in this effort was the work of the New York Bureau of Municipal Research, an organization composed of engineers, accountants, trained administrators, and social workers. The Bureau pointed to poor fiscal procedures as the main source of governmental inefficiency. Rather than being a tool to provide detailed information on the expenditures of different departments, the budget had become an imprecise vehicle of appropriation, obscuring more than it revealed. In the first place, information as to uncollected revenues was unavailable and control over collection was most defective. Furthermore, receipts and expenditures were recorded with wasteful repetition, but there was little statistical data to guide administrative policy as to both. In some instances, departments failed to indicate the functions performed and the distribution of money among the various services. Together, these practices, the Bureau noted, prevented effective control over expenditures and perpetuated a pattern of discretionary authority in municipal administration.[33]

Admirably complementing this critique of existing practices was the plan designed by the Bureau to inject uniformity and responsibility into the fiscal tissues of the government. Central to the scheme was the belief that officials needed precise data to accurately gauge input requirements and output potentials. Given this data, they could determine the relative efficiency of various operations. The Bureau proposed a budget on a unit cost scheme or "segregated budget" which would classify the activities of departments into integral parts. Along with this system of classification went standardization of functions within departments, enabling the board of estimate to exercise intelligent and effective control over departmental requests. In short, reorganization of the budget would substitute careful planning for an uncoordinated system.[34]

Convinced that this budget plan was the best way to obtain an increase in funds and show the community what was needed, New York City's health department invited the Bureau in 1907 to devise a budget for the following year. Since the department's work directly affected the entire community, the Bureau welcomed this opportunity to introduce its methods into government. After a detailed investigation of the organization and duties of the department, the bureau drew up a functional classification of salaries and expenses and presented it to the board of estimate in October 1907. Influenced by the fact that this form of budget permitted the consideration of requests on the basis of proposed service and specific activities, the board accepted the proposal and instructed the finance department to submit estimates for the next year's budget so as to show work done in 1907 and work contemplated for 1908 in every department. To the Bureau this response of the board was recognition of the fact that budgeting was being directed to "taxpayers who wish to know what benefits their taxes buy and to municipal officers who wish to obtain public support for efficient, far-seeing administration."[35]

One such officer was the comptroller, Herman A. Metz, who headed the department of finance. Inviting the Bureau of Municipal Research the same year to reorganize his department, he wrote: "To further postpone the reorganization of the department on a logical basis, whereby its various functions will be efficiently discharged . . . will, in my judgment, prove inimical to the best interests of the city."[36] Deprived of adequate accounting procedures, Metz found it extremely difficult to ascertain the honesty of personnel handling revenues, coordinate departmental records with those of his office, and figure with accuracy the cost of public services. By 1908 the bureau had helped reorganize the comptroller's office and provided data that won for Metz permission from the New York City civil service commission to appoint several accountants to the finance department. They, along with bureau personnel, analyzed the structure of six other departments and worked out a system of central accounting control. By 1909 budgets in these departments had been segregated according to function. In addition, the finance department introduced cost accounting systems into various departments. Thus, top officials could spend appropriations as they wished within the limits of the functions of the departments, but no official could divert funds voted under one title to purposes included in another title.[37]

Confined to these administrative procedures, efficient government and dishonesty could be both read from the ledgers of public expenditure. Speaking in 1909 before the National Tax Association, an organization of prominent middle-class fiscal reformers devoted to the efficient management of public finance and limitation of government expenditures, an official of New York's department of finance declared: "A rational system of analytical accounting, carried into every department and framed along such uniform lines as would make possible significant comparisons, would prove and test the economy and efficiency of administration in the various bureaus and departments of a city. . . . Such a system of uniform analytical accounting would eventually prove of great value to the modern municipality."[38] Other political reformers agreed. In the same year the Association of American Government Accountants heard its president assert: "No friend of efficient government can rest content until every government official is aroused . . . to the value of accounts as the measure and test of efficiency, as well as of dishonesty." William H. Allen, a director of the New York Bureau of Municipal Research, similarly informed a meeting of the National Municipal League in 1910 that the "most important of all benefits from adequate municipal accounting is that it puts a premium on efficiency which, in turn, is a soil unfavorable to the growth of graft."[39]

This emphasis on accounting controls revealed an ambivalence in fiscal reform. Political reformers in the 1880s saw little difference between economy and efficiency since both were expected to produce honest government. But in the evolution of structural progressivism there appeared to be basic differences in strategy: viewed in one way, economy as expressed in the introduction of accounting procedures could produce efficient, honest administration; in another light, efficiency as expressed in the reorganization of municipal offices could produce frugal, honest administration. Both notions of financial responsibility were mutually reinforcing and there was seldom a clear line between them. The end in view for middle-class elites and their reformist spokesmen was the insulation of fiscal authority from the virus of machine politics.

Boston furnished a microcosm of this consensus. Typical of cities under the sway of political bossism, Boston had a government filled with party regulars whose performance was questionable and whose handsome salaries were proving to be a costly drain on the city's treasury. In seeking to alter this situation Walter Webster, a reform lawyer and chairman of the Committee on Metropolitan Affairs in the state legislature, recommended in 1906 the appointment of a commission for investigating fiscal conditions in the Bay City. Hoping to take most of the bite out of the charges that his administration was one of the most corrupt in the city's history, Mayor John Fitzgerald welcomed the proposal and asked for a commission appointed by the city council to investigate the government: "What is required is a business examination of the subject by a body of such representative, able and impartial citizens of Boston that our taxpayers will have full confidence in the soundness of any conclusions which they may reach." The council, in response, authorized the mayor in 1907 to appoint a finance commission with members from leading commercial and civic associations. Included in the commission were representatives of middle-class organizations such as the board of trade, the chamber of commerce, the Boston Merchants' Association, and the Real Estate Exchange.[40]

From 1907 to 1909 the commission held public hearings and employed accountants, engineers, and lawyers to investigate all branches of the government. Provided with extensive testimony from several officials and considerable data on the activities of various departments, it pointed to the "excessive number" of clerical employees and day laborers as the main source of "waste and inefficiency" in the city government. In the years from 1895 to 1907 the population of Boston had increased by 22.7 percent, while the number of clerks had increased by 75 percent. At the same time, salaries continued to rise and by 1907 they were being paid three times more than those employed for similar work by the state government and private companies. These conditions resulted from the "continual pressure from political sources" upon departmental heads to create new offices for those clerks near the head of the civil service lists. In addition, most of the clerical employees repeatedly solicited "political influence" to secure a raise in salary. The commission asserted that this expansion of the city payroll took place "regardless of the amount of work to be done, the appropriations for the year, or the ultimate loss to the public."[41]

These conditions were more evident in the employment of day labor. Since 1895 the number of workers employed by the city had increased by 50 percent. By 1907 the efficiency of labor had declined to a point where the work done per man was half as much as it had been before 1895. According to the commission, this development resulted from the fact that "pay rolls were swollen for the political purposes of the administration for the time being. For similar reasons all pretence of discipline in the larger departments had been abandoned. Incompetency ... and insubordination were seldom visited by suspension, still less frequently by discharge." Party leaders had tolerated this situation and saw large numbers of immigrants and native workers on the public payroll as being in the "general interest" of municipal labor. However, the commission also pointed to the continual effort of the professional politicians of the parties to "get men on the pay roll who will help them to be elected or re-elected to public office." Moreover, various devices, such as employment of "emergency men" and "provisional" appointments, enabled the mayor and departmental heads to evade the civil service rules.[42]

Equally disturbing was the "outrageous waste of public money" in noncompetitive contracts. In the city charter there was a provision requiring heads of departments to invite public bids on proposed work costing more than $2,000 unless the mayor gave his written permission to dispense with public competition. During the years from 1895 to 1907 this permission was easy to secure and as a result the provision was "practically nullified." By 1907 the department heads were receiving orders from the mayor to secure his approval of a contract without competitive bidding. Furthermore, there was little competition in the awarding of contracts under $2,000. The commission pointed out that the "work was handed out to selected contractors, often members of the city council in disguise, always friendly to the administration. These were called 'gift' contracts, and as they were obtained by favor, the inspection was lax, the performance often poor, and the cost always excessive."[43]

Such practices were not confined to Mayor Fitzgerald's administration. The commission argued that the "politicians" in control of public monies had not devised "all the schemes of misgovernment, but they took advantage of, improved upon, and added to those which they found in operation."[44] John F. Kennedy, the representative of organized labor on the commission, contended in a minority report that all of his colleagues owed their appointment not to individual competence but to the leading business interests of Boston. He also pointed out that the slashing of public payrolls was inimical to workers since these expenditures resulted from "direct employment of labor by the city, or giving municipal work only to fair contractors," and thus were "sound economically and beneficial to the whole community." On the other hand, there was a considerable amount of evidence indicating a breakdown in the administrative machinery of the government. Kennedy stated: "We have all, including the active politicians themselves, been the victims of a bad system."[45] By 1909 recommendations from the commission resulted in the enforcement of economies in various departments and passage of a law requiring certification of payrolls by departmental heads with approval of the city's civil service commission. The payroll inspector of the civil service commission reported in September of 1909 that "thousands of dollars" were being saved to the city by "keeping off the lists false 'emergency men' and others whose employment in previous years the commission had no means of detecting with promptness." Moreover, large numbers of partisan incompetents had been discharged from some departments and city expenditures had declined by nearly $1 million since 1907.[46]

In addition to these achievements, the report of the finance commission revealed serious defects in the city charter. Among the weaknesses were the cumbersome structure of the council with its two chambers, division of responsibility for various appointments between the mayor and council, partisan nominations and elections, and the uncertain tenure of departmental heads. Feeling that the principle of executive responsibility intended by the amendments of 1885 should be carried to its logical conclusion, the commission submitted a new charter to the legislature. In 1909 the general court passed an act embodying the recommendations of the commission and the bulk of amendments went into effect without reference to the electorate. At the same time two proposals for reorganizing the city council and fixing the term of the mayor were submitted to a popular referendum. Plan One called for a mayor elected for two years and a single legislative chamber with one member from each ward to be elected for two years and nine members to be elected at large for terms of three years. Plan Two, which contained the recommendations of the finance commission, extended the mayoral term to four years, established a single legislative chamber of nine members elected at large, and provided that all party designations be excluded from the ballot and nominations for mayor be made by a petition containing 5,000 signatures.[47]

Convinced that the second proposal would "abolish the municipal boss" and the "wasteful division of public funds," the reformers pushed hard for the plan and it won by a narrow margin. In line with the charters of Baltimore and New York, the Boston document provided for the separation of executive and legislative powers and lodged responsibility for administration in the hands of the mayor, whose term of office was extended to four years. The mayor could appoint and remove heads of departments without obtaining the confirmation of the council. At the same time he was required to submit the name of his nominee to the state civil service commission with a statement certifying that the appointee was "specially fitted by education, training or experience" for the position. If within thirty days the commission found the nominee to be qualified, it was to file with the city clerk a certificate of approval and the appointment became effective. Departmental heads were to be appointed for terms of four years. This executive responsibility was further increased by giving the mayor an absolute veto over all acts or ordinances of the council. No appropriations could be passed by the council except upon the mayor's recommendation. It could decrease or omit items in the budget, but could not increase any item or add new ones.[48]

Supplementing this executive financial control were provisions to eliminate the sources of extravagance uncovered by the finance commission. Public bids were required for all contracts amounting to $1,000 or more. The mayor could dispense with public advertisement only if the department head furnished him with a statement giving the reasons for not inviting public bidding. This provision was supplemented by one which made it illegal for a member of the council or city employee to make any contract with the city unless he notified the mayor in writing of the nature of the contract. In addition, municipal officials were not to exceed appropriations "except in case of extreme emergency involving the health and safety of the people or their property." Finally, the charter provided for a permanent finance commission. Appointed by the governor and independent of the city government, the commission would periodically investigate "any and all matters relating to appropriations, loans, expenditures, accounts, and methods of administration . . . and report . . . to the mayor, the city council the governor, or the general court."[49]

Given the opportunity, Boston progressives had done more than pinpoint fiscal inefficiency; they had overhauled the lines of power in municipal administration. Chicago followed a similar pattern. Drawing on earlier attempts to investigate the revenues of the city, Charles E. Merriam, professor of government at the University of Chicago and member of the city's board of aldermen, introduced a resolution in 1909 providing for the creation of an organization to investigate fiscal conditions. To the delight of reformers the resolution passed unanimously and in October the mayor appointed the Commission on City Expenditures. Composed of three members of the council, the comptroller, and seven leading businessmen, the commission looked into three areas: budget procedures, letting of contracts, and city payrolls. Out of their inquiry emerged new devices of administrative control in the city's government.[50]

Convinced that the key to fiscal efficiency lay in control of the budget, the commission ignored its intention to focus on one department and with the cooperation of city officials, particularly the mayor and comptroller, proceeded to revise the city's budget system. "It was put into force so quickly and so quietly," declared Merriam, "that nobody realized exactly what had happened." Like the budget procedures in New York and Boston, the new system provided for the groupings of expenditures of departments according to functions and the "segregating" of those functions according to expenses. There were accounts in the comptroller's office with corresponding code numbers, thus enabling the comptroller to keep an effective check on particular appropriations.[51] Together, these procedures were giving Chicago what Merriam described as the "most scientific and up-to-date budget which we have ever passed in our city."[52] In addition, there were changes in the letting of city contracts and the purchase of materials and supplies. After its investigation of various departments, the commission concluded that a "demoralizing condition" was evident throughout the government. Among the sources of this situation were defects in specifications, failure to secure wide competition from a number of bidders, and failure to enforce the terms of contracts due to "inefficiency of inspection or because of collusion with contractors." Provided with various proposals from the commission, the city adopted some changes which included expanding the staff of inspectors of the board of local improvement, revision of paving specifications, and the transfer of auditing bills in some departments to the comptroller's office.[53]

Behind this administrative organization lay the effort to eliminate machine partisanship from public office. To the chagrin of the commission, the appointments and promotions in various departments continued to be a question of political persuasion rather than individual qualifications. Meanwhile, there was little effort by the city's civil service commission to remove this image of public employment. Faced with this situation, the commission pressured the government into establishing an "efficiency division" within the civil service commission. During the next two years the division assisted departmental heads in installing improved methods of organization, devised a uniform scale of salaries based on efficiency records, introduced new accounting procedures for various departments, and helped prepare the city budget of 1911.[54]

These developments in Chicago mirrored the strategy and goals of the efficiency movement in general and fiscal reorganization in particular. For most political reformers, extravagance, corruption, and incompetence were less an outgrowth of personal avarice and loyalty and more a result of confusion and disorganization within areas of administrative authority. True, campaigns for efficient, economical government were often couched in the traditional rhetoric of a struggle between the forces of honesty and the "plunderers" of public treasuries. But fiscal responsibility in public affairs appeared to be determined mainly by the structure of local government and hence not to be attained by simply reforming the characters of men. Charles E. Merriam stated the case: "The three great sources of loss are outright graft or stealing, political favoritism, and lack of proper system. . . . We may say that . . . with a proper type of system, both political favoritism and theft would be made more difficult."[55]

This emphasis upon structural reform meant more efficiency in the collection of local revenues as well as in the spending of public funds. "The selection of local tax boards or assessors by popular vote has serious drawbacks," Judge Oscar Leser of Baltimore's appeal tax court told the National Tax Association in 1908, "among which may be mentioned the liability to political pressure, the greater danger of interrupted tenure, and the general evil effects of associating offices of this kind in the public mind with partisan politics. . . . The modern trend of opinion is toward a centralized control of administrative offices, and no good reason has been put forward why the tax department should be [an] exception."[56] More importantly, public taxation policy was being transformed in Northern cities and states. Fiscal officials, academic experts, and middle-class reform groups sought to modernize the tax system and develop various forms of income taxation as the main sources of governmental revenues. Their work included the separation of state and local revenues, appointment of assessors, extension of corporate taxation, use of personal income taxes, and centralization of administration at the state level.[57]

Some reformers, on the other hand, did not see fiscal reorganization as just a medium through which public administration became a tight businesslike operation serving primarily the interests of the middle classes. They also felt that new procedures of financial control would bring government closer to the needs of all urban residents. "The subversion of revenues, the taking of public goods or the theft of time and service which is paid for by the municipality is a direct loss to the weak rather than to the strong," wrote Professor Frederick A. Cleveland in 1908. "This is necessarily so for the reason that persons of wealth can protect themselves with wholesome food and wholesome surroundings. For these, persons less fortunately situated must depend upon governmental regulation and control. Their hope lies in efficient and the most painstaking care in the application of public resources to public use."[58] LeGrand Powers similarly told the National Municipal League in 1909 that the uniform budget was the "only possible basis of providing the people with advance knowledge concerning ... proposed financial transactions and their effect upon the interest and welfare of the masses."[59]

From this standpoint, economical government did not simply mean hacking budgets to the bone. Some prominent structuralists protested against the spirit of intolerance and narrow-minded economy in fiscal reform. Addressing the City Club of Philadelphia in 1910, Boston's Robert Treat Paine, Jr., told his audience that it was wrong to promote efficiency simply as a matter of lower expenses and taxes: "In our city, and in your city, the bulk of the people ... see that the expenditure of public money brings work and that it increases convenience and comforts. So we must look at the city as a whole from a social or community point of view if we as business men are going to win in the control of elections. We must put ourselves in the place of the humbler citizen." A director of the New York Bureau of Municipal Research likewise argued that property holders should "interpret waste and inefficiency in terms of deprivation of beneficial service" and added that the end of efficient government was to "advance the welfare of all the people of the city ... and not merely those who directly pay taxes."[60]

These sentiments revealed clashing viewpoints in political reform on the nature and aims of fiscal efficiency. One saw rational, nonpartisan financial procedures as the answer to spoils, wasteful budgeting, and padded contracts. This older view touched all sections of political progressivism. There was also the insistence upon more executive control of public expenditures to produce maximum returns for a minimum input of monetary resources. This notion appealed particularly to some administrative reformers, business groups, and taxpayers' associations.[61] Still another view was the conviction of young professionals in administration, accounting, and social work that fiscal policy should be adjusted to the needs and wants of the urban masses. Which of the three or what blend of the three would constitute the prime emphasis in progressive structural reform? The reconciliation of these positions meant a priority struggle between increased services and the cost of governmental operations.

Chapter VI

RESEARCH AND REFORM

> It is perhaps through the employment of a relatively
> small staff of independent, privately-supported ex-
> perts to scrutinize public administration, to set stan-
> dards and to provide continuous material for public
> opinion that democracy may hope most directly to
> acquire the permanent service of experts within the
> municipal departments.

Rufus E. Miles
"Municipal Research—A New Instrument of Democracy"
Proceedings of the Cincinnati Conference for Good City Government
(1909)

Fiscal reform, like the enforcement of civil service regulations, involved a basic restructuring of municipal administration. In the
process, erratic means of controlling expenditures were being
replaced by careful allocation of administrative powers and functions. Upper-income groups who had a stake in this development
shared what one historian has described as a "legal-rational"
culture as opposed to a "traditional" political culture. Those party bosses and their constituencies who shared the latter culture
were mainly concerned with the way civic policy affected individuals. There was thus little attempt to bureaucratize formal
decision-making, for this would interfere with the use of personal
influence in public affairs. Such values were not prevalent in the
legal-rational culture of structural progressivism. Rather, there
was greater concern with questions of bureaucratic efficiency and
innovative administration. This led to the demand for more
detailed and uniform planning in resource allocation and com-

munity programs. Related to these considerations was the belief
that persons with advanced training and experience should be
continually involved in the implementing of public policy, especially in the management of social welfare services.[1] Those
reform-minded professionals dedicated to this philosophy settled
upon the notion of "research" and proceeded to gather empirical
information on governmental machinery and city life. Such
material became the basis of programs designed to improve the
operations of local government and provide urban dwellers with
new and better services.

Most important in this stage of political progressivism was the
activity of the New York Bureau of Municipal Research. In
keeping with its contributions to fiscal reorganization, the
Bureau worked to redirect reform aims and strategy away from
changing the governing personalities toward learning how new
officials could govern cities more constructively. The success of
the Bureau requires some discussion of the agency's origins. After
earning a doctorate from the Wharton School of the University
of Pennsylvania under Simon Patten, William H. Allen worked
for the New Jersey State Charities Aid Association and came to
New York City in 1903 to serve as general agent for the Association for Improving the Condition of the Poor. Drawing on his
experiences with large-scale relief, Allen uncovered a correlation
between systematic records and humane and efficient charity
organizations. He suggested to R. Fulton Cutting, a prominent
financier and president of the Citizens' Union, the establishment
of a nonpartisan agency of experts that would "apply the dis-
interestedness of research, and the techniques of business
management, to public affairs and civic problems." Cutting persuaded his colleagues, Andrew Carnegie and John D.
Rockefeller, to help him in financing such an organization as part
of the Citizens' Union, and established the Bureau of City
Betterment in 1905.[2] Henry Bruere appeared to be the best person to manage the agency. After graduating from the University
of Chicago, Bruere went to Harvard Law School and became a
resident of Boston's Denison House. He often visited the settlement houses in Chicago and New York, and in 1903 he joined
the staff of the AICP. By 1905 Bruere had conducted several
studies on various municipal services. Allen picked him to direct
the new Bureau of City Betterment.[3]

Bruere's most dramatic project was the examination of the Manhattan Borough's office in charge of public works. His staff obtained sufficient material to show incompetence and waste in the office. Few city officials, however, were interested in the Bureau's evidence. Undeterred, the agency issued a report that would eventually end in the removal of the borough president from office. More important, this investigation brought considerable publicity to Bruere's organization. The Bureau joined forces with Mayor McClellan's Commission on Financial Administration and Accounting in investigating the city's confused business records. Bruere worked closely with Frederick A. Cleveland, who headed the commission. Their relationship led to a memorandum drafted by Cleveland for the organization of an independent "bureau of municipal research." Upon receiving the document, William Allen wrote letters to several leading business and professional men in which he asked their opinion as to the need of such an organization. They endorsed the proposed agency and agreed to help support it. The Bureau of Municipal Research emerged in 1907, financed mostly by Cutting, Carnegie, and Rockefeller.[4] Among the original trustees were Cutting; Richard Watson Gilder, editor of the *Century Magazine;* Carroll D. Wright, former U.S. Labor Commissioner; editor Albert Shaw; and E.R.A. Seligman, the prominent economist at Columbia University. Allen, Bruere, and Cleveland served as the bureau's directors and undertook to "promote scientific methods of accounting and reporting the details of municipal business, with a view to facilitating the work of public officials."[5]

While dedicated to the economical administration of city government, the men of the Bureau of Municipal Research, unlike earlier urban reformers, did not equate efficiency with economy. The bureau defined efficient government in a broader context to include the maximum utilization of all administrative resources. It therefore sought to quantify efficiency by gathering and interpreting "facts" on how a department or office functioned as opposed to what its officers stated. "Although good men and good intentions are in the majority, desire for good government is ineffective for want of information as to the actual methods and results of government," announced the bureau in 1907. "Even leaders in philanthropy have failed to see that inefficient municipal government can cause more wretchedness, sickness and incapacity in one year than beneficence can alleviate in ten years."[6] Bureau directors intended their agency to employ a staff of specialists to promote administrative reform. They would help develop the full potential of city management and provide top officials with information on how their departments might operate more effectively.[7]

These principles of the Bureau gained official recognition with the removal of Manhattan Borough president Ahearn from office. Enraged by the charges of Henry Bruere and his staff that he was an incompetent and wasteful administrator, Ahearn asked Mayor McClellan to investigate the allegations. He ordered William B. Ellison, the city's corporation counsel, to conduct an inquiry and he in turn appointed John Purroy Mitchel, a young reform lawyer, as special counsel. Delighted with the opportunity to acquire more legal experience, Mitchel spearheaded the investigation and was appointed a commissioner in the office of the commissioners of accounts. With the help of several accountants, engineers, and other specialized professionals, he confirmed the charges against Ahearn and with Bruere's aid wrote a report condemning the borough president's administration for its waste and inefficiency. Governor Charles Evans Hughes, after a series of public hearings, removed Ahearn from office.[8] This was the first time that a leading New York official was dismissed from office for mismanagement without evidence of dishonesty. The Bureau proudly proclaimed in 1907 that American cities had "discovered a direct and effective way of securing administrative publicity and of promoting administrative efficiency."[9]

Closer to the mainstream of structural progressivism was the Bureau's emphasis on the corporation as the model for bureaucratic reorganization. It assumed that the technical side of running a government could be analyzed and developed on a factual basis in the same way as a business.[10] But this did not mean that business was inherently more efficient than government. In the Bureau's opinion there was little evidence for accepting the assumption that there was something about the term "private" that resulted in responsibility and efficiency, while the term "public" implied mismanagement and waste. The city deserved something "better" than business had, since many capitalist ventures failed "for want of efficiency."[11] Bureau spokesmen, reflecting the newer tendencies in corporate thought and practice, recommended the application of the philosophy of scientific management to municipal administration. Developed by Frederick W. Taylor and introduced by his followers into various manufacturing firms, scientific management included specialization, planning, quantitative measurement, and standardization. These concepts added up to "efficiency," which largely meant the maximization of output for a given input. In the Bureau's program, the governmental counterpart of this work-efficiency was the reorganization of offices based on accurate data and rationalization of operations to carry out specific policies. Bureau men particularly emphasized "statistical method" as the key to governmental reconstruction. This involved the comparison and classification of various activities in municipal departments and agencies.[12]

While drawing upon the ideas of scientific management, however, the Bureau adopted a different perspective. True, there was continual interchange of views and people between the two movements. But to see the Bureau's principles as mainly an offshoot of Taylorism is to overlook the crucial fact that municipal research was another important stage in the evolution of governmental efficiency. Indeed, urban political reformers had talked about efficiency long before the appearance of scientific management. More importantly, there was a key difference in the strategies of both movements. In pressing for more rational decision-making in the factory, Taylor and his disciples assumed that what was good in the corporate world was good for society as a whole. But there was little suggestion in their work that efficiency experts had an "outside" role in directing supervision and production, except through the workings of the marketplace. The Bureau of Municipal Research proceeded on different grounds. It operated as an independent agency to permit individual citizens to tell with some accuracy what was going on in city departments.[13] "There is one thing ... about our major premise which is new in New York," William H. Allen told the City Club of Chicago in 1908, "and that is the assumption that the great problem in municipal government is not to stop graft, is not to head off the politician, and not to get good men into office, but rather to keep the public informed of what public officials are doing.... So it is our very first and our exclusive motive, in the Bureau of Municipal Research, to bring about a method of talking about government and a method of government that will keep you and me currently informed as to what our community needs."[14]

From this standpoint, fiscal reform became much more than a cold statement of facts or a control on corrupt politicians. In the Bureau's eyes it was also the medium through which progressives could advance social betterment. To be sure, fiscal reform was essentially seen as the means to run government in accordance with middle-class notions of economy and efficiency. But the Bureau also felt that it could awaken citizens to the reality that governmental efficiency closely affected their welfare. The Bureau therefore focused on publicizing the budget and stressing its connection with the lives of all residents of New York.[15] In 1908 it sponsored the first budget exhibit in the United States. Civic groups, taxpayers' associations, and municipal departments contributed material relating to public expenditures and their effect on the economic and social conditions in the city. During the exhibit the Bureau pointed to needless expenditures and argued that this extravagance reduced amounts available for such basic services as education, health, and recreation. Taxpayers' groups saw this waste as simply an obstruction to economical government, whereas charity and philanthropic organizations suggested alternative channels for the revenues. Meanwhile some city departments used the exhibit as a means for advertising their services and securing more appropriations. Though the public could expect little immediate benefit from the exhibit, it did gain from the display of government operations. City administration appeared not to be a mysterious matter but could be observed and understood. The project drew about 50,000 citizens from various areas of the metropolis.[16] By 1911, the government had assumed responsibility for publicizing the budgetary process. More than two million people attended the municipal budget exhibits in this period. The resultant publicity helped some departments, particularly the health department, secure larger appropriations.[17]

In conjunction with these developments, the Bureau of Municipal Research pressed for more efficient administration.

We have seen its impact on the government in helping the finance department install new fiscal procedures from 1907 to 1909. Another avenue of influence in this period was the office of the commissioners of accounts. Commissioner John Purroy Mitchel invited the Bureau to study the office to discover ways of making it more capable to examine city agencies and departments. After a detailed investigation it recommended the establishment of uniform accounts, cost and efficiency records, time sheets, a technical staff, and an engineering bureau.[18] It also expressed displeasure with the city's civil service system and with the performance of public employees. It pointed out that there was too much emphasis on keeping undesirables out of appointive positions and not enough concern with maintaining efficiency standards for city employees; as a result, civil service procedures proved inadequate in relation to functional shifts among administrative personnel and the removal of incompetent municipal workers. Henry Bruere noted that civil service reformers were "more intent on competition before appointment than upon performance after appointment."[19] Without proper records of employee service, the merit system lacked rational procedures to determine fitness for promotion. Employee service records and comparison time reports, however, could stimulate municipal employees to work more efficiently. The bureau pressured the civil service commission into installing efficiency records and time sheets which served as more reliable bases of promotion as well as removal.[20]

Complementing these tangible achievements was the use of the survey method for determining facts in civic management regarding community services. Luther Gulick recalled that "survey" was used as a term because it "conveyed the idea of the inclusive, objective, and scientific approach which the Bureau applied to its work."[21] Particularly significant were the investigations of the city's public school system. Alarmed at the steady growth of the school budget, the Bureau demanded that cost accounting controls be enforced in the department of education.[22] More comprehensive were the surveys of general city administration. The Bureau of Municipal Research felt that other urban problems could not be resolved until there was a marked improvement in the government's methods of operation. With the cooperation of various officials the bureau staff obtained data relative to revenues, budget making, accounting and auditing, public works, and the police, fire, and other operating departments. After a close examination of the data they submitted suggestions for changes in administrative organization and met with the heads of departments to discuss the merits of their program. In the process municipal research became another crucial link between reform-minded officials and upper-middle-class elites outside local government. When party-minded personnel were unwilling to implement the proposals, the Bureau often released its findings to the public in the hope that popular pressure would bring about more competent government.[23]

To the chagrin of the Bureau, considerations of efficiency lent substance to the growing suspicion that the organization functioned within a range of limited goals, particularly with its emphasis on regulating municipal expenditures. Giving considerable credence to this belief was the uncomfortable fact that it was greatly dependent upon the support of leading businessmen. Consequently, the Bureau sought to remove the image of a tight-fisted, business-minded organization. In 1909 R. Fulton Cutting declared that the Bureau was not "setting up retrenchment for retrenchment's sake as its ideal," but was seeking to "prevent waste in municipal administration only in order that funds available for social betterment be increased."[24] "The government research movement was not a penny-saving or penny-pinching proposition at all," William Allen recalled.[25]

In the context of municipal research efficiency was not simply a question of rationalizing the processes of government. Rather, it could also be the key to an expansion and improvement of public services. In conjunction with the reorganization of fiscal practices, the Bureau, purporting to be a team of investigators with a "constructive social point of view," focused on questions of social welfare. It campaigned for free medical inspection in schools and helped establish the bureau of child hygiene in the department of health. It insisted that the health department centralize its inspection procedures, especially in municipal markets, and abolish the unsanitary practices of slaughterhouses. It asked that the tenement department intensify its campaign against violations of housing regulations. By 1911 the Bureau of

Municipal Research had issued several bulletins which described economic and social conditions in the city.[26]

Behind this concern for the well-being of the masses was the conviction that reformers could no longer rely on philanthropy as the panacea for municipal problems. William Allen informed editor Albert Shaw in 1908 that philanthropy was "being un-necessarily taxed and obstructed" because of "inefficient municipal government." Two years later, R.F. Cutting suggested that the wealthy could best alleviate suffering and end "criminal injustice to the poor" by redirecting their generosity to the Bureau of Municipal Research. Both looked forward to sub-stituting for a system of private charity an enlightened and in-novative government committed to a broad program of social reform.[27] Henry Bruere pointed out that municipal research was rooted in an effort to develop the "potential forces" of city ad-ministration for "social betterment" because of the "conviction that only through efficient government could progressive social welfare be achieved," since private efforts to "remove social han-dicaps" were a "hopeless task."[28]

For those top officials who interpreted efficiency in terms of social control, this precocious image of a welfare state was not the main factor attracting them to municipal research. They looked with approval upon the Bureau because it invariably recommended increasing the power of administrative authorities, supplying them with more information, and tightening up the lines of control within their bailiwicks. The Bureau lent members of its staff to various departments and agencies to assist in reorganization. As a reflection of this mutual cooperation, bureaus of efficiency appeared in some departments. Further, ad-ministrative officers often selected committees to meet with representatives of the Bureau to discuss questions of both policy and procedure. Even Tammany officials displayed a surprising friendliness. Asked by boss Charles Murphy about his attitude toward the Bureau, one Tammany official told him: "Those peo-ple have the right to the facts. They know fact from a guess when they see it and apparently they have enough money to keep themselves alive until they get the facts."[29]

In their efforts to redefine and restructure the concepts of efficient government, the Bureau was moving to the front ranks of urban political progressivism. Particularly significant for the *New York Times* was the effort to "substitute knowledge for indignation as the force" in municipal reform. In 1908 the *Boston Herald* lauded the Bureau for its "constructive criticism rather than hit or miss denunciation," and a leading newspaper in Cleveland noted that the Bureau was not "content with pointing out evils and deficiencies" — "along with the diagnosis a remedy is suggested." The *Chicago Tribune* felt that the Bureau was "helping untrained democracy to become efficient." Pointing to the municipal governments' "habit" of hiding "their extravagance and inefficiencies," the *Los Angeles Examiner* looked upon municipal research in 1909 as "a very good idea."[30]

Provided with such widespread publicity, the Bureau became a model for reformers in other cities. Requests poured into New York and by 1913 the Bureau had conducted studies in more than fifteen municipalities. Considered first as a temporary departure and despite a feeling that expansion would divert resources from work in New York, the Bureau's "outside" activities became a permanent function and provided a substantial source of income.[31] Although the Bureau did not initiate the trend toward efficiency in municipal government, its work lent further dimension and direction to the movement.

Impressed with the Bureau's influence in New York, a committee of businessmen in Philadelphia asked in 1908 for assistance in establishing a similar organization. After a preliminary visit by Allen, a number of Quaker City citizens came to New York and were entertained at a dinner by R.F. Cutting. Following this soirée and a number of more formal meetings, the Philadelphians pledged $12,000 for a six-month period and the Bureau proceeded to organize an institution for municipal research for their city in November 1908. Under the direction of Bruere and staffed largely with people from the Bureau in New York, the Philadelphia Bureau sought access to the offices in city hall. Suspicious of its intentions, Mayor Reyburn refused to cooperate with the new organization. By the end of six months, however, the Bureau had enlisted support from the city's board of trade, chamber of commerce, and manufacturers' association. Provided with a guarantee that two trustees of the Bureau would come from each of these three organizations, businessmen in Philadelphia pledged $25,000 per annum for the next five years, and in 1909 the organization became a separate entity.[32] Like its parent in New York, the Philadelphia Bureau of Municipal Research bore little resemblance to a social organization. Instead, there was a paid staff of engineers, accountants, statisticians, and administrators, most of whom worked full time for the Bureau. Seeing itself as a "non-partisan, scientific agency of citizen inquiry," the Bureau undertook to promote governmental efficiency through the adoption of "business methods" and proposed to "collect, classify, and interpret the facts regarding the powers, duties, limitations and administrative problems" of the city government.[33]

Behind these objectives lay the Bureau's conviction that efficient government should be based upon "adequate knowledge and consideration of community needs." It investigated and gathered data on social and economic conditions in the city. Drawing on the Bureau's survey of public education and subsequent recommendations, the board of education introduced special schools, reorganized the department of school supplies, and prepared a complete digest of laws and regulations pertaining to public education. Meanwhile, an exhaustive study of milk inspection resulted in the establishment of a commission which adopted the Bureau's proposals for complete revision of milk regulations and a reorganization of inspection procedure. After an investigation of Philadelphia General Hospital, the Bureau recommended a modernization of procedure and the hospital authorities adopted new techniques such as stores control and standardization of specifications. In cooperation with the University of Pennsylvania, it surveyed the conditions under which foodstuffs were sold in the city and in 1911 devised new controls for the city's handling of foods.[34]

Complementing these reforms were proposals to improve the operations and performance of city departments. The Bureau introduced efficiency records into the police department as a basis for promotion and discipline and brought about the establishment of a school of instruction in the bureau of fires. With the assistance of the director of the department of supplies, it introduced a system of centralized purchasing and formulated standard specifications for supplies bought by the city.[35] Witnessing this impressive program, the comptroller felt that new fiscal procedures were needed and invited the Bureau to revise the city's accounting system. The accounting methods of the municipal departments were merely records of cash transactions, and the assets other than cash belonging to the city were not under systematic record or control. Bureau men quickly introduced into the comptroller's office a general ledger designed to show the city's assets and liabilities, revenues and expenses, set aside for contracts. In addition, there were separate balance sheets indicating assets and liabilities which were applied to the city's current operations and the acquisition of permanent properties. By 1913 this system was extended to all departments of the city government and current transactions of the departments were under central accounting control.[36]

In conjunction with these innovations, there was the effort to replace, as one reformer described it, "the old grab-bag planless budget with one along more modern scientific lines." Like their counterparts in other cities, the heads of departments in Philadelphia submitted their estimates without any control or review by a responsible authority. During the period from 1912 to 1915 the Bureau and officials in the comptroller's office prepared a uniform classification and systematic budget program. In the new system there were requests of each department according to general functions and a detailed account of past and present expenditures. One leading newspaper noted that such procedures, coupled with a new accounting system, were helping to "remove" the strain of blundering inefficiency . . . fastened upon Philadelphia by amateur accountants and crooked politicians."[37]

Paralleling this thrust for more responsive government in Philadelphia was the work of political reformers in Cincinnati. In 1909 members of the Commercial Club, Business Men's Club, and chamber of commerce subscribed funds to set up the Cincinnati Bureau of Municipal Research. To direct the new organization, its board of trustees brought in Rufus E. Miles, formerly of the New York Bureau, and recruited a team of "experts" from the University of Cincinnati.[38] Like the organizations in New York and Philadelphia, the Bureau was "spawned by the civic organizations' passion for facts, their confidence in the ability of experts to accumulate and interpret correctly those facts, and their faith in the competence of a properly informed and educated public to act on this information in the interest of efficient public service."[39] The Bureau focused upon fiscal reorganization as the key to efficient government. In 1910 the Bureau drafted an ordinance which regulated the deposit of city funds and devised and helped install accounting systems in a number of departments. Drawing on proposals from the Bureau, the mayor's efficiency bureau prepared a uniform expense classification for all departments and introduced a plan for the standardization of salaries. The Bureau assisted the city's auditor in the reorganization of the purchasing methods of the city. Finally, with the cooperation of officials, it prepared five annual appropriation ordinances and also drafted the budget for Cincinnati in 1913 and 1914.[40]

As in New York, Philadelphia, and Cincinnati, considerations of economy were shaping the structure of municipal research in Chicago. In 1909 the city council, as we have seen, had appointed a commission to investigate public expenditures. After the investigation members of the commission noted that a number of "local jurisdictions" escaped examination. Confronted with this situation, the City Club seized upon the idea of a research bureau to continue and expand the program of the commission. "Inasmuch as its sole purpose is to aid in establishing sound business principles in the administration of our local government," said a spokesman, "it is confidently expected that the Bureau will appeal strongly to the businessmen of the community.[41] Easily persuaded by such logic, a group of wealthy Chicagoans pledged financial support and the City Club established the Bureau of Public Efficiency in August 1910. Composed of prominent business and professional people, the Bureau's board of trustees picked Herbert Sands to direct the program of the new organization. Sands reached into the ranks of the New York agency for investigators and recruited experts from business and government in Chicago.[42]

Designed to be an agency for the "rigid scrutiny of all the complicated schemes of local government," the bureau narrowed its perspective in the hope that better results would come from focusing upon specific problems. Finding the park governments to be "inefficient," it emphasized the need for consolidating them. Provided by the Bureau with data on the expenses of offices under their jurisdiction, the judges of the circuit court reduced the number of employees in these offices. Following the disclosures in 1912 and 1913 of losses in interest on funds handled in the county treasurer's office, newly elected officials agreed to keep books and records which would be open to public inspection. Two years later the Bureau published a report which showed that inefficiency was largely a consequence of the multiplicity of overlapping taxing bodies with many elective officers.[43] Delighted with the numerous requests for its report, the Bureau exuded confidence: "The publicity which the Bureau investigations have given to many defects in governmental organization and administration should ultimately bring about fundamental changes in conditions which will result in enormous savings and much better service to the public."[44]

Few political reformers in Milwaukee would have quarreled with these expectations; indeed, their city was the first one to have a research bureau supported by the municipal government. In 1910 the Social Democratic party captured the mayoralty and other leading positions in the city's government. Convinced that municipalities as well as corporations should have expert assistance, the Socialist administration organized the Bureau of Economy and Efficiency and called upon Professor John Rogers Commons to direct its work.[45] In the period from 1900 to 1906 Commons, along with other notables from the University of Wisconsin, held important administrative posts in the reform administrations of Governor Robert M. LaFollette. By the time he came to Milwaukee he was a leading advocate of the "Wisconsin Idea," which stressed the contributions of academic expertise to scientific management of government and public services.[46] Drawing on the skills of men from business, the professions, and the university, the Milwaukee Bureau minimized the distinction between the "expert" and the "reformer" and enlisted both in the service of the government. Serving the Bureau as consultants were Harrington Emerson, efficiency engineer from New York, and Charles Hine, organization expert of the Harrison Railroad Lines. Among its academic personnel were three deans from the University of Wisconsin, the head of the Department of Public Health at the Massachusetts Institute of Technology, and an authority on public finance from Wisconsin. These "consulting experts" organized a staff composed of accountants, economists, engineers, and administrators. Backed by their approval, the directors of the Bureau, as Commons pointed out, "could confidently recommend and publish the findings of the staff."[47]

From the outset, the Milwaukee Bureau looked upon municipal government as a social corporation designed to promote the "health, welfare and prosperity" of its inhabitants. It sought to measure efficiency in reference to an expanding program of community services. "If the city wastes its resources in one direction by bad organization and poor economy," declared the Bureau in 1911, "the effect is seen at some other point in the misfortune, ill health or economic handicap of its citizens. The social investigation is directed toward discovering these points in order that the efficiency investigation may find remedies for them."[48] Provided with additional funds and assistance from various civic organizations, the Bureau gathered data on housing conditions, infant mortality, milk supply, unemployment, and public health. At the same time it investigated the departments of health, water, and public works and found all of them to be "unbusiness-like, wasteful and inefficient." By 1912 the common council was enacting many of the Bureau's recommendations into law and city officials were reorganizing departments, installing techniques of cost accounting, and introducing segregated budgets. With special concern for public health, the council adopted a program which included improved sanitary facilities and inspection in the city's factories, improved resources for isolating contagious diseases, new standards in milk supply, and municipal backing for the campaign against infant mortality.[49]

Returning to office in April 1912, a bipartisan government of independent Democrats and Republicans moved to abolish the Bureau of Economy and Efficiency. By this time, however, the idea of municipal research was entrenched in the political system. Faced with this situation, the new administration scrapped the Bureau and replaced it with an organization called the Bureau of Municipal Research.[50] Writing to reformer Morris L. Cooke in 1914, Frederick Taylor related a conversation with Commons in which the Wisconsin professor informed him that "wonderful economies" still prevailed in the city in spite of the "gang . . . . now back in power."[51] In the same year Randolph Bourne, the noted reform journalist from New York, described his impressions of Milwaukee: "Social service loses its hectic, priggish note here. It's been worked into the life. A hard-headed Socialist administration of practical idealists and efficient Laborites gave a tone to the place."[52]

Behind these statements lay the disturbing ambivalence in political reform in general and municipal research in particular. Initially defined in terms of economical government, the movement was largely an effort to reorganize fiscal authority along the lines of the corporation. In fact, the bureaus were being financed and maintained by the dominant elements of the business community. By providing government with proper systems of accounting and budgeting, the bureaus were encouraging and maintaining centralized government. To business groups this process was most important in terms of political influence. Confronted with the complexities and decentralized structure of party government as expressed in machine politics, they were often hampered in their efforts to bring about concerted implementation of their programs. The pursuit of fiscal efficiency constituted an accommodation of the strategy and goals of middle-class elites in government with political values and trends in corporate and professional life.

Linked with this development was the emphasis upon "social efficiency." In their conviction that the broad programs demanded by the bureaus would make for greater efficiency and perhaps lessen class antagonisms, business leaders were being led in the direction of increased planning and even toward social reform. By 1912 the efficiency movement appeared to be separating along two paths: while businessmen continued to use the language of the budget and social control, the research agencies were talking more in terms of economic fairness and social welfare. The New York Bureau of Municipal Research reported in 1911 that its program for city departments had "both the moral and financial support of the poor, whose health and education and earning power suffer from misgovernment, as much and more than the rich man's pocketbook."[53] George McAneny, a trustee of the Bureau and president of the Manhattan Borough, argued in a similar vein before a Yale University audience. "The relief of the poor was an official function long before our industrial era began, and some of our other public benevolence may be traced to an equally early origin," McAneny declared. "The differences in our present-day practice are differences of form only. We are bent on reducing the volume of misery or dependency in the city through a correction, so far as possible, of the conditions that breed misery."[54]

This effort, however, did not imply a radical redistribution of economic power in the city. Meyer Lissner, a wealthy lawyer and leader of political reform in Los Angeles, wrote in 1911: "No matter how much artificial conservatism we [Progressives] may assume, our natural tendency toward radicalism will produce enough results to satisfy our own people and thoroughly justify the movement." Theodore Roosevelt similarly told Charles D. Willard, editor of the reformist *California Outlook*, in 1912 that social and economic reform necessitated a "steady, healthy, progressive movement, at once resolute and temperate."[55] The political progressives sought to achieve a balance among interest groups without arousing class tensions and to advance the welfare of the entire community. One student of Los Angeles reform has described the situation: "Some progressives, both within and without Los Angeles, advised their fellows that the way to alleviate if not eliminate class stratification was not to ignore the existence of classes but to propose and carry into effect measures that would make the city more nearly a social and economic as well as a political democracy."[56]

In this context, the notion of public interest among urban progressives was not simply a function of what two authorities on American city government describe as the expression of a "middle-class ethos" of public policy as opposed to an "immigrant ethos" of interest-group politics.[57] It was also growing out of an increasing demand of all classes for more social programs and the efforts of structural reformers to provide the institutional basis for these services. The task before them was the synthesizing of the traditional emphasis on economical government with social efficiency. But this was a problem for which there was no ready solution. Viewed in terms of fiscal reform, efficiency played somewhat the same role in government and business in attempting to maximize the attainment of certain ends with the use of limited resources. In this context it was usually seen as a "neutral" element defined in units of time or monetary costs. From the standpoint of social reform, however, efficiency appeared to involve the substitution of human costs in public administration for money value of output as a measure of values underlying the growth of public services. But, given the anti-political bias of governmental efficiency, there was little chance that the values which these services were expected to further would also be the criteria underlying specific decisional problems. On the other hand, the substitution of "value-indices" for the values themselves could ultimately result in the ends of social efficiency being sacrificed for the familiar campaign to acquire more political power through structural innovations.[58] In both situations the reformers, in their efforts in behalf of public welfare, were carrying an approach rather than a solution.

Against this background, the municipal expert emerged as the central figure in political progressivism. To business elites efficiency meant a safer, cleaner, and more economically managed community. For the professionals manning research bureaus, it promised the continual improvement of city administration and an ever widening range of social services. Trained civil servants could show the way for both groups of structural reformers. "We are gradually learning that municipal government is a complex matter, and that we need men who are not only honest, but competent," Clinton R. Woodruff told a gathering of the National Civil Service Reform League in 1911. "I can easily recall the time when honesty was the sole platform of reform campaigns. Now honesty may be taken for granted; and efficiency is the demand of the enlightened progressive."[59] William Dudley Foulke, president of the National Municipal League, spoke more precisely: "It is not the politicians, not even the people at large who have initiated the great modern improvements in city governments, but experts, sanitary and civil engineers, architects and landscape gardeners, bacteriologists, physicians, educators, and philanthropists. No city can hope to stand high in municipal progress unless it secures the best expert service for its municipal work."[60]

Most political reformers agreed. In the belief that public affairs should be managed in accordance with principles of community interest apart from machine politics, they objected to the bosses' penchant for filling various appointive offices with well-intended but unskilled party followers. This objection, however, reflected a basic structural similarity of attitude toward the distribution of power. Both party machines and the efficiency-minded bureaucracies of reform governments furnished disciplined hierarchies of authority and sought greater influence over functional areas of policy making. Still, standards and practices in many city administrations remained inadequate as a result of supervision by ill-trained, partially qualified bureaucrats. "The supposed expert administrator[s], for the most part," reported Boston's Richard Henry Dana III to the National Municipal League in 1909, "are men without the necessary education, training, or experience, whose chief bringing-up has too frequently been in the saloons and ward politics."[61]

Mrs. E.H. Harriman offered a remedy to this situation. On various trips to Europe Mrs. Harriman, whose famous husband had been a generous supporter of municipal research, closely observed public employment in countries such as England and France and was quite impressed with the professionalism in the civil service. After several American universities rejected her proposal to endow a school of public service to train government experts, she turned to the New York Bureau of Municipal Research for assistance. It proceeded to organize the Training School for Public Service in 1912. Charles A. Beard, noted history professor at Columbia University, Luther Gulick, an administrative expert, and W.H. Baker, widely experienced in charity work, served as directors.[62] They shared the conviction of other structuralists that local civil service commissions cared little about how well public executives were trained in the administration of civic services.[63]

This perspective of the school was indicative of the changing outlook of professionals in city planning. Since the 1890s civil engineers, landscape architects, social workers, and other experts had worked to impose land-use and other public controls over the urban physical environment, where few had existed previously. Their activity included the establishment of tenement-house regulations, rearrangement of buildings and streets, development of open areas and parks, and extension of landscaping and beautification throughout the metropolis. By the second decade of the twentieth century, professional planners were adopting the philosophy of the governmental efficiency movement. In so do-

ing they became more preoccupied with various technical
matters relating to law, finance, capital expenses, zoning, and
transportation.[64]

Similar concerns motivated students in the Training School.
Most of them had previous experience in city government and
enrolled to prepare for top-level administrative positions. The
school stressed technical competence and made books on scientific management required reading. More importantly, it devoted
attention to the relationship between public service and the fields
of political science, engineering, law, sociology, finance, school
administration, and public hygiene. Through classroom instruction supplemented by work in municipal departments, students
could keep in "touch with the efficiency movement in both
public and private business." Graduates of the school would then
serve as combination technicians and reformers to fill the growing need for expertise in local government and civic organizations
that worked closely with municipal officials.[65]

"The full meaning of scientific management," declared
Frederick A. Cleveland in 1911, "is comprehended in the word
'planning' and in the phrase 'the execution of plans.'"[66] Martin
H. Ray went from the Training School to the Philadelphia
Bureau of Municipal Research to help apply efficiency methods
to the buildings, fire, and police departments. His work resulted
in a comprehensive reorganization of the police department, the
removal of several partisan incompetents, and the establishment
of recruiting schools for policemen and firemen. Other students
conducted surveys of the health departments and public schools
in several Eastern cities. By 1914 graduates of the Training
School had obtained positions in municipal departments,
chambers of commerce, public education associations, city clubs,
and research bureaus throughout the country.[67]

Complementing this progress was the expanded program of
the Bureau of Municipal Research. Henry Bruere recalled: "We
would go to different cities either for the purpose of addressing
meetings and sitting down in conference with business men and
other civic leaders, or to conduct a survey at the expense of a local
group."[68] In 1911 Meyer Lissner, describing Los Angeles as
"about as progressive a community as there is in the United
States," invited the Bureau to make a study of the city's

governmental structure.[69] After a thorough examination the Bureau pointed out that inadequate controls stemmed from a decentralized accounting system, lack of department efficiency records, and little job standardization. This information led to the passage of a city ordinance which created an efficiency commission in 1913 to assist top officials in administrative reform.[70]

Similar services were exported to other cities. The Bureau advised the governments of Springfield, Massachusetts, and Dayton, Ohio, on public health programs. It examined the public works of Newark, New Jersey, and Grand Rapids, Michigan. It aided officials in Pittsburgh, St. Paul, and Portland (Oregon) in establishing new accounting and budget procedures. The Bureau also conducted educational surveys in Schenectady and Milwaukee. By the end of 1914 departmental operations and services in city after city were being modernized through the advice and expertise of the New York agency and other research bureaus.[71]

This extensive reform, however, could not permanently insulate civic management from partisan influence and informal networks of power within city politics. Most municipal researchers underestimated the ability of political bosses to extend lines of interest into restructured departments and offices. Furthermore, they overlooked the potential for dissension between department authorities and subordinate employees over duties, policy, and goals. In public school governance, for example, structural reorganization offered no lasting relief from old-style machine politics and intrabureaucratic conflict.[72] Administrative reform counted heavily, however. The research agencies had contributed considerably to the transformation of the moral precept of honest government into the scientific notion of efficient business management. Civic morality was now being measured according to more precise standards of bureaucratic efficiency.[73] In this environment, trained professionals and reform-minded officials extended the rationalization of government functions, introduced more professionalism into public administration, and established new social-welfare agencies and regulations. Together, these structural reforms enabled both inner-city ethnic groups and suburban middle classes to exert more effective pressure on municipal officials without the con-

tinual intervention of party leaders. Whether the form of government to which they gained access could remain more responsive
to them than the local machine depended mainly on the loyalties
and values of civil servants at all levels of city administration.

Chapter VII

THE BUSINESSMAN AS ADMINISTRATOR

> No improvement in the form of American city
> government can remedy the existing abuses and evils,
> unless the change of form be accompanied by the
> selection of a different sort of man to conduct the
> new government.
> Charles W. Eliot
> "City Government by Fewer Men"
> *World's Work*, 14 (1907): 9425

In the evolution of municipal research, businessmen, while financing the bureaus, preferred to stay on the sidelines and let the "professional" reformers carry the banner of governmental efficiency. Because of the existence of many subcommunities in the metropolis, it was difficult for them to sustain campaigns involving city-wide action. Consequently, they had to rest content with research bureaus and other civic organizations through which they could exert influence from outside government. But in the smaller cities businessmen could exercise considerably more influence. Here their close ties enabled them to develop strategies from which they could assume direct control over both the formulation and execution of public policy. In no area was this process more evident than in the movement for commission government.

Before the advent of the commission system, many political reformers in journalism and the professions shared the complaints of mayors such as Hazen S. Pingree and Tom L. Johnson about the passivity and often hostility of various business groups to changing drastically the lines of political power in urban society. In their eyes this was a consequence of a system of graft involving personal arrangements between businessmen and professional politicians.[1] But this view distorted the "politics" of corruption. Like their counterparts in large cities, businessmen in smaller municipalities were being denied easy access to the machinery of government and often forced to accept other procedures through which they could exercise formal power. "Unless there is a boss," wrote Henry Jones Ford, "government lacks consistency and purpose; there are no settled conditions upon which enterprise can rest; no competent authority with which business interests can negotiate."[2] In this context, the machines provided the best avenue to economic advancement and public recognition for many elements in the business community. Consequently, the relationship of businessmen to local government became a set of institutional accommodations between business groups and party bosses.[3]

By the late 1800s, however, this political system was being challenged in the large cities by an executive-centered coalition devoted to efficient administration and an economical program of public services. Similar developments were taking place in small and medium-sized localities. Confronted with the growing importance of the public functions of the city, business groups sought a broad program of continuous services that would be inexpensive. Despite the logic of this goal, they found themselves competing with the professional politician's conception of municipal policy that tended to be extravagant, sometimes wasteful, and generally uncertain.[4] In their search for alternatives to this situation, business leaders seized upon the commission plan.

Commission government first emerged out of the currents of political reform in Galveston, Texas. Desiring more efficient management of local affairs, representatives of leading commercial and professional interests formed the Good Government Club in 1894 to elect qualified businessmen to office. Charter revision provided the opportunity. A joint committee of the city council and chamber of commerce, backed by the Good Government Club, sent a new charter amendment to the state legislature and it was approved in 1895. The amendment replaced the election of aldermen by wards with a twelve-man council to the selected from the city at large. This system enabled the Good Government forces to elect a majority to the council. In the elections of 1897 and 1899 candidates of the Citizens' Club, which had succeeded the Good Government organization, gained seats in the legislature. This sequence of victories, however, did not bring business dominance of the government. Shortly after assuming office in 1899, six members of the council joined with Mayor Robert C. Jones to oppose the Citizens' Club aldermen. In the face of this opposition the club attacked the seven-man majority for partisanship and inefficient administration. Galveston businessmen saw these conditions as the breakdown of responsible leadership and vowed to gain full control of the municipal government. Their opportunity came quickly.[5]

In September of 1900 a hurricane and tidal wave virtually demolished Galveston. The council could not cope with the disaster and resigned from office. In the emergency, the Deepwater Committee, an organization of leading bankers and corporation officials, devised a plan for new city administration capable of quickly rebuilding the town. The committee introduced a charter bill before the state legislature which proposed that the governor appoint five men to manage the city. Encountering support for the measure from all social classes in Galveston, the legislature approved the bill in April 1901. The new plan provided for a five-man commission, with three of its members appointed by the governor and two elected within the city. Each commissioner headed a municipal department, and together they served as the policy-making council. The commission assumed both legislative and executive powers.[6]

Inheriting a bankrupt Galveston, the commission accomplished much more at less expense than its predecessor. By 1904 the city had been entirely rebuilt. In this period the commission collected back taxes which had remained unpaid, secured interest on city moneys in various banks, and reduced departmental expenses. This fiscal program provided the government with the bulk of money for vital projects such as the building of a giant sea-wall, new bridges and sewers, and the raising the grade of the city.[7] The achievement of these improvements, however, ended the state of emergency in Galveston. The Texas courts declared in 1903 that the appointment of commissioners was unconstitutional. The legislature proceeded to approve charter amendments providing for the election of all five commissioners.[8]

Galveston's success with the commission plan soon attracted

considerable attention. It appeared that a city could function under the new reform as essentially an administrative machine with few conflicts of interest. In Houston, business leaders secured a commission charter in 1904 and the city started operating under it the following year. Other Texas cities soon adopted commission government. By 1907 the new system had spread to Dallas, Dennison, El Paso, Fort Worth, and Greenville.[9]

This growth suggested that the commission plan would be best adapted to small communities containing high percentages of old-stock inhabitants with above-average incomes. In their recent examination of the political environment of urban progressivism, Richard M. Bernard and Bradley R. Rice provide an empirical model with which to differentiate commission cities of at least 25,000 population from their unreformed counterparts. Their findings indicate that the commission plan was more likely to be adopted in smaller, new cities with relatively large numbers of native white-collar workers and home owners.[10] Such localities were dominated by a view of the public interest which Oliver P. Williams has described as "promoting economic growth." Here government policies are directed toward the maintenance of an image of stability, honest administration, sound fiscal status, and cordiality toward business interests.[11]

Business advocates of the commission plan, tightly organized, could expect to achieve success in this kind of political environment. James G. Berryhill, a lawyer from Des Moines, Iowa, returned home from a trip in 1907 as an ardent supporter of the "Texas idea" of city government. Addressing the Commercial Club of Des Moines, he told of discovering in Galveston a "city approaching the ideal," in which the commission managed the city as a "board of directors manages a bank." The club quickly formed a "Committee of 300" to draw up a specific proposal. After the legislature approved the plan, the committee launched a campaign for electoral approval of the charter. Opposing the efforts of this organization were the "City Hall gang and the corporate politicians." In June 1907, by a narrow margin, the committee persuaded the electorate to accept the commission form of government. The charter provided for a five-man commission to manage the city. There were also provisions to entrust the voters with the power to initiate legislation, veto laws, and remove officials—the initiative, referendum, and recall. One reformer noted that these devices "hung like a sword over the head of every commissioner, reminding him constantly that he must answer to the people for his every act." This "Des Moines plan," reflecting a precarious balance between centralization and popular control, became a model of political reform for other cities. In 1909 the Iowa legislature approved a law permitting cities in the state with populations from 7,000 to 25,000 to adopt the new plan.[12]

Influenced by political developments in Iowa, the Illinois legislature sent a special committee in 1909 to investigate the workings of commission government in Houston, Galveston, and Dallas. Seeking the opinion of "all classes of citizens," the committee found the enthusiasm for the system to be "hardly describable." Under the commission system these cities were entering upon an "era of great prosperity" with the "full confidence" of the citizenry in the "efficiency" of commission government.[13] Responding to this enthusiastic report, the Committee on Municipalities in the legislature drafted a bill permitting commission government, and it became law in 1910. The law eliminated the ward system and the distinct powers of the mayor and council. Responsibility for municipal government lay with a council consisting of a mayor and four elective commissioners. Moreover, nominations for these offices would come from nonpartisan primaries.

In the winter of 1910–11 cities in Illinois discussed the merits of the recent law. John A. Fairlie, professor of government at the University of Illinois, observed that a "notable feature of the discussions was the activity of the business men's organizations . . . in favor of the commission plan," while the "local politicians" were opposing it. Subjected to incessant propaganda from the business community and generally dissatisfied with the personnel in office, the electorates in various cities opted for the new system. By 1912, as debate continued in some cities on the merits of the commission system, 18 had adopted it.[14]

Modeled upon the Des Moines plan, commission government was spreading to other parts of the East. Searching for the medicine to cure the ills of local government in Pennsylvania, the Pittsburgh chamber of commerce seized upon the commission plan. In sensing the new political consciousness among business groups, the Pittsburgh businessmen organized a convention of representatives of commercial organizations of all second- and third-class cities in the state, which met at Williamsport in 1910. After hearing various businessmen describe the advantages of commission government, the delegates voted to support legislation to permit the adoption of charters. Returning home to do battle with local machines, the delegates launched a vigorous campaign for the new political system. Following two years of agitation by leading bankers, merchants, and manufacturers in the state, the Pennsylvania legislature passed an act in June 1913 requiring all cities of the third class to adopt commission charters.[15] Limited to a specific group of cities, however, the Pennsylvania law left business groups with the uncomfortable question of whether the glass was half full or half empty. To the delight of businessmen in New Jersey, their state legislature removed this source of anxiety. Though the bill was "vigorously opposed by the special interests and the old time leaders of both political parties," the legislature passed a law in 1911 permitting every municipality in the state, after special elections, to adopt commission government. Governor Woodrow Wilson confidently told a group of municipal reformers that the new system would mean a "business-like, nonpartisan, economical, efficient government."[16]

Influenced by developments in Texas, Illinois, and New Jersey, other states were passing general commission laws. Enacted in 1907 and applying to first- and second-class cities, a Kansas law contained provisions for a commission, civil service, and the initiative, recall, and referendum. Welcomed in various cities as a means of destroying a "particularly unscrupulous ring," commission government spread rapidly through the state. By 1909 there were 24 cities in Kansas operating under the plan. In the same year Wisconsin, Minnesota, and California enacted laws permitting their cities to adopt commission government. Though differing in particular provisions, the laws followed the lines of the Des Moines plan. In the period from 1910 to 1912 other states, such as Massachusetts, West Virginia, Alabama, and Washington, passed laws permitting the establishment of the commission system.[17]

At the same time business groups in other cities pushed hard for commission government. Determined to abolish the excesses of political partisanship, businessmen in Huntington, West

Virginia, persuaded the electorate to accept the new plan in 1909. In Nashville, Tennessee, the Commercial Club submitted a commission charter to the legislature in 1912 and it was approved the following year. In Buffalo, New York, businessmen from the city's Municipal League pressured county legislators into endorsing a commission charter and secured its adoption in 1914. Three years later the chamber of commerce in Charlotte, North Carolina, led a successful movement for commission government in the city.[18]

Behind these developments lay the more important effort to place more wealthy businessmen in office. In line with their counterparts in large cities, many politically oriented capitalists in smaller communities were young representatives of advanced segments of relatively new industries which had come to dominate urban economic life. They felt that public policy should be consistent with the inherent rationalization in corporate systems and sought to bring more order to metropolitan life. Toward this end they sought to reduce the influence of lower- and middle-income groups in public decision-making. Before the adoption of the commission system, the typical ward-elected alderman was a small businessman, skilled artisan, or unskilled worker. But now upper-class businessmen were determined to change the social background of city officials.[19] In Des Moines, for example, the Committee of 300 selected a slate of wealthy businessmen to be the commissioners in 1908. Confronted with intense opposition from organized labor, the president of the committee defended the reform ticket on grounds that "professional politicians must be ousted and in [their] place capable business men chosen to conduct the affairs of the city."[20]

F.E. Chadwick, a retired naval officer and leader of political reform in Newport, Rhode Island, spoke more precisely: "We have deprived the true stockholders ... of any representation whatever. I thus hold that to give property some voice in the control of a municipal corporation is but sense and justice. Moreover, it is true democracy, not the shadow under which we now labor."[21]

From this standpoint, the goal of the commission movement was far from democratic in the traditional sense of proposing more popular control over public policy. In the minds of business leaders, the issue was not to make representative decisions.

Rather, it was a question of having the right people in government to make the correct decisions. One authority on urban politics notes that the positions of prominent businessmen in the social structure "make them visible targets for recruiting agencies and give them an edge if they choose to pursue a political career."[22] The first commission in Galveston included a banker, a merchant, and a real estate broker. In Janesville, Wisconsin, businessmen dominated the commission. Most members of the commissions in Illinois were experienced businessmen described by one reformer as "a distinctly better class of public officials."[23] In cities where businessmen were not in the majority, commissioners still remained under their influence. "As long as a proposition is based on good business principles and in no way compromises the interests of public," declared Oklahoma City's chamber of commerce, "there has been no question of difference between the commercial organizations and the city officials." The secretary of the Houston chamber of commerce likewise reported that there was "no phase of our city life which has required the attention of the chamber of commerce in which the city administration has not been willing at all times to cooperate."[24]

Developed and led by business groups, the commission movement was integrating the methods and values of the corporation into urban government. Operating on the principles of reducing costs and increasing services, the new system met the obvious needs of local business. To other representatives of the middle and upper classes who staffed the commissions, it represented an important advance in urban political reform. It was not only the movement's commercial efficiency, with its suggestions for tax cutting, that they had in mind, but also the possibility of a redistribution of power in local affairs. The businessman's commitment to fiscal efficiency fitted closely with this objective and shared its implications. For those entering local government, the new plan meant the emergence of a polity in which commissioners would define and determine policy according to middle-class social values.

From the outset, the commission plan permitted increases in the services provided by the city at little extra cost and sometimes at considerable savings. We have seen that the first commission in Galveston labored under extraordinary conditions and placed the

city on a sound financial basis. In Des Moines the commission
worked to eliminate "graft and extravagance" inherited from the
previous administration and showed a saving of $184,000 after
one year. Gradually new buildings appeared, the civic center was
landscaped, and the river banks were walled. Similar considerations shaped the reforms of other commission cities. In
1907 the commissioners of Leavenworth, Kansas, found the
city's funds to be "completely exhausted" and proceeded to
adopt a program of economy recommended by the Greater
Leavenworth Club. Provided with funds from the club, the commissioners reduced expenses in their respective departments and
introduced modern bookkeeping methods into the government.
Meantime, the city returned to a sounder financial basis and the
commission expended funds for improvements such as lighting
and paving of streets and construction of new buildings. Similarly, Haverhill, Massachusetts, recorded considerable savings after
one year of commission government despite the expense of new
services.[25]

This development of economical government resulted partly
from the retirement of city bonds and reduction in taxes. In
Dallas, commissioners inherited a debt of $129,575 and reduced
this sum by $50,000 within a year. San Diego cut off $59,200 of
indebtedness and at the same time lowered taxes from $1.48 to
$1.30 per $100 of valuation. Similarly, after one year the commission in Gloucester, Massachusetts, showed a savings of
$18,000 and slight reduction in the tax rate. Of course, the failure
of previous administrations to provide sufficient funds for future
expenditures forced many commission cities to raise taxes in particular periods. It was expected that substantial economies in administration would result in a future reduction of tax rates.
Ernest S. Bradford, a statistician of the Department of
Commerce and Labor and member of the National Municipal
League's committee on commission government, reported that
the "results so far secured under the commission form" showed
"a clear improvement over those attained under the former common type of municipal government."[26]

Most businessmen in commission cities agreed. Like their
colleagues in the large metropolises, they wanted continuous services and resented increasing taxes that took away with one hand
benefits they were producing with the other. By 1910 the com-

mission system had altered this situation considerably. The business community was enjoying indirect gains in the form of improved services and utilities at little or no extra cost.

While the burden of the defense of commission government fell on business organizations, structural progressives in other areas of urban life greeted the new plan with considerable enthusiasm. In an address to the National Municipal League in 1907, William B. Munro, professor of government at Harvard University, argued that the "cardinal advantage" of the system was the possibility of ending the "intolerable decentralization of responsibility which now characterizes American civic administration." This centralization of authority would facilitate the entrance of "higher type of men" into municipal office. Munro reminded his audience that there was "plenty of room" for the infusion of more "business principles" into municipal government. Silas Allen, a leading figure in the movement for commission government in Des Moines, told the same meeting that the new plan centered the work of the city in a "deliberative body of men" and this enabled citizens to be the "judges of efficiency" in city government.[27]

Other reformers stressed this concentration of responsibility and intelligibility to voters as sufficient grounds for supporting commission government. Casting an admiring glance on the new political system in America, one English student of municipal affairs wrote that commission government "inescapably enlists the personal and sustained interest of the ordinary citizen" and thus made him a "conscious power for good government." Similarly, reporter-reformer Ray Stannard Baker informed a gathering of businessmen in Grand Rapids, Michigan, in 1910 that the remedy for partisan mismanagement lay in the commission plan with its capacity for efficiency and simplicity.[28] Four years later the noted reform journalist Herbert Croly described the commission system as the "most encouraging expression of a desirable tendency to combine a simple, strong, and efficient government with a thoroughly popular government."[29]

Complementing these aspects of the new system were the implications for machine government. Under the plan reformers expected to see the demise of bossism with the shift from ward to city-wide elections. The 1910 convention of the League of California Municipalities listened to Berkeley's mayor declare:

"Abolition of wards removes . . . the incentive for a councilman to favor the . . . dominant of the section which elected him."[30] Ernest Bradford similarly defended central representation on the grounds that "under the ward system . . . the ward receives attention, not in proportion to its needs, but to the ability of its representatives to 'trade' and arrange 'deals' with fellow members."[31] But the ward-based machine had also functioned as the medium through which the urban masses could influence the city government. Political reformers outside business were, perhaps unconsciously, contributing to the erosion of the structural bases of popular democracy and the power of lower-class elements which lay behind it.

Equally important was the connection between businessmen and the rationale of commission government. "Business, with its developing sense of efficiency, management, and even planning, provided the public picture of the democrat governing himself," Barry D. Karl writes. "Professional self-government was a difficult concept to define in America except by analogy; and for the moment the businessmen could provide the analogy."[32] In 1907 Charles W. Eliot told the Economic Club of Boston that local government meant "nothing but good, intelligent conduct of business." Clinton Woodruff likewise praised business for "contributing . . . its effective form of organization . . . to city government."[33] Charles A. Beard put the point more precisely:

From the standpoint of pure business administration the commission form of government has many features to commend it. It centralizes power and responsibility in a small group of men constantly before the public and subjected to scrutiny of public criticism; it coordinates the taxing and spending powers, thus overcoming the maladjustment so common to American public finances, and it throws down that multiplicity of barriers behind which some of the worst interests in American municipal politics have screened their anti-social operations.[34]

But there were some urban progressives who saw the commission plan as a threat to popular democracy and a betrayal of the basic principles of efficiency. In evaluating the course of political reform in American cities, the *Independent* praised the Galveston plan for its "high level of efficiency," but saw the Des Moines plan as an expression of "true popular government."[35] Respected figures in municipal reform agreed. "Men speak of the Galveston plan and the Des Moines plan," wrote Brand Whitlock in 1909, "as if they were one and the same thing; whereas they are wholly different; the Galveston plan is autocratic, the Des Moines plan is democratic."[36] Tom L. Johnson similarly described the provisions for popular control in the Des Moines plan as the "best political machinery so far devised." Another reformer saw both forms of commission government as "benevolent paternalism that confesses incompetency in representative government."[37]

These statements suggested a disturbing ambivalence in the commission system. In one sense, the new reform meant a government closer to all urban dwellers. It placed authority in the hands of a few people and thus made officials more accountable to the citizenry. On the other hand, commission government was facilitating the large-scale movement into public office of commercial and upper-class elements who were generally unsympathetic, if not hostile, to the demands of the lower classes. "If the members of the commission have got to ... preside over the heads of complicated and technical city departments," declared reformer Richard S. Childs before a gathering of New York mayors in 1911, "they have practically got to belong to the employer class. ... Such a limitation is, I think, undemocratic, and we might more wisely have the administrative work done by appointees."[38] Moreover, with no separation of powers, a commission was not large enough to provide the critical evaluation of officials which most reformers conceded as essential to any system of representative government. The relationships of the commissioners were mainly on a personal basis, and they often preferred mutual accommodation to criticism of a colleague's policies.[39]

Few political progressives, however, were especially worried about these shortcomings of the commission plan. In keeping with the emphasis on nonpartisan administration in large cities, they were more concerned about the possibility of commissioners forming an "organization" to keep themselves in office. One reformer contended that it was "highly probable that the place of political parties [would] be taken by parties of office seekers, surely more dangerous and destructive than political parties." In 1909 a convention of the League of American Municipalities listened to a former official of Des Moines government tell about an "irresistible machine" which the "best element" in a city would not be able to overcome.[40] Furthermore, there was the problem of partisanship within the system itself. The commission plan, unlike the executive-centered system in large cities, did not provide for a top official answerable for all administrative operations. Instead, each commissioner could move in his own direction without having to consider the effects of his policies upon other departments. Ansley L. Wilcox, a wealthy lawyer from Buffalo, informed the National Municipal League in 1910 that the new system was "not a sufficient step in the direction of concentrating authority and fixing responsibility."[41]

Developments in commission cities were confirming the suspicions which some structuralists had about the "political side" of the new reform. In Wichita, Kansas, for example, the desire for a larger share of appropriations brought about considerable conflict among the commissioners. A close observer of the system reported that there were "five separate governments in the city." After an investigation of Des Moines's government the Norfolk, Virginia, chamber of commerce noted the inability of the commission to view the "affairs of the city as a whole and plan and direct them as a whole."[42] Similarly, in Galveston and Houston commissioners found themselves divided over various questions of public policy.[43]

Such discord mirrored the recurrent weakness in the movement for efficient government. In line with the pursuit of administrative reform in large cities, the commission plan was designed to divorce politics from administration. Most commission charters, however, did not provide for the incorporation of the merit system into the government. In the few cities with civil service laws, many offices were exempt from regulations. Commissioners, therefore, could use their immense patronage for building organizations to secure their reelection.[44] The remedy appeared to lie in a total reorganization of the system. Given the popularity of the plan, however, reformers felt that a more sensible approach was to stress particular "defects" in the system.

Focusing on the power of commissioners, some structuralists directed their criticism at the combination of executive and legislative functions. In 1911 Dunbar F. Carpenter, a reform lawyer from the commission city of Colorado Springs, Colorado, urged his colleagues to "abandon the idea that because a man is a successful lawyer or merchant, he will ... make a successful municipal administrator." Civic management, he argued, required knowledge and ability "far above that required for an ordinary business."[45] Similarly, President A. Lawrence Lowell of Harvard University, writing on the role of expertise in popular democracy, saw the commission plan as a "very poor way" of getting competent administrators because the public had "neither the means nor the leisure for the careful scrutiny needed to estimate . . . professional qualifications."[46] Other political reformers agreed. In their eyes, the plan was not much different from the weak-mayor system. True, commissioners shared collective responsibility as the policy-making council of the city. But the election of incompetent, partisan administrators revealed the "dangers" of combining executive and legislative functions in the commission. The reformers felt that individual commissioners paid less attention to developing responsive administration and more to consolidating their positions in the government.[47]

From this standpoint, even the city-as-business concept drew criticism from progressives outside the corporate world. They pointed out that city administration was a complex system of aids and services not reducible to neat profit-and-loss calculations. "Advocates of the commission plan attempt to draw an analogy between the city and a business corporation," wrote reformer Vincent Starzinger in 1910. "But there is a vast difference between the two. The prime object of the latter is private gain, and its efficiency is usually dependent upon the spur of personal interest. On the other hand, the city ... presents a problem of government in which the human element, such as the everyday well-being, schooling, hygiene, and the general happiness of a vast community of men, women, and children, is ever present."[48] Walter G. Cooper, a reform lawyer from Atlanta, charged in 1911 that "the idea so common among business men that a city council should be reduced to a few men ... is a dangerous error, sedulously propagated by special interests which are politically organized on a large scale."[49] Given these attitudes and the general disenchantment with the performance of commission governments, the goals of structural reformers in the professions were far broader than what one urban historian sees as "government by businessmen serving the interests of the business community."[50] Certainly the experience of wealthy capitalists in large and small cities was significant in shaping their political aims and programs. But the reformist model of efficient government did not simply mean the retooling of administrative machinery to fit the needs of modern business. Governmental efficiency, as we have seen, also involved the creation of a modern system of social security for the urban masses.

Investigating the governments of ten commission cities in 1912, Henry Bruere focused on this issue. In keeping with the emphasis in municipal research on the social needs of the city, he pointed out that efficient city service required the development of services based upon a "complete and continuing understanding of the special social and economic requirements of the community which it serves."[51] From this standpoint, the commission system was quite deficient. "You can count on the fingers of your hands the number of commission officials of the cities visited who definitely conceive a city government as an agency for promoting public welfare," wrote Bruere. "None of them is activated by a program which seeks to equalize opportunity among citizens for health, for economic welfare, for education or for recreation."[52] Furthermore, there was little evidence to indicate that the movement was bringing a "revolution" in municipal administration. Several commissioners did not come from business or the professions, but were experienced officeholders. Even those who could be classified as "new types" in municipal government were reluctant to develop efficiency in existing services. Both groups of officials lacked the kind of executive ability which their public positions demanded. "Citizens have yet to learn that commission government will in the long run be no better than any other government unless it adopts a constructive social policy and introduces methods of scientific business management," Bruere concluded.[53]

These observations summarized the disillusionment with commission government. With the speed of a fad the commission movement moved across the nation and in less than a decade some 160 cities had adopted the scheme. Promising economy, simplicity, and responsibility, it was one of the most attractive plans dangled before the eyes of the structuralists. But after a few years experience many of them had become suspicious, if not resentful, of the system. Despite what seemed a logical development in political progressivism, the commission plan revealed an opposition between two conceptions of executive power. Developed and led by reform-minded mayors in large cities, efficiency was characterized by the effort to construct a unitary executive in the form of a strong mayor and an administrative apparatus with technical skills and responsibilities. In contrast to this scheme, there was the system of the multiple executive or commission plan. Those in favor of the rigid separation of executive and legislative powers looked upon the plan as a reshaping of inefficiency in urban public affairs. On the other hand, there remained a consensus among reformers on the class origins of decision makers. Commission government had enabled more people from the upper classes to gain access to office at the exclusion of lower-class representation. In witnessing this development, political progressives, particularly those in academic circles, were only complaining about the amateur administration in commission cities. They continued their search for a system that would come closer to their model of efficient, service-oriented government.

Chapter VIII

THE POLITICS OF BUREAUCRATIZATION

> Being a career man under civil service relieves the administrator of the necessity of participating in party politics, but it does not relieve him of the necessity of making decisions which are politically significant.
>
> Edward C. Banfield and James Q. Wilson
> *City Politics* (1963)

Along with the growth of commission government, the efficiency movement had scored successes in the large cities. The revolution in administration and in the transmission of empirical knowledge had undermined the parochialism of local political life. In the process, progressive structural reform had evolved into what one historian has recently described as "popular elitism." According to this polity, in having highly trained men in office there was nothing inconsistent with the more general tenet that government should reflect more directly the wishes of the people. Because of the growing complexity of urban life, management required special techniques if it were to be ordered for the advancement of public welfare.[1] Thus, democracy to reformers became less a system of stimulating greater individual participation in the decision-making process and more a method of making decisions which insured efficiency in civic administration while requiring some measure of responsiveness to public opinion.

Such a perspective suggested a new kind of civil servant. The functional needs of an urban-industrial society, reformers felt, demanded the skills of the professional bureaucrat. It followed that mass democracy, with its emphasis upon equality and lay participation, was a disruptive force on all levels of American government. Decisions and programs were mostly matters for administrative deliberation rather than legislative divisions and electoral alignments. In 1914 Walter Lippmann, associate editor of the *New Republic* and later a distinguished political journalist, wrote that men were moving away from the "old democratic notion that any man can do almost any job" and looking instead to the "infusion of scientific method, the careful application of administrative technique, the organization and education of the consumer for control." Herbert Croly likewise charged that one of the "great weaknesses of professional democrats" had been the tendency to see democracy as "essentially a matter of popular political machinery." Popular government, insisted Croly, had to become "intelligent and purposive" and only a "permanent body of experts" in administration could bring this about.[2] This reconciliation, however, rested upon the assumption that the people would tolerate such a system. Political progressives were optimistic. "Democracies may be honest, they may be noble," A. Lawrence Lowell told a gathering of the National Municipal League, "but they cannot be efficient without experts; and without efficiency, nothing in this world can endure."[3]

In promoting these views, progressive reformers looked across the Atlantic again for inspiration. For them cities in Europe remained the best examples of municipal efficiency because of the high degree of trained intelligence in public life. Beverly L. Hodghead, former reform mayor of Berkeley, California, admiringly reported in 1912 that in most European cities administrative authorities possessed the "training and expert skill which the importance and complexity of the duties require."[4] More importantly, reformers were impressed with the alleged dedication of top officials to their work and willingness to advance community welfare as well as personal interests. "In spite of the autocratic nature of German government, her cities have developed the most democratic administration in the modern world," proclaimed Frederic C. Howe in 1913. "The efficiency of Germany is largely traceable to the big vision of the city, to an appreciation of the necessity of controlling the predatory greed of the few for the welfare of the many."[5]

This was an inaccurate description of German local government but an accurate description of the hopes of political progressives. They envisioned the emergence of a professional public bureaucracy composed of socially conscious officials. In public office an administrative expert, Herbert Croly felt, would be "the custodian not merely of a particular law, but of a social purpose of which the law is only a fragmentary expression." Walter Lippmann similarly argued that the growing complexity of an urban-industrial society required the leadership of those equipped with "expert knowledge and creative will" to promote reform because their intuition of society's "dynamic purpose" revealed it as necessary to the welfare of all citizens.[6]

These arguments mirrored a crucial development in city administration. In the late nineteenth century most efficiency-minded mayors, while not rejecting reform notions of merit, had usually appointed socially prominent individuals with good general abilities to top administrative posts. These "best men" were selected mainly because they could satisfy the demand of the mayor's middle-class supporters for economical government. After a decade that witnessed the emergence of commission government and research bureaus, the trend in reform was toward the "best" as the expression of merit or job-oriented skill in city management. Reform mayors would now find their department chiefs among specialized professionals such as doctors, engineers, and social workers. In the process, the center of administrative control shifted away from the neighborhood-based party bureaucracy toward appointive officials who derived their authority from city-wide constituencies. This gradual transference of power enabled top civil servants to be what Fred W. Riggs sees as semiadministrators and semipoliticians having considerable influence over both policy formulation and execution. Here administrative power becomes the dominant expression of an "officially based partisanship" as opposed to the "spoils-based partisanship" of a party-run polity.[7] Municipal administrators constituted a new political force in urban society.

This redistribution of power, however, revealed a dilemma for big-city mayors. Deprived of adequate resources for effective departmental control, they could lose power to cabinet specialists, who were in a position to thwart particular policies. In attempting to avoid this situation a mayor would find himself identifying with the emerging reformed bureaucracy. This in turn could invite more resistance from departmental heads to centralized control. In both situations, the chief executive was

faced with the problem of achieving efficiency and at the same
time making policy responsive to his own and his supporters'
goals.[8] Consequently, there was an increased dependence upon
professional experts. Some mayors selected job-oriented executives from the city bureaucracy and officialdom. Other
mayors chose men from professions and business organizations.
Still others reached into both areas for top administrators.

Political developments in various cities reflected the effort to
maintain an executive-centered order. Confronted with uncovered corruption and dismissed officials, Charles F. Murphy,
head of the Tammany organization, searched in 1909 for a
respectable candidate for mayor and finally settled upon William
J. Gaynor, long-time justice of the State Supreme Court. As in
the anti-Tammany movements in 1901 and 1903, reform-
minded lawyers and businessmen organized a "committee of one
hundred" and joined with the Citizens' Union and Republican
party behind a slate of fusion candidates. This ticket included two
nominees for major posts, John Purroy Mitchel for president of
the board of aldermen and William A. Prendergast for comptroller, who were closely associated with the government
research movement in the city. Gaynor was elected, but so, with
the exception of the candidate for borough president of Queens,
was the entire fusion slate.[9]

Following a pattern established by his predecessor, George B.
McClellan, Jr., Gaynor would not accept dictation from Tammany and pursued an independent course. "A public official
should act from a sense of official responsibility only," wrote the
new mayor. "This does not mean that he should ignore
politicians or party leaders, or refuse to consult with them or
listen to them, but only that in the end he should follow his own
enlightened official judgment in every official act."[10] Many of his
beliefs paralleled those of the political reformers, especially those
pertaining to expertise and administrative efficiency in local
affairs. In line with the gradual shift in recruitment patterns, there
was a greater degree of professional representation in the government. To head the board of health, the mayor selected Dr. E.J.
Lederle, who had served the city so well in Low's administration.
Rhinelander Waldo, a university graduate and member of one of
the wealthiest families in the nation, became fire commissioner.
Similarly, an engineer, Kingsley L. Martin, was chosen as com-

missioner of bridges and Calvin Tompkins, a member of the chamber of commerce and authority on dock facilities, as commissioner of docks and ferries. Gaynor appointed Raymond Fosdick, former resident at Henry Street Settlement and assistant commissioner of accounts during Mayor McClellan's second administration, as chief commissioner of accounts.[11] Given a free hand by the mayor, Fosdick and his staff proceeded to investigate the activities of municipal departments. They uncovered considerable graft and malfeasance in a few agencies and borough governments. This evidence led to the indictment of several public works administrators and the removal of some officials in the Queens borough from office.[12]

At the same time, Mayor Gaynor pressed for efficient and responsible management. He dismissed numerous party hacks from the city payroll, reduced the operating expenses of departments, and made strides to end indiscriminate convictions in the magistrates' courts. More dramatic were improvements in law enforcement. Gaynor abolished police blackmail of saloonkeepers and suppressed indiscriminate clubbing and mistreatment of citizens by irresponsible patrolmen. He also ordered that all appointments and promotions in the police and fire departments be made in numerical order from the civil service eligibility lists.[13]

No less significant were developments in the area of school administration. In 1911 the board of education and Superintendent William Maxwell, arguing that they dealt with both measurable and nonmeasurable units of expenditures, chose not to provide the fusion-controlled board of estimate with a detailed explanation of various items in their proposed budget. Anxious to apply more efficiency to the school system, the Bureau of Municipal Research persuaded the board of estimate to appoint the Committee on School Inquiry to survey public education. Paul H. Hanus, a professional educator at Harvard University, directed the educational survey in 1911 and 1912. Meanwhile, William Allen submitted a report on organizations cooperating with public schools to the school committee. In this document, he attacked the respected Public Education Association as ineffective because of insufficient information, lack of funds, and little central direction of programs. This criticism precipitated a fundamental reorganization of the PEA in which leadership was assumed by a small group of the city's business and financial elite. These progressives transformed the PEA into a more effective and professional instrument of school reform.[14]

Closer to the hearts of structural reformers were advancements in fiscal administration and efficiency. "To divorce politics from city financing is the present duty," Comptroller Prendergast told a gathering of the New York State Bankers' Association in 1910, "and to prosecute that duty to the utmost is the obligation to which I have addressed myself."[15] He centralized the auditing and inspection procedures of the finance department and extended uniform accounts to all city departments. Complementing these changes was the reconciliation of the comptroller's accounts with those of outside agencies, bureaus, and departments. Prendergast also worked with the board of estimate to complete the fiscal reforms begun under Herman Metz in 1907. They required department heads to submit daily reports on expenditures, established a unit-cost system in all departments, and devised a new general ledger for periodic statements on the city's financial transactions. In addition, Prendergast prepared the city's first corporate stock budget that provided for central accounting control over revenues obtained from the sale of long-term bonds. He also established a commission of standardization to devise procedures for a central purchasing system.[16] In all of this reconstruction, the accounting division of the Bureau of Municipal Research lent its personnel. Prendergast wrote that he had "not hesitated to enlist the services" of the bureau and found its aid "both generous and skillful." New York's structural reformers had made the first successful attempt to modernize the machinery of city finance.[17]

Other cities followed the same pattern of reform. In May 1911, Henry T. Hunt, Democratic county prosecutor in Cincinnati, secured indictments against Republican boss George M. Cox and 123 of his associates during an investigation of political corruption and organized vice. Four months later the Democrats, searching for a candidate acceptable to all party factions and anti-machine Republican business and professional men, chose Hunt as their mayoralty candidate on a reform ticket. Hunt conducted a vigorous campaign in which he denounced bossism as a threat to the welfare of the entire city and promised more economical and equitable management of local government. Drawing support from the lower-middle class wards near the core of the city and those in the wealthy suburbs, Hunt defeated the regular Republican candidate by a wide margin and all of the other offices went to his progressive colleagues.[18]

Like his counterparts in other large cities, Hunt saw city government as a profession for experts with training in the administration of civic services. For public service director he chose Henry M. Waite, the city engineer. Dennis Cash, a lawyer who had helped obtain the indictment of Boss Cox, was named director of public safety. Similarly, Dr. Otto P. Geier, a wealthy physician who had organized the Association of American Industrial Physicians and Surgeons, was selected to head the newly formed department of charities and correction. Hunt also enlisted the advice of the heads of business and civic organizations on the city's social needs. Drawing upon the suggestions of these people, Hunt developed a program of efficient government with emphasis on fiscal organization. In 1911 the administration drew up a proposal which showed departmental expenses and what the expenses were for. Several thousand copies of the proposal went to various organizations along with an invitation to public hearings. Out of these hearings, in which officials considered suggested additions or reductions, came a budget which included expenditures for several new projects. The administration set aside $500 for a municipal employment bureau, $2,475 for a bureau of information and complaints to maintain communication between the voters and public officials, and $10,000 for a bureau to conduct "efficiency and economy surveys" in city departments.[19]

By the middle of 1912, however, city revenues were not covering public expenditures. Required by law to hold a referendum to secure an increased levy, Mayor Hunt invited Dr. L.D. Upson of New York's Training School for Public Service to organize a budget exhibit for the purpose of getting public support for tax increases. The exhibit ran for two weeks and was the first in any large city outside New York. Various officials, with the help of the Cincinnati Bureau of Municipal Research, prepared charts and models which illustrated the activities of the government.[20] "In the place of textbook theories, the municipality suddenly became a reality of streets and lighting, of big mercantile projects, of extensive charities, of a management marked with both great efficiency and inefficiency," reported Upson. "Public officials became interesting men who were more than willing to explain the details of the department, and whose interest in their work was augmented by the public interest in it." The electorate approved the tax increase by a wide margin.[21]

The budget exhibit represented Hunt's commitment to efficient, socially conscious government from 1911 to 1913. In charge of the house of refuge for delinquent and dependent children, Dr. Geier did what he could to put this ideal into practice. He instituted a parole system, abolished the old rule of military discipline, reopened the manual training shop, and built new playground facilities. More dramatic was the work of his department's bureau of social investigation and relief. The agency secured the abolishment of the corrupt Overseers of the Poor and participated in the mayor's campaign to eliminate the exploitation of lower-class citizens by loan sharks. Meanwhile, Hunt attacked sanitation, health, and fire hazards in the central city. He forced owners of large buildings to install fireproof stairways and halls and required that public markets meet health department regulations. These measures were accompanied by new housing standards. City councilmen passed an ordinance which established a division of housing in the health department and provided the chief inspector with the powers of the building commissioner. The department proceeded to enforce municipal building codes and examine all plans for new tenements.[22]

Hunt's administration mirrored the conviction of urban progressives that governmental efficiency meant more social programs as well as economy measures. In this context, his mayoralty does not fit either of Melvin Holli's popular "social reform" or elitist "structural reform" types of city administrators.[23] True, Hunt was preoccupied with considerations of efficiency and thus imposed middle-class ideals on the masses of workers and poor. His brand of social reform, however, fell in line with the positions of most efficiency-minded executives who saw no inconsistency between the rationalization of city administration and increasing public services. They defined the mayoralty as the center of formal decision-making which would mediate between the power blocs of the upper-middle classes and those of low-income constituencies within the central city.

Notable among reform mayors dedicated to this conception of executive leadership was Los Angeles's George Alexander, who served from 1909 to 1913. Elected on the ticket of the Good Government League, Alexander, a former county supervisor who had opposed the local Republican machine, sought to promote a program of humanitarian service and at the same time advance middle-class notions of economy and efficiency in city government. Division over the main goals of structural reform existed, however. Some political progressives were unreceptive to the desire of labor groups for new welfare services and demanded a more economical administration of the government. Others insisted that efficient management had to be integrated into a broad program of social reform if citizens were to be served effectively and class stratification was to be alleviated. Seeking to reconcile these contrasting viewpoints, Mayor Alexander focused upon those policy areas which appeared to cut across class lines and give the impression that his administration acted on behalf of all Los Angeles residents. He dismissed several municipal commissioners for alleged partisan incompetence and replaced them with people who had some training in their areas of service. Eager to make city administration more effective, these appointive officers worked closely with the mayor in expanding the scope of departmental operations and services. By 1911 the government had modernized the police and street departments, built new fire and police stations, and launched a reconstruction of city parks. It also reequipped the fire department, secured approval of a $6.5 million bond issue for electrical power development, and crushed the exploitation of city employees by underworld loan sharks.[24]

These accomplishments, however, did not attract more working-class support for Alexander's administration. In the conviction that social and economic reform would never be fully implemented under a mayor committed to middle-class definitions of efficient government, the Union Labor Political Club joined forces with the Socialist party to challenge the progressives in the election year of 1911. They selected Job Harriman, an attorney for organized labor, as their candidate for the mayoralty. The Good Government organization renominated Mayor Alexander and the Republicans chose former city auditor W.C. Mushet. In the primary, Harriman polled a plurality of votes and Alexander secured the second spot. Shortly before the runoff, however, two labor organizers confessed to the bombing of the *Los Angeles Times* in late 1910 and Harriman, who had been one of their defense lawyers, lost his chance for victory. Alexander, drawing support from party regulars and business groups who were more fearful of trade unions and socialism than of progressivism, won the election by a considerable margin. The mayor now devoted more attention to a program of social reform that acknowledged the wants and needs of the city's working-class population. He advocated various welfare services such as public markets, tenement inspection, free municipal baths, and public ownership of all utilities. Unfortunately for the mayor, the city council was under the thumb of conservative reformers reluctant to place higher expenditures on the shoulders of middle-class taxpayers. By 1913, however, Alexander and his administrative staff had instituted tenement regulation, carried out sewer-construction projects, expanded public recreation facilities, and established a municipal electric power system.[25]

This reform program was in keeping with the overriding goal of political progressivism to bridge the cultural chasms between various areas of the industrial metropolis. A socially responsive mayor, buttressed by an administrative elite, was able to exercise more influence over policy making, educate the voters, and transcend class and ethnic conflict. Elsewhere such behavior generated crucial realignments in the political parties. Impressed with the organizational skills of reform executives like Gaynor and Hunt, party mayors sought to build and manage machines of their own that would appeal to all the major interest groups of their cities.

Boston politics furnished one microcosm of this strategy. James Michael Curley, a ward boss who directed the powerful Tammany Club of Ward 17, served on the board of aldermen from 1904 to 1909 and then became a member of the new city council. By 1913 Curley had broken relations with leading figures in the Irish machine and was presenting himself as a reform Democrat dedicated to both pragmatism and principle in government.[26] "Instead of soliciting their [the political bosses'] support, I warned them that when I became mayor," recalled Curley, "I would put an abrupt end to ward bossism in the

Athens of America. There was a time when the ward boss performed a needed function. . . . But the institution was outmoded by 1911, and was breeding party strife, petty animosity and cheap political chicanery, and was a roadblock in the way of enlightened city government."[27] In the campaign he vowed to remove those "machine" politicians and promised that there would be more schools, playgrounds, parks, and jobs under his administration. The machine candidate, Thomas J. Kenny, a lawyer and former president of the city council, meanwhile promised to reduce the tax rate and thus drew additional support from various civic organizations. Curley came in contact with almost every group in the city and secured a victory in which he carried 16 of the city's 26 wards.[28]

True to his campaign promises, Curley brought the government closer to his conception of it as an efficient, humanitarian corporation. In the first few months he removed a number of machine appointees from office. City Hall quickly opened up to those who would consult the mayor personally about jobs or favors. Gradually, the payrolls became padded with mayoral favorites who, in turn, furnished Curley with the support denied him by his choosing to pursue a course outside the traditional avenue of party politics.[29] In similar fashion, the administration moved away from the business notion of fiscal efficiency. Like Hunt, Curley felt that a great mayor could not be bound by "pinch-penny economics" and pointed to the "desperate need" for better health, transportation, and recreational facilities. To secure the revenues for these projects the administration raised assessments on business properties. Curley recalled the reaction: "Bankers and industrialists who had lauded me for putting out of business their former political bedfellows—the ward bosses—suddenly took a dim view of Curley."[30] Yet this response did not deter the mayor from his commitment to public welfare. By 1917 the administration had extended public transit systems, expanded hospital facilities, replaced slum sections with parks and playgrounds, and filled in swampy lowlands to provide beaches for lower-class groups.[31]

In seeking reelection Curley repeatedly pointed to these public improvements. This time, however, he encountered a well-organized coalition of businessmen and bosses who brought about his defeat. Still, his machine-backed successor did not turn back the clock. While he prevented the padding of payrolls with personal favorites, the new mayor expanded Curley's policy that taxation was merely the cost of the public service apportioned among the people. By 1920 the city was being provided with a program of public services larger than that of the previous administration. In the process the Democratic party was thinking more of the city as a whole, of general problems of health, safety, and sanitation.[32]

The pattern of reform in Cleveland was similar. In the period from 1912 to 1916 Mayor Newton D. Baker, a brilliant lawyer and the most respected official in the Johnson administrations, paid less attention to nonpartisanship and focused on increasing party responsibility. Baker would not join the nonpartisan Citizens League because he felt it undermined the value of parties, whereas he found himself "coming more and more to believe that true progress lies in strengthening political parties and building up their respectability and power." It was his firm intention to make efficiency mean the same thing for the Democratic party in Cleveland that it meant for reform organizations. He refused to pass out the jobs to "the boys" and insisted upon merit as the sole criterion for office. He brought in an expert from another city to head the newly formed division of recreation. Similarly, he chose an engineer to head the important department of public utilities. In other cases Baker adhered closely to the civil service system, limiting the discretion of his officials and ordering them to select the top man on eligibility lists. One close observer of the administration noted this insistence by Baker on merit was largely responsible for the "non-partisan support he received from independent Republicans."[33]

Complementing this program was a rational reorganization of public services. Mayor Baker continually pressed departmental heads to restructure their operations and supervised their progress. Under this tutelage the department of public safety added a hundred men to the police force, introduced new fire equipment, and modernized the police department. In addition, the newly formed department of public welfare, which had replaced the board of health and the department of charities and correction, expanded its operations. The department instituted milk inspection, free legal aid, free medical examinations, and other social services. An office was also created to assist the unemployed in finding work and give relief to newly arrived immigrants. Meanwhile, the public services department carried out an extensive program of liberal improvements. It built a municipal light plant, constructed new sewers, improved parks, built a filtration plant to insure the supply of pure water, renovated bridges, and extended garbage collection to all parts of the city. Together, these achievements brought Cleveland closer to Baker's conception of it as a model of social efficiency and humanitarianism.[34]

In contrast to the progressive ideal of nonpartisanship, the administrations of Curley and Baker were vivid indications that one avenue of reform lay in the harnessing of the machine to the wagon of efficient government. Long before the structural reformers were talking in terms of public welfare, party bosses, as has been mentioned, provided vital services to the urban masses in the late nineteenth century. After two decades of administrative reorganization, this traditional role was reemerging in a political system through which social efficiency was gradually replacing private notions of welfare reform. "An American political boss," wrote Frederick A. Cleveland in 1913, "is commonly one of the most intelligent and efficient citizens that we have. . . .'The boss' is the only one who makes it his business to know what is necessary to supply the community needs which are brought home to him."[35] Henry Bruere similarly told a gathering of New York mayors in 1914 that "some of our Tammany friends" were a "good deal" like reformers in that they also had "the idea that the business of city government is service."[36]

These statements reflected the changing attitudes of some political bosses toward structural reform. They sought to make city government more responsive by installing methods of administrative control to cut through partisan incompetence and factionalism. For example, "Boss" Edward H. Crump, who was mayor of Memphis from 1910 to 1916, succeeded in reorganizing city administration along the lines of efficiency and responsibility. He saw to the employment of nonpartisan experts, tightened up the tax system, improved various services, and reduced waste in the government by the extension of audited purchasing. Similarly, Frank Hague, head of Jersey City's Democratic machine, led a successful movement for commission government in the city. Elected commissioner of public safety in

1913, he disciplined derelict employees in the police and fire departments and cracked down on organized vice.[37] More important, many candidates of the machine were now coming from more "respectable" quarters of urban society. Charles Murphy of Tammany Hall explained that he encouraged the selection of young men for public office "who would develop character and a reputation which would do credit to themselves and reflect favorably upon the organization and my leadership."[38]

In analyzing this gradual alteration of party policy and strategy, leading students of progressivism have presented two general interpretations. Some stress the decline of political institutions at the ward level and the emergence of corporate decision-making systems in extra-community social organization. This larger environment of political activity forced party bosses to select candidates who could appeal to the majority of voters. In the process, slates of nominees for office were drawn from the top echelons of the major functional groups of the metropolis.[39] Other scholars have examined the electoral basis of reform and found that major changes in the support for progressivism took place in the second decade of the twentieth century. With the passage of extensive social legislation, middle- and upper-class electors drifted away from reform to consistently support party regulars and the bulwark of progressive electoral strength shifted to working-class and immigrant voters. Such realignment led to the transformation of progressivism from a narrowly based middle-class crusade into a broader reform movement sustained by "urban new stock lawmakers" who represented growing lower-class populations.[40] Viewed in a wider perspective, however, this interrelationship also resulted from the fact that the political and social programs instituted by a progressive mayoralty were seldom reversed by the succeeding machine administration. The structural reformers and professional politicians were operating within a new liberal polity that included what Otis A. Pease has described as "a record of social concern for the working ethnic population, reinforcing a middle-class revolution in the effective governing of a city."[41] Most structural progressives, however, continued to see machine politics as the intrinsic malady in civic management. True, they had embraced the tactics of bossism to promote their programs. In the large cities, as we have seen, progressive mayors had transformed loose coalitions of ethnic interests, political independents, and nonpartisan administrators into organizations as efficient and dedicated as those maintained by the bosses. These reform "machines," however, were not trying to capture control of the regular party organizations. In 1911, for example, Theodore Roosevelt congratulated Los Angeles progressives on their effort to "withstand the very human temptation to pay the machine reactionaries back in their own coin.... We cannot afford to do what our opponents so cynically and continually do." Meyer Lissner expressed the same thought but with a different emphasis: "Before many years have passed the old party lines will have been abolished and we will have rational party divisions along the lines of progressiveness and conservatism."[42] There were also the recurrent differences between progressive and machine politics in the allocation of political values. For most party bosses, the criterion for distributing governmental services to individuals was not a matter of their having special skills or falling into a category prescribed by law. Rather, it remained a matter of what they could contribute to the success of the machine. In the process the bosses continued to tie governmental outputs to the survival of their organizations. Reformers, on the other hand, sought the complete separation of the input and output processes of urban public affairs. In the establishment of new lines of administrative authority, they could maintain the emphasis on eliminating the structural roots of graft and incompetence and exercise more control over the resources of city government.

Most important in this development was the growing interest in scientific management. Harrington Emerson served as an efficiency adviser to the Socialist administration in Milwaukee and his brother Samuel worked for the city governments of Pittsburgh and Seattle. Another of the Taylorites, Hollis Godfrey, served as head of the gas bureau in Philadelphia.[43] But it was the work of Morris L. Cooke that brought scientific management into the mainstream of municipal progressivism. Capitalizing upon dissension within the Republican machine of Philadelphia in 1911, the Keystone party, an organization of reform-minded independents, secured the election of Rudolph Blankenburg, a manufacturer and long-time participant in civic causes, to the mayoralty.[44] In his determination to provide a "strictly business administration," Blankenburg went to

Frederick W. Taylor for assistance and came away with Cooke, an industrial engineer, as his director of public works. Taylor informed Cooke: "I told the mayor that . . . you would accept it with the distinct idea of being able to introduce our methods."[45]

Cooke quickly became the driving force of the administration. In 1911 Taylor had told him that there was "no better opportunity for the application of scientific management than will be given your position in Philadelphia." Cooke sought the advice of Taylor, who recommended the hiring of various efficiency experts in the engineering profession and academic circles.[46] During the next four years Cooke employed the services of more than sixty experts from the Society of Municipal Engineers and from colleges and technical schools. This brought upon him the hostility of local politicians and some political reformers. To party leaders the outside appointees were "carpetbaggers," while some reformers protested his appointments of assistants who were not required to take standard examinations. In defending his policy Cooke expressed the view of most political reformers that the methods of civil service commissions were inadequate when it denied officials the latitude to fill various posts with experts who happened to be outside the ranks of the classified service.[4] This opposition, however, did not deter him from developing an efficient program of public services. He set up a planning board in the department of public works and devised a program of "functionalized management." The department forced garbage collectors to give better, cheaper service. In addition, a half million dollars was saved by the bureau of water with improvements in the filter system helping to purify the water system. Similarly, the bureau of highways introduced test roads that checked the durability of materials and modernized specifications.[48]

During the course of this work, Cooke dismissed more than a thousand men for inefficiency and political activity. In the highway bureau, for example, he found in 1912 only one trained engineer among 1,000 employees. By 1916 the city had nearly 200 engineers in the bureau. Cooke instituted paid vacations for full-time employees. Social workers employed by the department visited the sick, ran a loan system, and responded in general to the needs of the department's 4,000 workers and their families. Upon Cooke's insistence, municipal complaint books were made available in various locations and all grievances were promptly investigated. All of this activity was an outgrowth of his conviction that political reform was a social issue as well as an experiment in administrative theory.[49]

This thrust for efficiency in the department of public works was matched in other departments. Determined to insulate the police and fire departments from machine influence, the public safety director, George D. Porter, set up a training school for recruits and abolished the political assessment of employees in both departments. Similarly, the director of supplies eliminated dual appropriations in city purchasing which had fostered collusion between contractors and councilmen. In the department of wharves, docks, and ferries the director, along with Cooke, negotiated contracts with the principle railroads serving the city. This resulted in an agreement between the city and railroads on sharing expenses to abolish hazardous crossings and relocate tracks for opening up new industrial areas.[50]

These accomplishments did not save the progressives from defeat in 1915. Mayor Blankenburg had alienated the Keystone party by refusing to dole out patronage to party members. Furthermore, the campaign was carried on in an atmosphere of controversy over the ability of the city to assimilate growing numbers of immigrants. The primary cause of the defeat, however, was the failure of local reformers to build a stable and permanent alliance for themselves. They organized the independent Franklin party and nominated George D. Porter for the mayoralty. Porter was beaten easily by the regular Republican candidate. Soon after the election, the progressives disbanded the Franklin party and returned to the Republican organization.[51]

With the eclipse of reform in the Quaker City, the administration of John Purroy Mitchel in New York emerged as the showcase of municipal efficiency. In 1913 a large group of prominent business and professional men initiated an anti-Tammany campaign and created a citizens' organization to nominate candidates. The Citizens' Municipal Committee, an organization composed of representatives of the City Club, the Citizens' Union, labor spokesmen, the Progressive party, and the local Republican party, nominated the thirty-four-year-old Mitchel for mayor, George McAneny for president of the board of aldermen, and William A. Prendergast for comptroller. As before in the case of fusion movements, most of the campaigning was couched in the jargon of reform politics. Mitchel asserted that Tammany represented "the system of spoiliation and graft" and promised to give the city a business administration.[52] This familiar rhetoric, however, did not simply mean government in the interests of the business community. One student of New York progressivism writes: ". . . when the young candidate argued that the chief issue of the campaign was Tammany and corruption versus honest business government, he did not suggest that such a government meant only businessmen or other well-meaning gentlemen in office, but the machinery, methods and processes . . . that could be used to achieve a better and more responsive municipal government."[53] Mitchel defeated the Tammany candidate by a substantial margin and all of the city-wide offices went to the fusion forces.[54]

Consistent with the recruitment pattern of William J. Gaynor's administration, Mitchel appointed department chiefs with professional training in their areas of service. Katherine B. Davis, who had been a head resident of College Settlement in Philadelphia and moved on to become a noted figure in prison reform, was named commissioner of correction. To head the health department Mitchel selected Dr. S.S. Goldwater, a prominent physician and expert in public administration. John Kingsbury, a social worker and former agent for the Association for Improving the Condition of the Poor, became commissioner of charities. Arthur Woods, a former police deputy with considerable experience in law enforcement, was selected to head the police department. Mitchel also chose professional leaders to manage the departments fundamental to the efficiency movement such as accounts, finance, law, and license.[55]

Out of these departments, aided by various experts from other cities, came studies designed to modernize further the city government. "I can say to you from the bird's-eye view I have been able to get in reading a number of . . . reports that we are going to effect a reorganization upon an efficiency basis," Mayor Mitchel told the City Club of Chicago in 1914, "and that we shall be able to render to the people of New York a very much larger and more effective service for the same amount of money than that which has been rendered during the past years."[56] Some reports led to the establishment of a central purchasing system and consolidation into one department of the licensing and inspection functions previously performed by various bureaus. Other administrative studies resulted in the creation of standing committees within the board of estimate and apportionment to prepare plans for new municipal improvements. The board of estimate formed two specialized staff agencies, a bureau of standards and a bureau of contract supervision, to examine problems of purchasing and using materials and personal services.[57] It also requested the Bureau of Municipal Research to investigate the city's budget system. After a detailed study the Bureau submitted a revision of budget procedures which provided for greater executive control over expenditures and a more precise financial statement of New York's business details. The Bureau also aided the committees and agencies of the board of estimate in standardizing municipal employment. This work included the systematic arrangement of salaries and titles so as to enable department authorities to supervise their personnel more closely.[58]

Complementing these efforts to increase municipal efficiency was the activity of the commissioner of accounts. Mayor Mitchel presented a bill to the 1914 session of the state legislature which provided for a restructuring of the office. When the legislators failed to act on the measure, he appointed Leonard M. Wallstein, a prominent reform lawyer, to the post. Wallstein, aided by the Bureau of Municipal Research, proceeded to investigate various areas of the city government. A detailed examination of the coroner's office uncovered considerable corruption and inefficiency. This evidence led to the passage of legislation which replaced the outmoded county coroner system with a board of medical examiners composed of physicians. On another occasion, Wallstein investigated the sheriff's office and the result was legislation that restricted the sheriff to his salary and put his fees into the city's treasury. Other investigations involved an examination of county government and a study of outside political influence on the board of elections. Wallstein also helped the city chamberlain, Henry Bruere, make a detailed analysis of the operations of city departments.[59]

More important was the activity of those professional bureaucrats who administered the vital health, crime prevention, and welfare functions of the metropolis. They worked to improve the physical environment so that the government could meet the social needs of the entire city. A noted historian of American educational reform, however, contends that "Bureaucracy inhibits reform. Its potent informal organizations mobilize resistance and frequently sabotage innovations."[60] Such an interpretation overlooks the capacity of a bureaucratic organization to operate also as an effective instrument of social innovation and change. Indeed, the municipal bureaucracies were in a constant state of change due to the adoption of new goals and the succession of top officials. "Innovation . . . is not absent from a bureaucratic system," Michel Crozier writes. "Curiously, the innovator seems to be the polar figure of the whole system and innovation the most envied achievement, the one for which people are most ready to fight."[61] New York's progressive government, like other big-city reform administrations, reflected these characteristics of modern bureaucracy. It was the professional administrator who largely determined whether or not to expand the range of a specific function to which the metropolis was already committed. "The impatient laymen who paid the taxes was apt to put down the expansive nature of a department or bureau to its desire for greater power, higher salaries, and more spoils," writes Ernest S. Griffith. "He overlooked the fact that the more professional and more dedicated a civil servant was, the more he would believe in his job and would want to expand its scope and effectiveness."[62] In this context, there was an expansion of services that benefited all classes. These included street-cleaning improvements, more efficient administration of police operations, prompt collection of garbage, fire prevention work, and aggressive public health service.[63] Furthermore, the special needs of inner city workers and tenement dwellers were not ignored. The government established an employment bureau and child welfare board and renovated the municipal lodging house. Mayor Mitchel also worked closely with the heads of the departments of charities, correction, and health in promoting better housing laws, more parks and playgrounds, rehabilitation of criminals, and special treatment for dependent children.[64]

Despite this extensive program of social reform, Mitchel went down to defeat in 1917 and Tammany regained control of the government. Mitchel's associations with the city's social elite left the impression that he was not a man of the people. His preoc-cupation with school economy invited widespread criticism and resentment. The introduction of the "Gary plan" of education, which enabled the mayor to cram more pupils into existing public schools, resulted in considerable resistance from New York parents and labor organizations.[65] The main cause of defeat, however, was inability of a reform administration in a brief period to construct an organization that could compete on equal terms with the local machine. As in Seth Low's administration, power had been dispersed to a range of officials, bureaucratic agencies, and outside civic groups. This made the distribution of resources quite difficult. Tammany's centralized structure of authority meant a return to a more reliable and rapid system of distributing material perquisites.[66]

Still, the reforms instituted by the Mitchel administration were not undone by Tammany. Expertise and scientific methods, although they had not ushered in a municipal revolution, had been integrated into the fabric of city administration and become accepted criteria for evaluating public service. In this sense, mayors like Blankenburg and Mitchel represented the highest ex-pression and fullest development of efficient government. Some historians, on the other hand, see structural progressivism in general and Mitchel's administration in particular as "captives of a modern business mentality" with reform as an end rather than being addressed to the "real needs" of the people.[67] True, Mitchel was dedicated to principles of economy and efficiency and thus was imposing, perhaps unconsciously, upper-middle class social values upon lower-class elements in the community. However, he and other efficiency-minded mayors in this decade realized that the implementation of various social programs necessitated the establishment of a modern administrative system capable of discharging new and better services to growing urban populations. The professionals in control of this bureaucratic machinery had succeeded in shifting the focus of governmental efficiency from one of relatively narrow considerations of economy to an emphasis upon the quantity of services provided by government. In the process, per capita expenditures rose con-siderably between 1910 and 1920 in cities with populations above 300,000. Most of these costs involved increased expenses for charities, education, health, sanitation, and recreation.[68]

Such concern for human welfare, however, could not attract a permanent mass following for structural progressivism. "The trouble with all movements," declared Edward A. Dickson, associate editor of the reformist *Los Angeles Express,* "is that leaders are developed who plunge to excess in governmental affairs. Efficient, economic, and honest government does not satisfy our people and the demand goes up for ultra-radical legislation."[69] In the same admonitory vein, Professor William B. Munro informed his fellow structuralists in 1916 that experts could "solve no difficult problems without steadfast popular support. The chief merit of free government is not the efficiency which it procures at the apex of the administrative pyramid; it is the initiative and intelligence which it develops at the base." The *New Republic* put the point more precisely: "Although the American people have consented to the aggrandizement of the administrator under the pressure of sheer necessity, they remind the expert whenever they get an opportunity of their lack of confidence in his ways and his ideas. He is being imposed on the American political system rather than being assimilated into it."[70]

Most political progressives had ignored these considerations. In their relentless effort to get more trained, anti-machine people into city government, they overlooked the crucial fact that the decisions of such civil servants were based on value judgments which did not always reflect the beliefs and aspirations of the urban masses. Herbert A. Simon has pointed out that an administrator in a democratic system "must give a proper weight to all community values . . . and cannot restrict himself to values that happen to be his particular responsibility."[71] Furthermore, the evolution of administrative reform under efficiency-minded mayors had produced new centers of political power in which those who controlled the bureaucratic agencies exercised as much influence as outside groups on official policy-making. But this disturbing disparity between popular government and expert administration did not indicate a major setback to the efficiency movement. Little noticed in the early years of this decade was a major breakthrough in structural progressivism. By 1920 the city manager would remove many doubts about the efficacy of governmental efficiency in American urban society.

Chapter IX

A NEW PROFESSION

The city manager plan represents a completer and
more effective unification of the administrative work
of the municipality; it makes possible the retention of
a permanent professional expert and therefore the
opening of a new career of the greatest possibilities.

Clinton Rogers Woodruff
"Of What Does Municipal Advance Consist?"
National Municipal Review 3 (1914): 4

Behind the thrust for expertise in large cities lay a significant shift
in urban progressivism. While administrative reorganization
carried much of the reformers' burden of concern with trained
and effective personnel, the elites in local government were determining the direction in which political reform would head. Pulling both dimensions of the efficiency movement into a structural
synthesis was the city manager system. To political reformers,
this system combined the supposed virtues of the strong executive and commission government and hence would facilitate
the entrance of more professional administrators into municipal
government. Specialization and expertise were becoming a
recognized part of urban life, and few reformers could see any
reason for not extending those principles in local government.

Implicit in the critique of commission government was the notion that the administration of municipal affairs could be best
handled by a professional manager. Recurrent weaknesses in
budgeting brought this idea into a clearer focus. To question
another commissioner's budget was to leave the critic's proposals
open to dispute. Consequently there was a general logrolling of
plans so that the city's budget became the sum of departmental
proposals. In 1912 the progressive city council of Los Angeles

appointed a committee of political reformers, headed by Meyer Lissner and Dr. John R. Haynes, to draft a new charter along the lines of the commission plan. Haynes proceeded to send inquiries to officials in commission cities on the performance of their governments. John S. Schnepp, mayor-commissioner of Springfield, Illinois, reported a typical situation: "One of the greatest difficulties with our Commission Form is the fact that each commissioner looks after his department and ... will naturally vote to let his fellow commissioners expend what they deem necessary in their departments."[1] Such conditions tended to offset the economies realized by the change in governmental organization.[2]

More distressing to the structural reformers was the continual lack of coherent and clear leadership. They often watched in dismay as individual commissioners interfered with administrative details. The commission system, as has been mentioned, permitted no one to coordinate the policies of the various departments. Deprived of institutional leadership, the city either ran the risk of disorganized programs or was dependent upon services developed outside the government. In this absence of executive centralization, party bosses were exerting considerable influence in some commission cities.[3] Moreover, many antimachine commissioners were quite willing to overlook questions of competence and award jobs to people as a reward for services rendered during campaigns. In 1912, for example, Mayor W.H. Gibbes of Columbia, South Carolina, informed John R. Haynes that "in some cases favoritism and not capability had induced certain appointments and displacements."[4] These conditions had already led most structuralists to the conclusion that the commission system required drastic reorganization.

Primarily responsible for formulating the manager concept was Richard S. Childs. Shortly after graduating from Yale University in 1904, he joined the Erickson Company and moved on to become general manager of the Bon Ami Company. In these years he became a vigorous advocate of political reform and in 1909 organized the National Short Ballot Organization, whose supporters included such luminaries as Theodore Roosevelt and Woodrow Wilson. Seeking to make municipal administration beholden to the elected executive rather than to the city boss, this organization carried on a campaign to reduce the long ballot or, as Childs called it, the "politician's ballot." By 1911 the short ballot was attracting a diverse group of reformers united in their belief in the inadequacy of the public when confronted by the complexities of municipal government.[5]

Encouraged by this response to the short ballot, Childs proceeded to indict commission government and the strong-mayor plan. In his eyes, the commission system was defective because of the "struggles of the people to select men of executive capacity who can administer complicated city departments ... and produce results from a business standpoint." The mayoralty form constituted a dangerous aggrandizement of political power in urban society.[6] More disturbing to Childs was the fact that boss politics continued under both systems of government. "In the last analysis," he wrote, "I think our complaint against our city governments comes down to this: that they have been oligarchies; that the office-holders have been under obligations to the little ruling class of politicians, and that government has consequently been in the interest of the politicians rather than in the interest of the people."[7] With the appropriate alteration in the formal machinery of government, Childs reasoned, the need for this informal role of the boss would end and local government could finally become unified and integrated. The result of these changes would be the emergence of a mechanically perfect democracy in which officials would be more sensitive and responsive to the demands of all groups in the city.[8]

Seeking to translate this vision of nonpartisan government into political practice, Childs drew up the "commission-manager" plan.[9] In line with the basic tenets of efficiency, the plan separated legislative and executive responsibilities by retaining an elective commission to make public policy, while providing for an appointed officer to exercise all administrative functions. Commissioners would no longer be required to have executive ability. The management of city affairs was now integrated under the control of a professional manager, who would be hired on a contractual basis to carry out policies formulated by the commission. He would serve for no definite term of office but rather at the pleasure of the majority of the commission or council. Childs then instructed H.S. Gilbertson, executive secretary of the Short Ballot Organization, to draft the plan in statutory form. Both men took the document in 1910 to the board of trade of

Lockport, New York, which was seeking a new charter for their community. Easily persuaded that the plan was essentially sound, the board sponsored it that same year. Particularly significant in the Lockport proposal, as Childs's plan was called, was the equation of the city manager form with business organization: "The chief improvement in this act over previous commission plans is the creation of this city manager, thus completing the resemblance of the plan to the private business corporation with its well-demonstrated capacity for efficiency."[10] Despite the persuasiveness of this argument and the efforts of the board of trade, the charter was defeated in the state legislature in 1911.[11]

Undeterred, Childs and Gilbertson continued to publicize the plan through their New York City offices. In 1912 the South Carolina legislature passed a bill permitting the plan to be adopted on a local referendum as an alternative to the regular commission system. Shortly afterward the city of Sumter adopted the commission-manager plan and it went into effect in January 1913. Later that year two cities in North Carolina, Hickory and Morgantown, also came under the new system.[12] While these cities furnished the basis for more extensive publicity on the part of Childs and his colleagues, they were not big enough to command the attention of the nation. This situation changed when Dayton, Ohio, adopted the manager system in August 1913. It was a city of more than 110,000 inhabitants and its governmental problems were typical of those in the large cities. Moreover, a terrible flood in March riveted national attention upon the city. Nothing better to dramatize the manager movement could have happened, and it occurred at the time when dissatisfaction with the commission plan had become widespread.

Prior to coming under the new system, Dayton was another example of municipal inefficiency because of incompetent and wasteful administration. The source of this situation lay in a "partisan political government" in which elected and appointed officials owed their positions to the support of the local machines. Such arrangements hindered the economical use of existing revenues and the government ended each year with deficits in operating expenses from various departments and agencies.[13] In 1896 John H. Patterson, Dayton's head of the National

Cash Register Company, had recommended that local affairs be "placed upon a strict business basis and directed, not by partisans either Republican or Democratic, but by men who are skilled in business management and social science."[14] Gradually, this familiar canon of political reform gained popularity among various business groups; by 1912 they were ready to sponsor a scheme which would alter the city's government. In that year the Ohio legislature approved a home rule amendment which permitted cities to frame and adopt their own charters. Shortly after the passage of the amendment, Dayton's chamber of commerce selected a committee to consider plans for a charter campaign. At the same time, the Dayton Bureau of Municipal Research joined forces with the business community in the drive for a new charter. Feeling that it should be more representative of various groups in the city, the chamber of commerce terminated its official role and the original committee was enlarged to 100 members. Dubbed the Citizens' Committee of One Hundred, it selected and promoted a slate of candidates for the charter commission who were pledged to the commission-manager plan. Opposing them were candidates nominated by the Democratic and Socialist parties.[15]

Convinced that the new system would liberate the city from the "meaningless, yet harmful labels" of party organizations, the citizens' committee campaigned vigorously for the manager plan and in the process created an organization "as elaborate as any party machine." Standing in the path of this effort was the stiff opposition of the parties who denounced the plan as a "scheme of business interests to gain perpetual control of the government." At this point nature intervened in behalf of Dayton's businessmen. Shortly before the charter election, the city experienced a devastating flood and when the government could not cope with the emergency, John Patterson took charge of relief activities. His factory became a great refugee station complete with dormitories, hospital, and eating facilities. As the waters receded, Patterson emerged as the city's leader and if the reformers needed a clinching argument for the new charter, he had provided it. Two months later Patterson and the other candidates promoting the new reform were elected to office and they quickly drafted a manager charter, which the electorate approved by a wide margin.[16] Thereafter, the "Dayton plan" spread rapidly and in the next seven years more than 140 cities came under the manager system.[17]

The structural reformers greeted the new system with the sort of acclaim once given the commission plan. In 1912 W.R. Williams, a member of the Los Angeles charter commission, recommended the inclusion of a city manager in the new charter so as to save the legislators "from the necessity of assuming administrative detail," adding: "I would have a City Manager the big subordinate man of any administration."[18] Herman G. James, professor of government and director of the Bureau of Municipal Research at the University of Texas, wrote in 1914: "Democracy need fear no setback through the introduction of this new form of administration; and efficiency . . . can come into her own at last." Similarly, the reformist *Outlook* announced that the Dayton charter provided for a government that would "yield more sensitively to the impulses of real public opinion than any other type known in America."[19] Most business structuralists, on the other hand, were not promoting the new reform as a revitalization of popular government. Democratic ideology, involving equitable representation to all social classes and geographic areas of the city, received little emphasis in their programs. What they sought was the replacement of the ward system of public affairs with a centralized administration that would organize municipal services according to the business view of what was good for the community. City manager government promised to accomplish all of this. Businessmen could then reduce the influence of lower-class groups in city government and advance their own notions of public policy.

Political environment determined whether these goals would be achieved. As in the commission government movement, proponents of the manager plan had a better chance of victory if their city was small and new and had a majority population of native whites of high socioeconomic status.[20] The manager system was well suited to such cities because the citizens considered the role of local government to be primarily that of "providing life's amenities." In consequence the primary task of government, as Oliver Williams has pointed out, was to furnish a high level of services designed to improve the comforts of urban life and benefit the productive activities of the city.[21] An effective organization of business elites could easily exploit these conditions. We have seen that the Lockport board of trade sponsored the first attempt to inforce the plan and the chamber of commerce in Dayton led the movement for manager government. Similarly, in Sumter, South Carolina, the local chamber of commerce sponsored the manager charter.[22] In La Grande, Oregon, a small trading city, charter reform began with businessmen's and taxpayers' groups. "The citizens back of the charter commission, as well as those composing it, were busy property owners who were ... striving to find a means whereby the city's critical financial situation might be met in a thorough, businesslike way without making large demands upon their own time," wrote a member of the Whitman College Bureau of Municipal Reference and Research. "Among this class of men the business-manager feature of commission government met with peculiar favor." La Grande adopted the manager plan in 1913.[23]

Other cities followed the same pattern. In Jackson, Michigan, the chamber of commerce pushed hard for a manager charter and secured its adoption in 1913 despite opposition from working-class districts. Business leaders in Lynchburg, Virginia, appalled by the lack of coordination and direction in city administration, led the movement for manager government in 1919. In Ames, Iowa, the Commercial Club sponsored the manager plan and it was adopted in 1920 despite the protests of local politicians. Similarly, reform-minded capitalists in Janesville, Wisconsin, drawing considerable support from upper-middle class wards, pushed through a manager charter in 1923. They expected that the new plan would keep the people "loyal to business and professional men" and away from the influence of "ward politicians."[24]

Most manager charters, as in the commission system, replaced the ward system with city-wide representation in which candidates were required to run on nonpartisan ballots.[25] Before this electoral revolution, representatives of labor and ethnic minorities often entered politics on the Socialist party ticket and served as councilmen and even mayor. Few of them, however, had the fiscal resources for city-wide campaigns. Moreover, the plan required more support than could be expected from local wards. These factors led to an upward shift in the class origins of municipal legislators.[26] In Dayton, for example, the Citizens'

Committee elected a "hand-picked business ticket" to office. Similarly, in Springfield, Ohio, five businessmen made up the commission, and in Jackson, Michigan, most of the councilmen from 1915 to 1920 were prominent executives and merchants. In Janesville the council was composed of business and professional men or what one student described as the "socially acceptable classes."[27]

True to their occupational values, these legislative bodies sought managers who shared their corporate or anti-political concept of the city. In La Grande, Oregon, for example, the council advertised in 1913 for a manager of "business character and ability ... sufficient to enforce the municipal law" who would "perform his duties and services for the best interests and welfare of the municipal government, and in a careful, prudent and businesslike manner." Similarly, the Dayton charter required that a manager be held responsible for the "efficient administration" of all departments and be appointed "without regard to his political beliefs."[28] Richard Childs put the point precisely: "The position of the city manager ... is the central feature of the plan and the ultimate theory of the scheme contemplates that he should be an expert in municipal administration, selected without reference to local politics, and even imported from out of town."[29]

Few managers in the years from 1912 to 1920, however, exactly fulfilled these requirements. In contrast to "professional" or "semiprofessional" managers of today, these executives belonged in the "amateur" category. While they had collegiate training in engineering and business administration, the managers had little or no experience in public administration.[30] Instead, their adult careers were confined to technically specialized branches of public management such as the directing of engineering projects for corporations and the supervising of electric and water utilities in particular cities. "The city manager," writes Barry Karl, "combined nonpartisanship, scientific skill, and the practical realistic personality of the business tycoon newly infused with an old fashioned moral sense."[31]

No manager was closer to this ideal than Henry M. Waite of Dayton. He was a civil engineer and had spent a number of years in railroad and mining engineering. In 1912, as mentioned earlier, he was a leading figure in Cincinnati's government as chief engineer of the city and had distinguished himself for an un-wavering commitment to efficiency in public administration. Quite impressed with this performance, Dayton's commission in-vited him to be city manager and he assumed the post in January 1914. "I insist that when I employ men for work in my depart-ment that they be selected for their efficiency and not because of any political affiliation or in payment of any political debts," asserted Waite, "and this same policy I expect to adhere to in Dayton."[32] He selected a prominent attorney to head the depart-ment of law. A local public accountant became director of finance. For director of public welfare he picked a minister who had been active in the community's social agencies. An engineer who had been associated with Waite in Cincinnati was named director of public service.[33] To the disappointment of local reformers, however, there was no wholesale dismissal of political appointees in the various departments. Waite gave these civil ser-vants an opportunity to meet higher standards of performance. In time, they displayed a loyalty toward the new government which was stronger than that which had bound them to the city's political machine.[34]

Provided with this consensus on administrative policy, Waite improved the methods of internal management. He adhered closely to the merit system and ordered the civil service commis-sion to select the top persons on certified lists. Both parties agreed that the manager would have final authority over the dis-missal of public employees. Gradually, the administration moved away from the old system of "political favoritism." At the same time, Waite introduced techniques designed to undermine the in-fluence of the bosses over public finance. The Dayton Bureau of Municipal Research devised a system of central purchasing and with the help of departmental officials it introduced a new and centralized bookkeeping system.[35]

Concomitant with this administrative reorganization was the establishment of a public welfare program. In the face of demands by labor groups and the local Socialist party for more public services, Waite instructed the department of public welfare to introduce new social reform measures. The depart-ment proceeded to institute milk inspection, free legal aid, medical examinations for children, a municipal employment agency, and other welfare services. In addition, the government promoted improvements which benefited all residents of the city. These included municipal garbage collection, new sewers and bridges, and park expansion.[36]

Although expected to be an executive who would manage the city on a purely business basis, Waite presided over a government which developed social as well as civil engineering.[37] Other managers adopted similar objectives. Confronted with paving conditions that threatened to turn parts of their city into an underground system of natural caves, the council in Staunton, Virginia, appointed Charles E. Ashburner in 1908 to the post of city manager. He had been an engineer for railroad and electric companies and had also worked periodically for the federal Bureau of Highways and the state bureau in Virginia. Feeling that the situation in Staunton required that he act without vacillation, Ashburner launched a public works program and selected "efficient" personnel to carry out the program. In the next three years the city was lifted from "mud to asphalt" and placed on a sound financial basis. The new government paved streets at ten times the former pace, improved the water supply and sewage systems, and installed better lighting.[38]

Considerably impressed with his record in Staunton, the city commission of Norfolk, Virginia, invited Ashburner to be city manager and he accepted the post in 1917. By 1920 the city had experienced an impressive growth in public improvements. During this period the government laid ten miles of new sewers and paved twenty-one miles of streets. It also built a huge water plant and established a municipal market. In all of this work there was little increase in public expenditures.[39]

Behind the work of Waite and Ashburner lay interesting developments in the manager system. Most structuralists saw the manager as a nonpartisan expert who would practice no political "favoritism" and concern himself with the details of administration.[40] In practice, however, he was also advancing programs that mainly helped businessmen in the form of improved facilities and services with little extra cost. This occurred because businessmen in the commissions and councils were rejecting the nonpartisanship that they had admired in theory; they wanted to eliminate the "wasteful" favors enjoyed by the lower classes through machine politics, but looked on their own privileges as essential to the "public interest" of the city. In the process, few managers were able to confine themselves to "non-political" operations and routine matters. Indeed, legislators looked to them for recommendations concerning policy and development of the city's public functions. "On some types of highly controversial issues, a manager, if he is prudent, will avoid taking a stand," write two authorities on modern city government, "but apart from these, it is his job to make recommendations and, in fact, to initiate policy recommendations.[41]

Some prominent structuralists outside the business community opposed this involvement. "It is not the city manager's function to govern," declared Richard Childs before the National Municipal League in 1915, "but only to administer. The occasional manager who favors fixed definite tenure and power to defy the commission fails to comprehend the higher aspects of the job. It is not his function to blow into town and immediately implant in city hall all the ideals of the bureau of municipal research from which he has graduated."[42] Similarly, a gathering of the American Political Science Association in 1915 heard Herman G. James speak about "the danger of giving too much prominence to the city manager as a factor in government and so inevitably making him a political issue." The following year Dr. Augustus R. Hatton, professor of government at Western Reserve University, told the City Managers' Association, which had been organized in 1914, that the "real authority is not the manager but the council," and added: "the council is determining the policy and your function is to carry out this policy."[43]

Other structural reformers, however, felt that such deference would undermine the manager's authority and prevent him from exercising broad administrative discretion. They also wanted the manager to help formulate policies of municipal improvement and public welfare. H.S. Gilbertson told the National Civil Service Reform League in 1913 that a manager "must be a person of vision and initiative with a constructive grasp on the destiny of American cities, for while he is in theory the servant of the council, he will be no errand boy." The manager of Beaufort, South Carolina, agreed. "If the council attempts to do things he cannot stand for," declared Harrison G. Otis before a gathering of the National Municipal League in 1915, "instead of rearing up and pushing them back the best thing he can do . . . is to get his councilmen one at a time into a corner and show them what is the right thing to do, and then get it done."[44] And the 1915 meeting of the City Managers' Association listened to manager M.H. Hardin of Amarillo, Texas, declare that the "greatest trouble" with the new system was the "usurpation of the power of the manager by the commission."[45]

Most structuralists shared misgivings about the social background of the commissioners. In 1915 Richard Childs complained about "a certain inadequacy in the representative side of the government. . . . Large sections of the people find not a single man on the commission who is of their own type." Henry Waite similarly told the City Managers' Association in 1916 that a "vast difference" existed between "the few of the public-spirited citizens traveling along with us and the entire community and their belief and understanding is far from being representative . . . of the mass of the public."[46] Two years later Clinton R. Woodruff informed the association that "considerable opposition" to manager government derived from the fact that "commissions are usually made up of so-called 'business men,' the result of which is that only one element in the community is represented upon the legislative body. That makes all the rest in the community . . . feel as if they are unrepresented in the city-manager cities."[47]

Most managers agreed. But they were not in a position to challenge the occupational origins of the commissioners or members of the council. Indeed, theorists like Childs and Woodruff overlooked the use of their model for achieving what the former system could not accomplish, namely, the movement of more commercial and upper-class elements into the centers of formal power. Hired to give efficient and economical administration, city managers could not function effectively if denied the confidence of the majority of these officials. More importantly, the managers saw the primary needs of the city as being largely of a business nature and thus bureaucratic and nonpolitical. They identified with the movement of structural reformers in large cities to insulate administrative decision-making from the pressures of machine politics.

Developments in various manager cities mirrored this thrust of political reform. Searching for a manager with "high business character and ability," the council in Jackson, Michigan, selected an engineer who had administered a small town in the state.

After four months of indecisive administration, the council reached into Dayton's government and came away with Gaylord C. Cummin, the city engineer. Cummin had also worked a number of years in various municipal projects and in 1917 served as president of the City Managers' Association.[48] Emulating his mentor in Dayton, he worked to bring the city closer to the council's conception of it as a business corporation. Feeling that "taxpayers should understand the finances of their government," he introduced the segregated budget and installed a system of cost accounting. In addition, he brought city purchasing under one agent. By 1917 these procedures were providing more "real knowledge" of expenditures and replacing what Cummin described as "long years of weird accounting and appropriation bills."[49]

Closer to the strategy of the efficiency movement was the assault on political patronage. Long before Cummin assumed his duties, the city had become accustomed to a system of patronage and privilege which enabled the bosses to exert considerable power in the government. By 1915 the government was filled with well-intended but unskilled amateurs who supported the machine. Seeing this system as a costly drain on public finance and wishing to "organize his work force," Cummin discharged more than half of the public employees and replaced them with a much smaller number of efficient personnel. He encountered stiff opposition from labor organizations and party leaders, who convinced their followers that the new form of government was elitist and unrepresentative.[50] "As the spokesman for the new system," wrote one student of Jackson's government, Cummin was "naturally not regarded as an impartial administrator, but, with the best intention in the world of carrying out the theory of council-manager government, he became a partisan official. It was impossible for him not to do so, since the rank and file of the voters regarded his basic political assumptions as highly controversial points."[51]

Such resentment did not discourage the manager of Dubuque, Iowa. In the period from 1915 to 1917, Ossian E. Carr, an engineer with experience in international projects, was manager of three cities and served a term as president of the City Managers' Association; he assumed his duties in Dubuque in 1918. Inheriting a considerable deficit from the previous administration, Carr moved quickly in the direction of administrative efficiency. Within the first month he removed a number of political appointees from office. These dismissals saved the city about $30,000 by eliminating "useless positions." Along with this policy went the collection of "delinquent taxes." In addition, Carr introduced an accounting system, reorganized various agencies, and brought the county and city health officers into one department. By 1920 the city was on a sound financial basis and there had been little increase in public expenditures.[52]

Louis Brownlow pursued similar objectives. Before coming to Petersburg, Virginia, in 1920 he had been a newspaperman in Tennessee and Washington, traveled around the world with the Haskin newsletter service, and, from 1915 to 1920, served as a member of the board of commissioners in the District of Columbia, in which office he had searched for the key to effective administration and the growth of professional public service. Petersburg provided an ideal setting for such a political synthesis.[53]

Finding little or no entrenched opposition from local interest groups, Brownlow quickly brought the government in line with the familiar principles of economy and efficiency. With the help of outside accountants, he instituted a budget system, prescribed uniform accounts, and created a central purchasing office. By 1921 this fiscal reform had resulted in considerable savings and a reduction of the city's debt. Meanwhile, there was a modernization of existing city services. Street-improvement operations and garbage collection were directed by the council's street committee, while the health committee of the council operated the city incinerator. With no separation of garbage, ashes, and cinders, the health committee had refused to accept municipal collections at the incinerator. Brownlow pressured the council into passing an ordinance which required the separation of incombustible material from other kinds of waste and divided the street-laboring force into a section for cleaning and repair and another to collect and dispose of refuse. He then transferred the incinerator to a new engineering department and launched extensive street repair projects. This work was accompanied by the installation of new machinery to perform familiar operations such as better methods of road building and more efficient water supply facilities.[54]

More significant was the introduction of new and better social services. Saddled with inadequate department facilities, the city's health officer recommended to the government the organization of a new health center. In response Brownlow, finding no suitable city-owned building, persuaded the council to lease a spacious downtown residence. The government moved the health officer and city bacteriologist to the center and established a well-baby clinic to fight the problem of infant mortality. By 1922 the number of infant deaths per thousand births among white people had fallen from 97 to 85 and among Negro families from 210 to 126. Brownlow secured the passage of a standard milk ordinance which created a bureau of milk inspectors within the health center. The council had also authorized him to direct the department of public welfare. Brownlow focused on public recreation and considerably expanded park facilities, especially in the lower-class areas of the central city.[55]

Given virtually a free hand in both the initiation and execution of public policy, managers like Carr and Brownlow were fulfilling the requirements of efficient government by more innovative leadership. They worked to modernize urban administration and institutionalize the ethos of social efficiency that had come to dominate structural progressivism. In this environment, city managership became more than just a tool of outside business elites devoted to cheaper government. Many of the commissions and councils were humanitarian and community-oriented, and these attitudes were shared by the professional managers. They, in turn, expanded utilities and services and spent more funds, though usually more efficiently, than the officials they replaced. As a result, taxes and per capita expenses rose in many middle-sized manager cities.[56] Other localities under the manager plan experienced substantial savings and better services with little or no extra cost. In Manistee, Michigan, for example, the manager inherited a budget of $104,000 in 1914. By 1916 the new government showed a savings of $20,000 over the old system. During this period ten miles of streets were paved and a new sewer system was built. In Abilene, Kansas, after two years of manager government, the manager had added twelve miles of new streets, reduced water rates by half, installed a storm sewer, and expanded social services. He had the streets cleaned at three times the former pace, extended garbage collection to every house, and enlarged the activities of the city's department of public welfare.[57]

Similar developments took place in other manager cities. In the two years from 1918 to 1920 Goldsboro, North Carolina, operated without higher taxes despite rising costs of labor and materials. The government improved police services, built new sewers and water mains, introduced modern fire equipment, and enacted new sanitary measures. Public improvements in Rock Hill, South Carolina, were also financed out of current revenue. The municipal authorities reduced water and electric light rates, expanded the parks system, and improved health services.[58] In San Jose, California, manager Thomas H. Reed, former professor of government at the University of California, found the city in considerable debt in 1916. He proceeded to install an executive budget, a centralized accounting system, and civil service regulations. By 1918 operating expenses had dropped considerably and the city was on a sound financial basis. During this period the government installed night auto patrols in residence areas, appointed a city bacteriologist to assist doctors in diagnosing contagious diseases, suppressed threatened epidemics, and established a purification system for park drinking water.[59] In Wichita, Kansas, after two years of manager rule, the government had, among other things, completed a five-mile sewer, established a free clinic for venereal diseases, increased the number of public health nurses, and organized a park board to improve public recreational facilities.[60]

This impressive growth of welfare services brought pleas from some prominent reformers for a far-ranging program of civic betterment. In 1917 the City Managers' Association heard Dr. Jesse D. Burks, director of the Los Angeles Bureau of Efficiency, describe professional administrators as the "advance agents of a successful and triumphant democracy and declare, "It's up to us to make good on a social program." Similarly, Richard Childs surprised the same meeting with his suggestion that the "great managers of tomorrow will be those whose ideals stopped at no line of dogma or tradition, but who pushed beyond the old horizons and discovered new worlds of service."[61] This advice met with mixed reactions among the managers at their 1918 meeting. "If we have saved money, conserved health, contributed to the growth and well being of our community in large contrast to previous government," declared Ossian E. Carr, "it is not due so much to our personal ability as it is to a form of government the principles of which are easy in operation."⁶² Others believed that the future success of manager government lay in more personal leadership in the areas of policy that directly affected the social welfare of urban residents. "I want to bring out the one point that a manager can perhaps 'get by' and even be called a good manager, though he may be passive," asserted H.H. Sherer of St. Augustine, Florida, "but that fellow who is actually performing a real service to the place where he is employed is the active manager."⁶³ Harry H. Freeman spoke more bluntly:

It seems to me that it is a duty on the part of the city managers who are engineers, if you please, to remember that engineering is but one of the functions of a city manager. We have to be careful to round ourselves out in city work, so as to take in the other fields. . . . In other words, we ought not to let pavements, sewers, lights and some of the other material things in city government become more important than the human beings whose happiness ought to be a prime object for which government exists.⁶⁴

These views mirrored the reluctance of many managers to restrict themselves to the housekeeping chores of municipal administration. By 1920 there was clearly a strong movement toward an aggressive policy that served the needs and wants of all social classes in the city. Some managers, to be sure, did not readily conform to this departure. In 1920 the manager of Sandusky, Ohio, informed a gathering of the Managers' Association that on "important bond issues" he stayed "in the background." Henry L. Waite, however, expressed the real feeling of the convention: "I would rather say that if the manager has not got enough strength of conviction and belief in the policy which he has helped to sell to the commission to go before the public and explain it, he is weaker than if he does go out and face the music."⁶⁵

This ambivalence over community leadership left city managers in a very precarious role. Like the professional executives who directed the reformed bureaucracies of large cities, they were engaging in behavior that included both functional and political responsibilities. True, loyalty to the ethics of their profession competed against dedication to any local faction or interest group. However, the managers were also clearly in the

political arena to the extent that they were involved in the making and selling of public policy. Their positions constituted a
tenuous mixture of bureaucratic, legislative, and partisan-action
relationships.[66] Professor Augustus R. Hatton outlined the reconciliation of these roles in 1920: "The city manager needs to understand that while he has no part in the fight for a municipal
policy, he is hired by the commission with the idea that he has his
mind on the solution of the problems of the city, that he has to
devote himself to thinking out far and wide constructive plans for
the city, and if he fails to do so, he will be considered a failure and
in the course of time be compelled to move on."[67]

Difference between business groups and their spokesmen in
commissions and councils on one hand, and the managers and
some political progressives on the other, continued to exist in
regard to the ultimate purpose of social and economic programs.
Their mutual dedication to efficient government, however,
blurred political dissension and permitted the rapid expansion of
the manager system. In 1923 some 270 cities were using it.[68] By
then, most managers had altered their "politics is business" approach to government and were viewing city hall as the place
where representatives of interest groups met to resolve their conflicts. In doing so the managers continued to participate in the
making of public policy with little immunity from political considerations.

Chapter X

EPILOGUE: THE MODEL AND POLITICAL REALITY

> Municipal democracy, and indeed efficient municipal administration, depend upon a system by which men who enter the public service shall have the opportunity to develop and strengthen their individualities, not merely in the technical performance of their duties, but in their conscious relation as public servants to the public whom they serve.
>
> Delos F. Wilcox
> "The Placing of Responsibility in Municipal Government"
> *Modern City* 1 (1917): 296

In stark contrast to his contention in 1888 that local government was the "most conspicuous failure" in the United States, James Bryce informed a gathering of the City Club of New York in 1911: "Your forms of government are far better over the country at large than they used to be. . . . In nearly all the cities the sky is brighter, the light is stronger." Seven years later Newton Baker confidently wrote that the "progress" of the cities in "effective reorganization" was the "most significant political development in recent American history."[1] But such praise overlooked serious shortcomings of political progressivism. Professor Albert H. Wright of the University of Pittsburgh reminded reformers in 1918 that at times "the whole social and economic structure of the governmental area should be examined, the standards and desires of all groups ascertained and then a governmental organization be framed in light of this information for the realization of democratic aims."[2]

From the perspective of a half-century later, the latter position seems more tenable. In pressing for efficient government, the structural reformers rejected group struggle as a central feature of municipal politics and sought to reduce the impact of partisan and socioeconomic cleavages upon formal decision-making. They therefore ignored the "mobilization of bias in preparation for action," as E.E. Schattschneider has termed it, in an environment where politics was (as it still is) a matter of continuous change in which the "upper-class bias of the pressure system" remained constant.[3] The progressive theorists saw municipal politics essentially as a static and formalistic process, and there is little evidence to suggest their model ever reflected reality in this regard. Meanwhile, there was a significant realignment of political power, especially in manager cities, under the banner of nonpartisanship. In 1880 members of the upper classes found that their wealth and status did not readily admit them to the formal machinery of urban government. By 1920 the structuralists had brought about the bureaucratic arrangements that facilitated the inflow into public office of middle- and upper-class people whom they believed the most capable and qualified to govern the metropolis. And down to the present day there is considerable evidence that nonpartisanship, particularly when it removes party labels from elections, favors members of upper-income groups.[4]

To the dismay of the reformers, these upper-class officials were not a guarantee that efficiency would remain the rule rather than the exception in municipal governance. They continually pointed to the alleged evils of machine politics as the source of administrative inefficiency and rigidity. But the explanation went much deeper than this argument. True, party-minded bureaucrats often put considerations of personal profit far ahead of the requirements of responsible management. Yet by 1920 many bosses had integrated the basic tenets of political progressivism into their programs and chosen to sponsor candidates dedicated to more efficient government. What the structuralists failed to comprehend was the complex nature of responsibility within an administrative organization. They depicted bureaucracy as a rational, monocratic system of firmly arranged levels of hierarchical authority flowing from superior to inferior roles. In practice, however, there were a number of functions and positions which brought professional experts and less specialized employees into various interdependent work relationships. Both groups of bureaucrats pursued more specialization as the means to increase their prestige and function. Such nonhierarchical activity led to continual competition for the control over the allocation of departmental resources. As a result, authority came to be derived less from specific offices and more from the qualifications and skills people brought to their respective positions. Thus, it would be quite difficult for administrative authorities to shape the strategy, much less the policy, of the government as a whole.[5]

More important was the fact that "politics" had not been exorcised from city management. Indeed, four decades of structural reform had intensified rather than depressed partisanship among administrative officials. They emerged as a new political force and derived most of their authority from such metropolitan constituencies as business interests, civic organizations, and research bureaus. In consequence, the machine bureaucracy, popularly based, was being replaced by career agencies, professionally organized. These reformed bureaucracies, while relatively free of corruption and malfeasance, constituted the new power centers in urban affairs and were more entrenched than the bases of power of the political machine. Future mayors would find it difficult, if not impossible, to manage effectively this "organized decentralization" of city government.[6] In the formal model of political progressivism, such matters were not relevant and hence seldom considered.

Likewise, the model distorted the function of leadership in a democratic society. For the structuralists the ultimate determination of public policy clearly rested with the forces of administrative rationality and centralization. In the process, the city's chief executive and his staff of professional civil servants were exercising greater control over all levels of public affairs, including the areas of finance, police, streets, public utilities, health and sanitation, welfare programs, and the like. But this polity rested on the naive assumption that the goals for administrative authorities were generally settled and that the main resources for achieving them were available. True, socially responsive government required more efficient procedures of communication and supervision. But the more important task before political reformers lay in the development of procedures which assured a closer interaction of officials and all groups in urban society. In effect, they were confusing the tasks of reshaping fundamental perspectives and relationships with a reform polity already committed to the tenets of scientific administration and cost accounting.

Given their reluctance to adjust new techniques of social control to the exigencies of mass democracy, it appears that the political progressives had serious doubts about the efficacy of popular government. In this study, there is sufficient evidence to buttress the view of some historians that the drive for governmental efficiency was essentially a program to develop and insulate the power of emerging metropolitan elites from sustained pressures from the masses as expressed in machine politics.[7] But such a conclusion overlooks another significant realignment of political power in urban society. In redirecting the goals of municipal efficiency from changing governing personalities to the establishment of better administrative methods, the structuralists made it easier for various "functional" organizations representing all occupational classes to gain greater access to government without the intervention of the machine and with the assurance that their goals would be more readily achieved. "The political party, the major instrument of political expression since the 1790's, an innovative and liberating development in its day," Samuel Hays writes, "had by the 1890's become an inhibiting and restrictive influence in political life. It was incapable of expressing the political demands arising from the new functionally based organizations."[8] In this context, the centralization of administrative authority permitted these groups to tell with some accuracy what was going on inside the government. They could thus exercise more pressure on officials in general and administrators in particular.

This development suggests the importance of structural changes in American city administration between 1880 and 1920. The progressive reformers correctly grasped that efficient organization was a prerequisite for more innovative and socially conscious government. "Democratic values require not only that social goals be determined by majority decision," write Peter M. Blau and Marshall W. Meyer, "but also that they be implemented through the most effective methods available—that is, by establishing organizations that are bureaucratically rather than democratically governed. The existence, therefore, of such bureaucracies does not violate democratic values."[9] During these years civil service reform helped increase the number of governmental positions in large cities, and filling these posts were persons with considerable skills and training. With the cooperation of reform-minded mayors, they devised budget and accounting systems, systematized the structure of municipal departments and offices, and professionalized the distribution of public services. Bureaus of municipal research provided a continual flow of information on all of these innovations and helped establish new regulations and agencies in the area of social welfare. And the sight of many small and medium-sized cities under the supervision of professional managers who interpreted efficiency in in terms of more humanitarian services as well as sound fiscal status was something quite new in urban society.

The following two decades witnessed further development of these innovations in local government. While there had been a significant shift in the techniques and rationale of urban administration, the great shift in scale, such as the emergence of public personnel systems, the widespread adoption of the executive budget, effective city planning procedures, and extensive regulation of private enterprise, would have to wait for efficiency experts in the twenties and the innovations of the New Deal.[10] But the basic concepts of modern municipal administration had been introduced in the late nineteenth century and translated into viable systems of governmental regulation in the next two decades. Furthermore, the efficiency movement had produced a concept of public interest which would be the rationale for the increasing emphasis upon welfare capitalism in later years. True, there remained limitations to political progressivism in the area of economic reform. Corporate regulation of public utilities was usually preferred to municipal ownership. But this position was in line with the overall effort of the structuralists to alleviate the social and economic ills of city life while maintaining the basic structure of American capitalism. They replaced nineteenth-century notions of laissez-faire and limited governmental functions with the concept of public responsibility for the welfare of all urban dwellers.

Serious problems remained unresolved, however. Most structuralists expected that rational management meant the ultimate eradication of personal ambitions and passions in city administration. A neutral bureaucracy could then deal more effectively with various community problems, especially in the area of social welfare. This has proven to be a very shaky assumption. Indeed, it appears that self-interest rather than altruism is the prime motivating force among appointive employees at all levels of municipal government. These officials are preoccupied with maintaining their own positions while pursuing at the same time career opportunities for advancement within city agencies. Such behavior produces continual intrabureaucratic competition for power and status. In this struggle, compromise solutions to goal conflicts often mean "a dilution of several positions into a form of nebulous, often ineffective policy."[11]

More disturbing is the failure of public bureaucracies to function effectively as an integrative force in the large metropolis. The progressive theorists firmly believed in the capacity of professional administration to coalesce municipal government and interest groups. Unfortunately, they overlooked the possibility of collective politics among public employees. There was and still is a rough egalitarianism in public service reform ideology, which holds that each candidate for tenure and higher-level positions should be measured against other competitors by the yardstick of merit and performance. As a result, city governments function with little experience and still less legal precedent for dealing with civil servants through municipal employees' unions and associations. These organizations, composed of middle and lower-level officials, control entry to specific agencies along ethnic lines and utilize civil service tenure as protection against outside reform pressures. Constant demands for salary increases and better working conditions compete with improvements in service as drains on the allocation of scarce resources among municipal departments. In the process, the city bureaucracies function as relatively autonomous centers of power in competition and conflict with one another. Their leadership is virtually self-perpetuating and not readily accountable to higher executive authority.[12]

Such dysfunctionalism has led to the perpetuation of certain inefficiencies in big-city administration. There is often little direction or guidance from department heads as to how certain programs should be managed. A process of "incremental" decision-making occurs, characterized by routine responses to a variety of problems and slow delivery of public services to clienteles. Further, municipal agencies are sometimes uncertain about who has jurisdiction and ultimate responsibility for the implementation of social programs. This lack of coordination and responsiveness generates interbureaucratic conflict, with agency protectionism often supplanting program goals.[13] Moreover, occasional "co-option" of regulatory and policy-making agencies by representatives of outside groups, particularly in the enforcement of laws against gambling and awarding of public contracts, produces corruption and inefficiency.[14] In the face of all these conditions, the mayor stands virtually paralyzed before municipal bureaucracies. He cannot get city agencies to deal on a concerted basis with such critical problems as air pollution, transportation, land-use patterns, social welfare, and the enforcement of civil rights legislation.[15]

Most of this insulated power of urban bureaucracy is the unfortunate legacy of the progressive structural reformers. To be sure, modern city governments are impressively competent, generally responsive, and decently humanitarian. Yet the legislative and executive offices reformed in the late nineteenth and early twentieth centuries are incapable of effectively wresting power away from the bureaucratic organizations established to implement the public policies that they were supposed to have been formulating. "Bureaucratization tends to insulate elites, shrouding their activities in a great deal of secrecy," writes J. Rogers Hollingsworth. "Within bureaucracies, professionals tend to be more concerned with the opinions of their colleagues in other communities, even other countries, rather than with the attitudes of their clients. Moreover, the norms of professionalization require that decisions be made according to professional standards—which may run contrary to popular opinion."[16] The remedy for this perversion of public decision-making is to be found in a diffusion of responsibility which inculcates among all urban dwellers a feeling that they have the power to determine important administrative policies which affect them and the common life of the community. Political scientist Vincent Ostrom speaks forcefully to the issue: "The practitioner of American public administration, if he is to contribute to the viability of a democratic society, must be prepared to advance and serve the interests of the individual persons who form his relevant public. His service is to individual persons as users or consumers of public goods and services and not to political masters. He respects the authority of governmental officials who help define and limit the scope of public endeavors."[17]

Furthermore, municipal governments are experiencing a fiscal crisis that was not evident in the early twentieth century. Government costs in areas such as health, welfare, housing, suburban mass transit, highways, public housing, and urban redevelopment have soared beyond the capacity of traditional sources of local revenue. Such expansion has precipitated a desperate search for new revenue sources. The property tax remains as the core of fiscal support of local administration, but urban governments have sought to expand their tax bases with income, excise, and sales taxes.[18] More importantly, state and national governments have assumed an increasing share of the growing costs of municipal services such as education, housing, welfare, and transportation. This intergovernmental activity, however, has resulted in a number of competing bureaucratic agencies and lack of coordination of federal aid programs. Out of the widespread dissatisfaction of public officials with these conditions has come the emphasis upon a more decentralized federal system. The program includes revenue sharing with cities and states and the replacement of existing categorical dispersements with block-grant projects. Both strategies permit urban communities to determine how they will use the funds for various development goals.[19]

The dilemma of size remains. Government reform efforts continue to originate with business and professional elites in the metropolis. Directing their criticism at bureaucratic fragmentation, overlapping jurisdictions, confusion of responsibility, and unregulated growth, they constantly stress the theme that community problems, particularly in the area of public finance, require supergovernments with metropolitan-area authority and functions. This system, reformers argue, will result in more administrative efficiency, coordinated city planning, more equitable dispersal of costs and benefits, and greater access to official decision-making. Low-income groups, however, look with disfavor on attempts to reorder the metropolitan political structure. Many Negro leaders regard metropolitan government as an effort to undermine the political influence of blacks in the central cities. Similarly, organized labor often resists reorganization proposals because it believes that the plans will only be to the advantage of the business community. Other low- and middle-income persons fear that metropolitan decision-making would result in tax increases and less representation. Furthermore, suburban officials and the entrenched administrative agencies in the area usually oppose area-wide government. The issue of governmental consolidation is not, therefore, simply a technical or administrative question. It is also a political matter that involves conflicting values and needs among residents and subcommunities in the metropolitan environment.[20]

Understandably, proposals for metropolitan restructuring are seldom fully implemented. The reformers overlook the fact that governmental reorganization, as was the case in the progressive era, alters the relative access of groups to policy making and administration and raises serious issues of political power. In this context, representativeness and responsiveness became more important considerations for the average citizen then technical questions of operational effectiveness. "Efficiency and economy may be furthered by the creation of a governmental unit of such large size that citizen control would be limited and popular participation discouraged," John C. Bollens and Henry J. Schmandt point out. "Or the type of representation . . . may increase overall effectiveness but deny meaningful access to minority groups. The same dilemma exists with respect to needs. The kind and size of the organization that may be best for areawide administration may be dysfunctional for the management of conflict or the protection of valid neighborhood interests."[21]

Given this situation, awesome chores stretch ahead for municipal administrators and their various business and professional ideologues. Effective political reform will require a reassessment of some cherished beliefs about the merits of centralized government. But it is important for those of us today who favor "participatory democracy" over the efficiency experts in city hall to keep a perspective on political progressivism. In an era of boss politics a reform administration, despite its short life, recovered a large amount of responsible civic management, instituted new forms of political leadership, and extended the welfare functions of the city. When the machine regained control of the government, those accomplishments were not lost; the people had been shown higher standards of public service which the boss wisely chose not to ignore. Forty years of reform agitation and machine counterpressure resulted in the establishment of a more flexible and socially conscious administration than would have been the case had the ideal of nonpartisanship been allowed to fully prevail in American cities. We, therefore, should look back on this period of urban political reform with charity and understanding. In securing the basic reorganization of municipal administration along the lines of middle-class definitions of democracy and efficiency, the structural progressives, while far from paragons, bequeathed to later officials better methods of meeting problems of social control and community welfare. Contemporary architects of efficient administration are not likely to be very effective if in imagination, political skill, and social outlook, they are the inferiors of their progressive predecessors in the painful quest for more humane and democratic city government.

Notes

INTRODUCTION

1. Blake McKelvey, *The Urbanization of America, 1860–1915* (1963), pp. 75–85; George M. Smerk, "The Streetcar: Shaper of American Cities," *Traffic Quarterly* 21 (October 1967): 571–79.

2. On the other hand, rapid growth of smaller New England cities during this period brought about a significant shift in attitudes toward government that generated more direct involvement of officials in the areas of public education, water supply, sewage treatment, street cleaning, and the like. See Michael H. Frisch, *Town into City: Springfield Massachusetts, and the Meaning of Community, 1840–1880* (Cambridge, Mass.: Harvard University Press, 1972), pp. 92–113, 157–75; Estelle M. Feinstein, *Stamford in the Gilded Age: The Political Life of a Connecticut Town, 1868–1893* (Stamford: Stamford Historical Society, 1973), pp. 49–69, 144–48, 162–85.

3. "A Typology for Comparative Local Government," *Midwest Journal of Political Science* 5 (May 1961): 152.

4. *The California Progressives* (Berkeley and Los Angeles: University of California Press, 1951), pp. 89–102.

5. *The Age of Reform: From Bryan to F.D.R.* (New York: Random House, Vintage Books, 1955), pp. 135–43. On the weaknesses of the status theory in analyzing the motivation of middle- and upper-class reformers see David P.

Thelen, "Social Tensions and the Origins of Progressivism," *Journal of American History* 56 (September 1969): 325–29.

   6. *The Search for Order, 1877–1920* (New York: Hill and Wang, 1967), pp. 112–29.

   7. Melvin G. Holli, *Reform in Detroit* (1969), pp. 161-80. I am indebted to Melvin Holli for his perceptive discussion of the structural reform movement. However, my interpretation of the strategy and goals of the structuralists will differ to a considerable extent from his analysis.

CHAPTER I. A NEW CONCEPTION OF POLITICS

   1. "The Failure of Universal Suffrage," *NAR* 127 (July 1878): 4, 7, 20.

   2. "The Sentiment of Equality in American Politics," lecture in Cooley Papers, pp. 51–52.

   3. "Municipal Reform," *NAR* 137 (July 1883): 228; see also C.E. Pickard, "Great Cities and Democratic Institutions," *American Journal of Politics* 4 (April 1894): 378, 385, 389–91.

   4. George L. Prentiss, *Our National Bane; or, The Dry Rot in American Politics* (1877), pp. 7–8.

   5. *Report of the Commissioners to Devise a Plan for the Government of Cities in the State of New York* (1877), p. 9; hereafter cited as Tilden commission, *Report*.

   6. Pp. 170, 508.

   7. Spencer Clinton, "Reform in Municipal Government," *Papers Read before the Cleveland Democracy of Buffalo* (Buffalo, 1886), p. 104.

   8. *The American Commonwealth* (1888), 2:96.

   9. "The Administration of American Cities," *International Review* 4 (September 1877): 634.

   10. "Failure of Universal Suffrage," p. 20. See also Thomas Cooley, "Lectures on Political Science," IV, "Protections and Securities in City Government," May 12, 1879, in Cooley Papers.

   11. "Why the City Government Is Bad," *Nation* 38 (January 10, 1884): 26–27. See also Diana Klebanow, "E.L. Godkin, the City, and Civic Responsibility," *New York Historical Society Quarterly* 55 (January 1971): 63–64.

   12. Frank P. Crandon, "Misgovernment of Great Cities," *Popular Science Monthly* 30 (1886–1887): 521.

   13. "Municipal Reform," *New Englander* 45 (February 1886): 158.

   14. "The Government of American Cities," *Forum* 10 (December 1890): 368.

   15. James Parton, "Municipal Government," *Chautauquan* 8 (January 188): 204; Crandon, "Misgovernment of Great Cities," p. 525.

   16. *The Ecology of Public Administration* (1961), p. 9. See also Herbert A. Simon, *Administrative Behavior* (1965), pp. 39, 179–82.

   17. "Administration of American Cities," p. 634.

   18. Kasson, "Municipal Reform," p. 221.

   19. Ibid., p. 226.

   20. "Misgovernment of Great Cities," p. 524.

21. "Outgrown City Government," *Forum* 2 (February 1887): 543, 545; idem., "Municipal Government," p. 204.

22. "Why the City Government Is Bad," p. 380.

23. *Politics as a Duty and as a Career* (1889), pp. 6–7, 14–15.

24. Theodore Roosevelt, "Phases of State Legislation," *Century* 7 (April 1885): 825.

25. *American Commonwealth*, 2: 37, 43.

26. Quoted in John G. Sproat, *"The Best Men": Liberal Reformers in the Gilded Age* (1968), p. 60.

27. J. Sloat Fassett, "Why Cities Are Badly Governed," *NAR* 150 (May 1890): 631, 634; Simon Patten, "The Decay of State and Local Governments," *Annals* 1 (July 1890): 27.

28. "Municipal Reform," p. 154.

29. White, "The Government of American Cities," p. 372; see also E. L. Godkin, "A Key to Municipal Reform, *NAR* 151 (October 1890): 431.

30. G. Edward White, *The Eastern Establishment and the Western Experience: The West of Frederic Remington, Theodore Roosevelt, and Owen Wister* (New Haven: Yale University Press, 1968), pp. 19–20. On the crucial role of the middle classes in restructuring power relationships in an urban-industrial society see Leonard Reissman, *The Urban Process: Cities in Industrial Societies* (New York: The Free Press, 1964), pp. 180–88.

31. Tilden commission, *Report*, pp. 33, 39–40.

32. "Protections and Securities in City Government," Cooley Papers; Ivins, "Municipal Government", *PSQ* 2 (June 1887): 303–4, 311.

33. *Report*, p. 11.

34. Crandon, "Misgovernment of Great Cities," p. 521; Fiske, *Civil Government in the United States Considered with Some Reference to Its Origins* (Boston: Houghton Mifflin, 1890), p. 132.

35. *The Letters of Theodore Roosevelt*, ed. Elting E. Morison (1951–54), 1: 57n; Richard W.G. Welling, *As the Twig Is Bent* (New York: Putnam, 1942), p. 42. Welling, one of Roosevelt's Harvard classmates, was a member of the Reform Club in the eighties and later joined the City Club of New York.

36. City Reform Club, New York, "Minute Book," October 10, 1882.

37. Roosevelt to Samuel J. Colgate, October 8, 1882, *Letters*, 1:57; "Minute Book," October 16, 1882.

38. Robert Muccigrosso, "The City Reform Club: A Study in Late Nineteenth-Century Reform," *New York Historical Society Quarterly* 52 (July 1968): 240.

39. To Francis Markoe Scott, October 30, 1884, *Letters*, 1: 84–85.

40. To Elihu Root and William H. Bellamy, October 16, 1886, ibid., p. 111.

41. Quoted in David J. Rothman, *Politics and Power: The United States Senate, 1869–1901* (Cambridge, Mass.: Harvard University Press, 1966), p. 225; see also pp. 226–31.

42. Geoffrey Blodgett, "Reform Thought and the Genteel Tradition," in *The Gilded Age*, ed. H. Wayne Morgan, rev. ed. (Syracuse, N.Y.: Syracuse University Press, 1970), pp. 63–64.

43. "The Government of American Cities," p. 369.

44. *The American Political Tradition and the Men Who Made It* (New York: Random House, Vintage Books, 1948), p. 247.

45. "Notes for a Public Lecture at the Johns Hopkins," March 2, 1888, *The Papers of Woodrow Wilson,* ed. Arthur Link and Associates (1966-), 5: 697.

46. *Congressional Government: A Study in American Politics* (Boston: Houghton Mifflin, 1885), pp. 255, 284.

47. Dwight Waldo, *The Administrative State* (1948), pp. 26n.

48. "The Study of Administration," *PSQ* 2 (June 1887): 212, 216, 218.

49. Ibid., p. 210.

50. Ellis B. Oberholtzer, "Home Rule for American Cities," *Annals* 3 (May 1893): 742-47, 763; Frank J. Goodnow, *Comparative Administrative Law,* (1893), 1: 223-31.

51. Parton, "Outgrown City Government," p. 544; Patten, "State and Local Governments," p. 27.

52. "Municipal Government," *Scribner's Magazine* 2 (July-December 1887): 487.

53. Harold C. Syrett, *The City of Brooklyn, 1865-1898* (1944), pp. 90-91; Edward M. Shepard, "The Brooklyn Idea in City Government," *Forum* 16 (September 1893): 41-42.

54. Quoted in Syrett, p. 92.

55. "Municipal Government," p. 490.

56. *Civil Government in the United States,* p. 131.

57. Syrett, pp. 105-8, 110-13; Low, "An American View of Municipal Government in the United States," in Bryce, *American Commonwealth,* 1: 628-29.

58. Ibid., pp. 623-24.

59. Bridenbaugh, *Cities in Revolt: Urban Life in America, 1743-1776* (New York: Knopft, 1955), pp. 292-331; Wade, *The Urban Frontier: Pioneer Life in Early Pittsburgh, Cincinnati, Lexington, Louisville, and St. Louis* (Chicago: University of Chicago Press, Phoenix Books. 1964), pp. 270-303.

60. Low, "Obstacles to Good City Government," *Forum* 5 (May 1888): 261; idem, "The Problem of City Government in the United States," *Outlook* 53 (April 4, 1896): 624-25.

61. Low, "The Problem of City Government," *An Address* (delivered to the students of history and politics in the Johns Hopkins University), April 1889, p. 7.

62. Low, "The Government of Cities in the United States," *Century* 42 (September 1891): 730.

63. "The Problem of City Government," p. 10.

64. C. K. Yearley, *The Money Machines: The Breakdown and Reform of Governmental and Party Finance in the North, 1860-1920* (1970), pp. 103-18. My view of urban politics and reform in the late nineteenth century has been influenced particularly by Yearley's study, a major work which says a great deal that is new and important about the period.

65. Storey, "The Government of Cities: The Need of a Divorce of Municipal Business from Politics," *Proceedings of NCSRL,* 1891, p. 63. See also

Lewis Janes, *The Problem of City Government* (New York: Appleton, 1892), p. 171.

66. "Municipal Government: Lessons from the Experience of Quincy, Massachusetts," *Forum* 14 (November 1892): 290.

67. "Why the City Is Not Well Governed," *Nation* 50 (March 12, 1890): 216.

68. "One Remedy for Municipal Misgovernment," *Forum* 12 (September 1891): 154-56.

69. Albert Shaw, *Municipal Government in Great Britain* (New York: Century, 1895), p. 4; idem, *Municipal Government in Continental Europe* (1895), pp. 289, 291, 304-5, 312-14, 323. See also Lloyd J. Graybar, *Albert Shaw of the "Review of Reviews"* (1974), pp. 79-82.

70. See, for example, Francois Vigier, *Change and Apathy: Liverpool and Manchester during the Industrial Revolution* (Cambridge, Mass.: MIT Press, 1970), pp. 6-9, passim; C.K. Yearley, "The 'Provincial Party' and the Megalopolises: London, Paris, and New York, 1850-1910," *Comparative Studies in Society and History* 15 (January 1973): 51-88.

71. "One Remedy for Municipal Misgovernment," p. 166.

72. Quoted in Geoffrey Blodgett, *The Gentle Reformers: Massachusetts Democrats in the Cleveland Era* (1966), p. 33.

73. "The Problems of Municipal Government," *Annals* 4 (May 1894): 865, 873, 879-81.

74. See, for instance, R. Hal Williams, "'Dry Bones and Dead Language': The Democratic Party," in Morgan, ed., *The Gilded Age*, pp. 129-48; Lewis L. Gould, "The Republican Search for a National Majority," ibid., pp. 171-87; Richard Jensen, *The Winning of the Midwest: Social and Political Conflict, 1888-1896* (Chicago: University of Chicago Press, 1971), pp. 154-77.

75. "How to Improve Municipal Government," *NAR* 153 (November 1891): 582-84, 587-88, 590, 593-94 (an article including observations on local government by the mayors of Boston, Baltimore, Buffalo, and St. Louis).

CHAPTER II. PATRONAGE AND POWER

1. Prentiss, *Our National Bane*, p. 7.

2. Quoted in Syrett, *City of Brooklyn*, p. 121.

3. Herbert Welsh, "The Influence of Spoils upon the Government of American Cities," *Proceedings of NCSRL*, 1894, pp. 58, 60.

4. Bryce, *American Commonwealth*, 2: 94-95.

5. *The Political Problem* (1890), p. 20.

6. *Thirty Years of New York Politics* (1899), pp. iii-iv.

7. Ari Hoogenboom, *Outlawing the Spoils* (1961), p. 1.

8. Sproat, *"Best Men"*, p. 258; Philip S. Benjamin, "Gentlemen Reformers in the Quaker City, 1870-1912," *PSQ* 85 (March 1970): 68.

9. Quoted in C. Stuart Patterson, "Municipal Reform and Civil Service Reform," *Penn Monthly* 13 (April 1882): 297, 299.

10. "Municipal Government," pp. 300, 311-12.

11. "Study of Administration," p. 210.

12. Hoogenboom, *Outlawing the Spoils*, pp. ix–x, 192–97.

13. Gerald W. McFarland, "Partisan of Nonpartisanship: Dorman B. Eaton and the Genteel Reform Tradition," *Journal of American History* 54 (March 1968): 806–12, 816.

14. Ibid., p. 813.

15. Eaton, "The Public Service and the Public," *Atlantic Monthly* 41 (February 1878): 250; idem, "Tenure of Office," *Lippincott's Magazine* 27 (June 1881): 588–89.

16. *Civil Service in Great Britain* (1880), pp. 389, 397–98.

17. Ibid., pp. 391–92, 400–401.

18. U.S. Congress, Senate, Committee on Civil Service and Retrenchment, *Report of the Committee of the Senate to Regulate and Improve the Civil Service of the United States*, 47th Cong., 1st sess., May 15, 1882, S. Rept. 576, p. 8. Drawing upon the testimony of prominent political reformers, this committee would draft the bill which became the Pendleton Act of 1883, establishing civil service regulations in the federal government.

19. Sproat, *"Best Men"* p. 269.

20. U.S. Congress, Senate, op. cit. (n. 18 above), pp. 96, 112–13, 159.

21. James Q. Wilson, "The Economy of Patronage," *Journal of Political Economy* 69 (August 1961): 370–79.

22. Blake McKelvey, *American Urbanization: A Comparative History* (Glenview, Ill.: Scott, Foresman, 1973), p. 73; John A. Garraty, *The New Commonwealth, 1877–1890* (New York: Harper Torchbook, 1968), pp. 201–2.

23. "Civil Service Reform," *Civil Service Record* 4 (January 1885): 68.

24. Eaton, *Civil Service in Great Britain*, pp. 389–90; see also Patterson, "Municipal Reform," pp. 300–301.

25. Henry Lambert, *The Progress of Civil Service Reform in the United States* (pamphlet, 1885), pp. 10–12; Hoogenboom, *Outlawing the Spoils*, pp. 187–89.

26. New York Civil Service Reform Association, *Purposes of the Civil Service Reform Association* (New York, 1881), p. 13.

27. William H. Tolman, *Municipal Reform Movements in the United States* (1895), pp. 121–22.

28. *Letters Addressed by the Civil Service Reform Association to the Various Candidates for the Governorship, and for Congress, the Assembly, and City Offices during the Campaign of 1882 with Replies to the Same* (New York, 1882), pp. 52, 53–54.

29. "Civil Service Reform in Municipal Government," *Civil Service Record* 2 (April 1882): 1. Published in the 1880s by the Boston and Cambridge civil service reform associations, the *Record* (later *Good Government*) was the magazine of the National Civil Service Reform League. It kept reformers apprised of the movement by printing articles and speeches of reformers, reports of civil service groups, and governmental publications.

30. Robert A. Dahl, *Who Governs?* (1961), pp. 31–34; Alexander B. Callow, Jr., *The Tweed Ring* (New York: Oxford University Press, 1966), pp. 116–31; Sam Bass Warner, Jr., *The Private City* (1968), pp. 86–91.

31. State of New York, Senate and Assembly, *An Act to Regulate and Improve the Civil Service of the State of New York*, 106th sess., chap. 354, May 4,

1883, in *Laws of the State of New York Passed at the One Hundred and Sixth Session of the Legislature* (Albany, 1883), pp. 530–35.

32. "The Year's Work in Civil Service Reform," *An Address* (delivered before the National Civil Service Reform League), August 6, 1884 (New York, 1884), p. 13.

33. "New Civil Service Regulations for New York City," *Civil Service Record* 4 (September 1884): 29–32; *First Report of the Civil Service Commission of the City of Brooklyn, Presented to Seth Low, Mayor, December 26, 1884*, p. 13; "Progress of the Reform in Buffalo," *Civil Service Record* 6 (July 1886): 7.

34. *First Annual Report of the Civil Service Commissioners of Massachusetts Together with the Civil Service Law, and the Rules and Regulations Relating Thereto, 1885* (Boston, 1885), pp. 15–22.

35. *Progress of Civil Service Reform*, p. 20.

36. Quoted in *Civil Service Record* 4 (August 1884): 23; Wheeler, "Civil Service Reform," pp. 66–68; *First Report of the Civil Service Commission* (n. 33 above), p. 4.

37. *An Autobiography* (1916), pp. 149–50.

38. Curtis, "The Situation," *An Address* (delivered before the National Civil Service Reform League), August 6, 1886 (New York, 1886), p. 20; Shaw, "Civil Service Reform and Municipal Reform," *Proceedings of NCSRL*, 1897, p. 129.

39. Quoted in *Address of the President and Report of the Secretary of the Civil Service Reform Association of Brooklyn, February 20, 1890* (pamphlet, 1890), p. 7.

40. Ari Hoogenboom, "Civil Service Reform and Public Morality," in Morgan, ed., *Gilded Age* (chap. 1, n. 42), p. 80.

41. Report, February, 1889, *Civil Service Record* 4 (October 1889): 46. Godkin and Wheeler were members of the board.

42. Bayrd Still, *Milwaukee* (1965), pp. 282–83.

43. *The New Citizenship: Origins of Progressivism in Wisconsin, 1885-1900* (1972), p. 29.

44. Yearley, *Money Machines*, pp. 103–4.

45. *New Citizenship*, pp. 30-31.

46. See Waldo, *Administrative State*, p. 192, and Frederick C. Mosher, *Democracy and the Public Service* (1968), p. 65.

47. Roosevelt, "The Merit System versus the Patronage System," *Century* 39 (February 1890): 628; Thomas A. Devlin, *Municipal Reform in the United States* (New York: Putnam, 1896), p. 85.

48. "Civil Service Reform from the Point of View of City Government," *Good Government* 13 (September 15, 1893): 30.

49. "Merit System versus the Patronage System," p. 632.

50. Devlin, *Municipal Reform*, p. 100; MacVeagh, "The Business Man in Municipal Politics," *Proceedings of the Louisville Conference for Good City Government and the Third Annual Meeting of the National Municipal League, May 1897*, p. 142.

51. *Democracy and the Public Service* (1968), p. 64.

52. John M. Dobson, *Politics in the Gilded Age* (1972), p. 77.

53. Prichard, "The Study of the Science of Municipal Government," *Annals* 2 (January 1892): 450, 452–53, 456; Wilby, "Municipal Reform Impossible under the Spoils System," *Proceedings of NCSRL,* 1894, p. 80.

54. Frank Morison, "Municipal Government, A Corporate Not a Political Problem," *Forum* 13 (August 1892): 793–94.

55. Tolman, *Municipal Reform Movements,* pp. 70–71, 115–16; Municipal League of Philadelphia, *What Is the Municipal League?* (pamphlet, 1894), p. 1.

56. Tolman, pp. 112–13; Thelen, *New Citizenship,* pp. 158–60.

57. Yearley, *Money Machines,* pp. 68–69, 71.

58. Herbert Welsh, "A Definite Step toward Municipal Reform," *Forum* 15 (1894): 179–85; Frank Mann Stewart, *A Half Century of Municipal Reform: The History of the National Municipal League* (1950), pp. 15–18.

59. Dobson, *Politics in the Gilded Age,* p. 79.

60. "The Relation of Civil Service Reform to Municipal Reform," *Proceedings of the National Conference for Good City Government,* January 1894, pp. 124–26, 128–29, 133; see also George Gluyas Mercer, "Municipal Government of Philadelphia," ibid., pp. 96–98.

61. Thelen, *New Citizenship,* pp. 163–64.

62. Joseph Bush Kingsbury, "The Merit System in Chicago from 1895 to 1915: The Adoption of the Civil Service Law," *Public Personnel Studies* 3 (November 1925): 306–11; *Fifteenth Report of the United States Civil Service Commission, July 1, 1897 to June 30, 1898,* pp. 498, 500–501.

63. "Municipal Affairs in Philadelphia," *Proceedings of the Louisville Conference . . . Third Annual Meeting . . . May 1897,* p. 187.

64. *Fifteenth Report* (n. 62 above), p. 501.

65. "The Changing Political Structure of the City in Industrial America," *Journal of Urban History* 1 (November 1974): 6–25.

CHAPTER III. STRENGTHENING THE EXECUTIVE

1. Scott Greer, *Metropolitics* (1963), pp. 9–10, 12.

2. Quoted in Claudius O. Johnson, *Carter Henry Harrison I* (1928), p. 246. Due mainly to a three-way struggle between Democrats, Republicans, and the Socialist Labor party, the election scattered enough votes to give Harrison the victory by a slim margin. For more information on the election see Bessie L. Pierce, *A History of Chicago,* 3 vols. (New York: Knopf, 1937–57), 3: 351–53.

3. The Illinois Municipal Act of 1872 provided mayors with powers of appointment and removal subject to confirmation by the city council and also gave them authority to veto items in appropriation bills. Edwin A. Greenlaw, "Office of the Mayor in the United States," *Municipal Affairs* 3 (March 1899): 53–54.

4. Willis J. Abbot, *Carter Henry Harrison: A Memoir* (New York: Dodd, Mead, 1895), p. 240; Johnson, *Harrison,* pp. 247–49.

5. Johnson, p. 251.

6. Abbot, p. 246.

7. Johnson, pp. 260–61.

8. *Inter-Ocean*, April 2, 1885, as quoted in Johnson, p. 264; *Mayor's Message for the Year, City of Chicago, 1887*, p. 5.

9. *Mayor's Message . . . 1887*, p. 36.

10. Quoted in Gerald Kurland, *Seth Low* (1971), p. 43.

11. Ibid., p. 44; Shepard, "Brooklyn Idea" (chap. 1, n. 53), p. 43.

12. Syrett, *City of Brooklyn*, pp. 111–13.

13. Ibid., pp. 132–33.

14. *First Report of the Civil Service Commission of the City of Brooklyn . . . December 26, 1884*, p. 3.

15. Kurland, *Seth Low*, pp. 41–42.

16. "Brooklyn Idea," p. 39.

17. James R. Bugbee, *City Government of Boston* (1887), p. 41.

18. Ibid., pp. 35–36; Thomas A. Reed and Paul Webbink, eds., *Documents Illustrative of American Municipal Government* (1926), pp. 151–52.

19. Bugbee, pp. 41–42.

20. E.V. Smalley, "The Philadelphia Committee of One Hundred," *Century* 26 (July 1883): 395–99; Edward P. Allinson and Boies Penrose, *The City Government of Philadelphia*, (1887), pp. 61–63.

21. Allinson and Penrose, pp. 64–65.

22. Wharton School of Finance and Economy, *The City Government of Philadelphia: A Study in Municipal Administration* (Philadelphia: University of Pennsylvania Press, 1893), pp. 20–24; Greenlaw, "Office of the Mayor," p. 51.

23. Allinson and Penrose, pp. 71–72.

24. Robert M. Fogelson, *The Fragmented Metropolis: Los Angeles, 1850–1930* (Cambridge, Mass.: Harvard University Press, 1967), pp. 30–31.

25. In the mayoralty campaign of 1886, Hewitt was the candidate of both Tammany and the County Democracy. The other candidates were Henry George, the nominee of Irving Hall (Brooklyn's counterpart of Tammany) and organized labor, and the young Theodore Roosevelt, the choice of the Republican party. Endorsed by a few business groups, Roosevelt had little chance to win. Frightened by George's socialist theories and his popularity with the Irish masses, many conservatives in the Republican ranks voted for Hewitt. See Everett P. Wheeler, *Sixty Years of American Life* (1917), pp. 333–34; Allan Nevins, *Abram S. Hewitt: With Some Account of Peter Cooper* (1935; reprint ed., 1967), pp. 460–69.

26. Nevins, pp. 401, 409; Matthew T. Downey, "Grover Cleveland and Abram S. Hewitt: The Limits of Factional Consensus," *New York Historical Society Quarterly* 54 (July 1970): 225.

27. Reed and Webbink, *Municipal Government*, pp. 132–34; Greenlaw, "Office of the Mayor," p. 49.

28. Nevins, pp. 482–83.

29. *Nation* 45 (August 11, 1887): 103.

30. Nevins, p. 489.

31. *Nation* 44 (June 23, 1887): 521; Wheeler, *Sixty Years of American Life*, pp. 336–37.

32. *Letters of Theodore Roosevelt*, 1: 148–49; Nevins, pp. 525–26.

33. Joy J. Jackson, *New Orleans in the Gilded Age* (1969), pp. 99–100.

34. Ibid., p. 101.

35. Ibid., pp. 102–6.

36. Winston, quoted in *Review of Reviews* 7 (February 1893): 17; Eustis, January 13, 1893, in Box 10, Albert Shaw Papers.

37. *Review of Reviews*, 7: 16.

38. Holli, *Reform in Detroit*, pp. 16–19.

39. Ibid., pp. 24–27.

40. Ibid., p. 29.

41. Hazen S. Pingree, "Detroit: A Municipal Study," *Outlook* 55 (February 6, 1897): 437–42; Holli, *Reform in Detroit*, pp. 33–100.

42. Holli, pp. 126–28.

43. Ibid., pp. 136, 145, 154.

44. Blodgett, *Gentle Reformers*, pp. 150, 158–59.

45. Nathan Matthews, *The City Government of Boston: Valedictory Address to Members of the Council* (Boston: Rockwell and Churchill, 1895), pp. 17–27.

46. Ibid., pp. 179–80. Woodrow Wilson had argued in a similar vein before a Brown University audience in 1889: "The chief characteristic of a city . . . is that of a business corporation. But it is by no means so simple as if it were only a business corporation. It is also an organ of government, a political body, and its complexity arises from this fact." "A Newspaper Report of a Lecture on Municipal Government," January 19, 1889, *Papers of Woodrow Wilson*, 6: 52.

47. Matthews, *City Government*, pp. 29–32; Moorfield Storey, "Municipal Government of Boston," *Proceedings of the National Conference for Good City Government, January 1894*, p. 69.

48. Samuel B. Capen, "The Boston Municipal League," *American Journal of Politics* 5 (July 1894): 7; Storey, "Municipal Government of Boston," pp. 66–67; Matthews, *City Government*, p. 118.

49. *Gentle Reformers*, p. 161.

50. "The Lexow Investigation," *Current History* 4 (July-September 1894): 607–12; Frank P. Pavey, "Mayor Strong's Experiment in New York City," *Forum* 23 (June 1897): 539–40; quoted material in George F. Knerr, "The Mayoral Administration of William L. Strong, New York City, 1895–1897" (Ph.D. dissertation, New York University, 1957), pp. 26–28.

51. Tolman, *Municipal Reform Movements*, pp. 85–91.

52. Pavey, "Mayor Strong's Experiment," p. 541; Knerr, "William L. Strong," pp. 36, 39–41; see also Richard W.G. Welling Papers, Box 23.

53. In early February 1895 Mayor Strong appointed a committee, headed by Carl Schurz, to investigate the policies and procedures of the police department. After a month of interrogating various members of the department, the committee reported that appointments and promotions were generally secured through "political influence" or by "absolute purchases" while civil service rules did not "interfere seriously with either practice." "Report of Committee to Investigate Appointment and Promotion in the Police Department, February 25, 1895," Shaw Papers, Box 3.

54. Pavey, "Mayor Strong's Experiment," pp. 542–45; Knerr, "William L. Strong," pp. 67–74.

55. To William L. Strong, April 17, 1897, *Letters of Theodore Roosevelt*, 2: 594. See also James F. Richardson, *The New York Police: Colonial Times to 1901* (New York: Oxford University Press, 1970), pp. 259–60.

56. Knerr, "William L. Strong," pp. 122–37; Richard Skolnick, "George Edwin Waring, Jr.: A Model for Reformers," *New York Historical Society Quarterly* 52 (October 1968): 359–60, 367–69.

57. Knerr, "William L. Strong," pp. 166–69, 191–92, 201–2, 208–10.

58. Sol Cohen, *Progressives and Urban School Reform* (1964), pp. 30–45; David C. Hammack, "The Centralization of New York City's Public School System, 1896: A Social Analysis of a Political Decision" (M.A. thesis, Columbia University, 1969), pp. 27, 51–78, 92–95.

59. James B. Lane, *Jacob A. Riis and the American City* (Port Washington, N.Y.: Kennikat Press, 1974), pp. 119–26.

60. Wheeler, *Sixty Years of American Life*, p. 358; "Memorandum of Good Government Campaign Headquarters," October 16, 1896, Welling Papers, Box 23.

61. Pavey, "Mayor Strong's Experiment," pp. 241–42; Knerr, "William L. Strong," pp. 272–74, 282.

62. Delos F. Wilcox, "The First Municipal Campaign of Greater New York," *Municipal Affairs* 2 (June 1898): 212–20.

63. To his father, December 15, 1894, in *The Letters of Lincoln Steffens*, ed. Granville Hicks and Ella Winter, 2 vols. (New York: Harcourt, Brace, 1938), 1: 108. See also Roswell P. Flower, "Is Non-Partisanship in Municipal Government Feasible?" *Forum* 23 (June 1897): 532, and John W. Keller, "Municipal Reformers in Party Politics," *Municipal Affairs* 4 (June 1900): 343–46.

CHAPTER IV. THE POLITICS OF NONPARTISANSHIP

1. *The Rise and Growth of American Politics* (1898), p. 301.

2. Blodgett, *Gentle Reformers*, p. 243.

3. Robert C. Brooks, "Business Men in Civic Service: The Merchants' Municipal Committee of Boston," *Municipal Affairs* 1 (September 1897): 492–93, 497–98, 504.

4. George C. Hooker, "Mayor Quincy of Boston," *Review of Reviews* 19 (May 1899): 576; "A Progressive Administration," *City Government* 2 (April 1897): 102.

5. Josiah Quincy, "Municipal Progress in Boston," *Independent* 52 (February 15, 1900): 426.

6. Francis C. Lowell, "The Municipal Service of Boston," *Atlantic Monthly* 81 (March 1898): 319–20. Quincy also promoted some social reform, including expansion of public bathing facilities and the city's playgrounds. Hooker, "Mayor Quincy of Boston," p. 577; Quincy, "Municipal Progress," pp. 424–25.

7. Blodgett, *Gentle Reformers*, pp. 248, 258–59.

8. Seeking a candidate who could win the support of the growing majority of lower-income ethnic groups, the Democrats nominated Harrison in 1897 on a platform which appealed to these social classes. Running against him were Judge Nathaniel C. Sears, candidate of the city's boss-ridden Republican organization, and John M. Harlan, former alderman and reform-minded independent. Harrison, capitalizing upon his father's popularity and promising to protect the cultural life-styles and personal liberties of the masses of Democratic voters from the efforts of upper-income pietistic Protestant Republicans to use the government for imposing their moralistic programs on the community, won over Harlan and Sears by a considerable margin. See his autobiography, *Stormy Years* (1935), pp. 103–4, 112–13, 118–20; also, Joel Arthur Tarr, *A Study in Boss Politics: William Lorimer of Chicago* (Urbana: University of Illinois Press, 1971), pp. 83–85.

9. *Stormy Years*, p. 162.

10. *Outlook* 58 (February 5, 1898): 309; Tarr, *Study in Boss Politics*, pp. 44–45.

11. Joseph Bush Kingsbury, "The Merit System in Chicago from 1895 to 1915: The Administration of the Civil Service Law under the Various Mayors," *Public Personnel Studies* 4 (May 1926): 154–56; Harrison, *Stormy Years*, pp. 108–9, 179–81.

12. Nick A. Komons, "Chicago, 1893–1907: The Politics of Reform" (Ph.D. dissertation, George Washington University, 1961), pp. 253, 255–56; Kingsbury, "Merit System in Chicago," pp. 158–59; Harrison, *Stormy Years*, pp. 177–78.

13. Kingsbury, "Merit System in Chicago," pp. 159–60; Kent to Steffens, June 9, 1904, Lincoln Steffens Papers, Box J-K.

14. Komons, "Politics of Reform," pp. 244–45; see also Willis J. Abbot, "The Harrison Dynasty in Chicago," *Munsey's Magazine* 29 (September 1903): 814.

15. H.H. Bowen to Shaw, March 10, 1900, Shaw Papers, Box 10.

16. Contrary to many municipal charters at this time, Baltimore's charter did not include civil service regulations and mayoral appointments required consent of the city council. James B. Crooks, *Politics and Progress: The Rise of Urban Progressivism in Baltimore, 1895–1911* (1968), p. 95.

17. Ibid., p. 99.

18. W.H. Tammen, "Changes Wrought by Baltimore's New Charter," *New York Times*, August 25, 1903, p. 6; Crooks, *Politics and Progress*, pp. 99–100.

19. "A Programme of Municipal Reform," *American Journal of Sociology* 1 (March 1896): 552–53, 562.

20. "American Political Ideas and Their Institutions and Their Relation to the Problem of Good City Government," *Proceedings of the Louisville Conference for Good City Government and Third Annual Meeting of the National Municipal League, May 1897*, pp. 76–78; see also James H. Hyslop, "Responsibility in Municipal Government," *Forum* 28 (November 1899): 473–74.

21. Dwight Waldo, "Development of Theory of Democratic Administration," *American Political Science Review* 46 (March 1952): 85–86.

22. "Democracy and Efficiency," *Atlantic Monthly* 87 (March 1901): 291.
23. Lurton W. Blassingame, "Frank J. Goodnow: Progressive Urban Reformer," *North Dakota Quarterly* 40 (Summer 1970): 23–24, 28.
24. Goodnow, *Politics and Administration* (1900), pp. 16, 23–24, 37; Henry Jones Ford, "Politics and Administration," *Annals* 16 (September 1900): 185–86.
25. Goodnow, *Politics and Administration*, pp. 24–25, 45, 79–80.
26. Goodnow, *Comparative Administrative Law*, 2: 140–43, and *Politics and Administration*, p. 85.
27. Frank J. Goodnow, "The Place of the Council and of the Mayor in the Organization of Municipal Government," *Proceedings of the Indianapolis Conference . . . Fourth Annual Meeting . . . December 1898*, pp. 71–81; Goodnow, *Politics and Administration*, pp. 81, 86–90; Blassingame, "Frank J. Goodnow," pp. 29–30. One close student of local government, on the other hand, saw the city council as the "proper repository" of administrative control and recommended that it be given more authority over public employees. E. Dana Durand, "Council Government versus Mayor Government," *PSQ* 15 (1900): 441, 450–51, 685–88, 699–703, 709.
28. *A Municipal Program . . . Adopted by the League, November 17, 1899* (1900), pp. iv–xi; Stewart, *Municipal Reform*, pp. 28–49.
29. Melvin G. Holli, "Urban Reform in the Progressive Era," in *The Progressive Era*, ed. Lewis L. Gould (Syracuse: Syracuse University Press, 1974), pp. 137–39.
30. *A Municipal Program*, pp. 169, 201, 204, 214–15.
31. Ibid., pp. 204–10, 215.
32. Edward M. Shepard, "The Second Mayoralty Election in Greater New York," *Atlantic Monthly* 74 (February 1902): 196–201 Feeling that the movement would be more clearly seen as nonpartisan if the Republicans supported a reform-minded Democrat, the Citizens' Union had initially preferred that Comptroller Bird S. Coler receive the fusion nomination. Writing to Edward Shepard on February 6, 1902, Everett Wheeler explained the shift to Low: "They [the Republican leaders] did undoubtedly say that he [Bird Coler] could not command the full vote of their organization. But he was very fully considered. And in my opinion he would have been nominated, if he had been willing to declare himself against the wrongdoings of the Tammany administration and pledge himself to reform them." Wheeler Papers, Box 3.
33. Shepard, "Second Mayoralty Election," pp. 202–8; Wheeler, *Sixty Years of American Life*, pp. 392–96.
34. *Review of Reviews* 25 (February 1902): 22–23; Kurland, *Seth Low*, pp. 145–46. On the impact of settlement workers on urban politics and public policy during the progressive era see Allen F. Davis, *Spearheads for Reform: The Social Settlements and the Progressive Movement, 1890–1914* (New York: Oxford University Press, 1967), especially chaps. 4, 8, 9.
35. Kurland, *Seth Low*, pp. 164–65.
36. *Review of Reviews* 25 (February 1902): 139.
37. "The New York Situation," *Proceedings of the Boston Conference . . . Eighth Annual Meeting . . . May 1902, pp. 134–35; also see Walter L. Hawley,*

"The Strength and Weakness of Tammany Hall," NAR 173 (October 1901): 482-85.

38. The Shame of the Cities (1904), pp. 211-12. Recently, historians have taken a more critical view of the social functions of the municipal machine. See Callow, The Tweed Ring, pp. 159-60; Crooks, Politics and Progress, pp. vii, 8-9, 19-21; Kurland, Seth Low, p. 203; L.E. Fredman, "Seth Low: Theorist of Municipal Reform," Journal of American Studies 6 (April 1972): 38.

39. Holli, Reform in Detroit, p. 167.

40. Kurland, Seth Low, p. 165.

41. Gustavus Myers, "The Results of Reform in New York City," Independent 55 (October 22, 1903): 2493; Kurland, Seth Low, pp. 166-68. For more information on the extensive reforms of the charities department under Homer Folks see Walter I. Trattner, Homer Folks: Pioneer in Social Welfare (New York: Columbia University Press, 1968), pp. 75-81.

42. Kurland, Seth Low, pp. 206-12.

43. Tom L. Johnson, My Story (1913), pp. 108-17; Robert H. Bremmer, "Tom L. Johnson: Reformed Businessman," American Journal of Economics and Sociology 3 (April 1948): 299-301, 308-9.

44. My Story, p. 167.

45. Ibid., pp. 118-19, 172-74; Eugene Murdock, "Cleveland's Johnson: The Cabinet," Ohio Historical Quarterly 56 (October 1957): 378-80.

46. Interview in 1905, Steffens Papers, Box J-K; My Story, pp. 179-84; Murdock, "Cleveland's Johnson," pp. 381-90.

47. My Story, p. 169. Years later, Lincoln Steffens described Johnson's ability to lure capable men to public service: "A practical businessman, he was a practical politician, too. He knew the game. He could pick and lead a team; men loved to follow him. . . . Resourceful and understanding of the economics of a fight, he could make clear to others what they were up against and what they had to do about it." The Autobiography of Lincoln Steffens (1931), 2: 478.

48. The Confessions of a Reformer (1925), p. 115; see also pp. 98, 109, 123.

49. My Story, pp. 123-30, 174-78, 182-83, 209-12; Edward W. Bemis, "Tom L. Johnson's Achievements as Mayor of Cleveland," Review of Reviews 43 (May 1911): 558-60.

50. George Cartwright to James A. Johnston, March 14, 1911, Tom L. Johnson Papers.

51. "The Basis of Present Reform Movements," Annals 21 (March 1903): 249-50.

52. Eugene M. Tobin, "The Progressive as Politician: Jersey City, 1896-1907," New Jersey History 91 (Spring 1973): 11-15.

53. Ibid., pp. 15-19.

54. Gordon H. Cilley, "Mayor Weaver's Work in Philadelphia," New York Times, September, 1903, p. 7.

55. "The Overthrow of the Spoils System in Philadelphia," Proceedings of NCSRL, 1905, pp. 152-59.

56. Thomas Raeburn White, "The Revolution in Philadelphia," Proceedings of the Atlantic Conference . . . Twelfth Annual Meeting . . . Annual Meeting . . . League, April 1906, pp. 140-47; William S. Vare, My Forty Years in Politics

(Philadelphia: Roland Swain Co., 1933), pp. 90–95. William Vare, along with his brothers Edwin and George, built the South Philadelphia machine which became the core of the city's Republican organization in the early twentieth century. See Warner, *The Private City*, pp. 215–19.

57. A. Julius Frieberg, "The Cincinnati Situation," *Proceedings of the Atlantic Conference . . . April 1906*, pp. 124–29; Zane L. Miller, *Boss Cox's Cincinnati: Urban Politics in the Progressive Era* (1968), pp. 182–92.

58. "The New Patriotism: A Golden Rule Government for Cities," *Municipal Affairs* 3 (September 1899): 460. For the work of Jones see Harvey S. Ford, "The Life and Times of Golden Rule Jones" (Ph.D. dissertation, University of Michigan, 1953).

59. Brand Whitlock, *Forty Years of It* (1914), pp. 188, 260–62; Jack Tager, *The Intellectual and Urban Reform: Brand Whitlock and the Progressive Movement* (1968), pp. 71–75, 82, 96–97.

60. Here I have drawn on Charles R. Adrian and Charles Press, *Governing Urban America* (1972), pp. 210–16, and Dahl, *Who Governs?*, pp. 186, 204–5.

CHAPTER V. FISCAL INSTRUMENTS OF EFFICIENCY

1. Fred W. Riggs, "Prismatic Society and Financial Administration," *Administrative Science Quarterly* 5 (June 1960): 37–38, relates the political context of fiscal reform and class connections.

2. Frederick R. Clow, *A Comparative Study of the Administration of City Finances in the United States, with Special Reference to the Budget* (1901), p. 14.

3. Ibid., pp. 26–27.

4. Ibid., p. 30.

5. Charles C. Williamson, *The Finances of Cleveland* (1907), p. 45; Clow, *City Finances*, pp. 30–31.

6. Gamaliel Bradford, "Our Failures in Municipal Government," *Annals* 3 (May 1893): 33–34; Frederick W. Kelly, "Responsibility in Municipal Government," *American Journal of Politics* 4 (May 1894): 459–60.

7. Frederick A. Cleveland, "Evolution of the Budget Idea in the United States," *Annals* 62 (November 1915): 22.

8. Edward D. Durand, *The Finances of New York City* (1898), pp. 253–54, 260–61.

9. Ibid., pp. 259–61.

10. Augustus R. Hatton, comp., *Digest of City Charters Together with Other Statutory and Constitutional Provisions Relating to Cities* (1906), pp. 99–100, 99–100.

11. Jacob H. Hollander, *The Financial History of Baltimore* (1899), pp. 363–64; *Digest of City Charters*, pp. 110–11, 147, 167–68; Clow, *City Finances*, p. 42.

12. "The Government of Greater New York," *NAR* 169 (July 1899): 95.

13. *Digest of City Charters*, pp. 280, 283–84; Williamson, *Finances of Cleveland*, pp. 34–35.

14. John A. Fairlie, *Essays in Municipal Administration* (1908), p. 190.

15. *Digest of City Charters*, pp. 285–86; Clow, *City Finances*, p. 83.

16. Charles Waldo Haskins, "The Municipal Accounts of Chicago," *Proceedings of the Rochester Conference for Good City Government and the Seventh Annual Meeting of the National Municipal League, May 1901*, pp. 307–13; Frederick A. Cleveland, "Chicago Accounting Reform," *Proceedings of the Detroit Conference . . . Ninth Annual Meeting . . . April 1903*, pp. 268–76.

17. Harvey S. Chase, "Uniform Accounting Applied to Boston, Baltimore and Other Municipalities," *Proceedings of the Boston Conference . . . Eighth Annual Meeting . . . May 1902*, pp. 310–12, 314–21.

18. Edward M. Hartwell, "Report of the Committee on Uniform Municipal Accounting and Statistics," *Proceedings of the Boston Conference . . . May 1902*, pp. 298–301; idem, "Report of Committee on Uniform Accounting and Statistics," *Proceedings of the New York Conference . . . Eleventh Annual Meeting . . . April 1905*, pp. 226–27, 233–34. Hartwell was chairman of this committee and secretary of Boston's statistics department.

19. *The Coming City* (1902), pp. 45–46.

20. *Finances of New York*, p. 273.

21. Ibid., p. 359.

22. Yearley, *Money Machines*, pp. 37–118.

23. "A Newspaper Report on Two Lectures on Problems of City Government," February 29, 1896, *Papers of Woodrow Wilson*, 9:469; Bird S. Coler, "Mistakes of Professional Reformers," *Independent* 53 (Juen 20, 1901): 1405, 1407.

24. Frederick R. Clow, "Suggestions for the Study of Municipal Finance," *Quarterly Journal of Economics* 10 (July 1896): 463–64; see also L.S. Rowe, "Public Accounting under the Proposed Municipal Program," *Proceedings of the Columbus Conference . . . Fifth Annual Meeting . . . November, 1899*, pp. 119–20.

25. *Historical Statistics of the United States, Colonial Times to 1957* (Washington: Bureau of the Census, 1961), p. 14.

26. U.S. Department of Commerce and Labor, Bureau of the Census, *Bulletin 20, Statistics of Cities Having a Population of over 25,000: 1902 and 1903* (1905), p. 4. See also Kenneth Paul Fox, "The Census Bureau and the Cities: National Development of Urban Government in the Industrial Age" (Ph.D. dissertation, University of Pennsylvania, 1972), pp. 144–46.

27. *Bulletin 20, Statistics of Cities . . . 1902 and 1903*, p. 6. Subsequent reports were for cities over 30,000.

28. Ibid., p. 49; see also Fox, "Census Bureau and the Cities," pp. 152–53.

29. Ibid., pp. 21, 48–49; Powers, "The Bureau of Census as an Agent of Municipal Reform," *Proceedings of the Pittsburgh Conference . . . Fourteenth Annual Meeting . . . November 1908*, pp. 330–31.

30. "Municipal Ownership as a Form of Governmental Control," *Annals* 28 (1906): 366. By this time many cities had been converted to the accounting system of the National Municipal League by state laws requiring uniform municipal accounting. See John A. Fairlie, "The Problem of City Government from the Administrative Point of View," ibid., p. 153.

31. *Special Reports, Statistics of Cities Having a Population of over 30,000: 1907* (Washington, 1910), p. 13.

32. Tyack, *The One Best System: A History of American Urban Education* (1974), pp. 126–28, 167–68.

33. "Report to the Sub-Committee on Accounting and Statistics of the Mayor's Commission on Finance and Taxation, Appointed by Mayor McClellan, January 1906," in Frederick A. Cleveland, *Chapters on Municipal Administration and Accounting* (1909), pp. 248–54. For the founding of the Bureau, see pp. 156–58.

34. Ibid., pp. 246–48, 255–56.

35. William H. Allen, "The Budget as an Instrument of Financial Control," *The Government Accountant* 2 (September 1908): 194–95; Bureau of Municipal Research, *Making a Municipal Budget* (New York: Bureau of Municipal Research, 1907), preface.

36. To the Municipal Civil Service Commission, March 17, 1908, Shaw Papers.

37. Herman A. Metz, "The Reorganization of Accounts and Methods of Transacting Municipal Business in New York City," *Government Accountant* 3 (May 1909): 176; "Some Results and Limitations of Central Financial Control," *Municipal Research*, no. 81 (January 1917), p. 206. Metz, the first major city official to ally himself with the Bureau, later contributed $10,000 to a fund to advance the study of municipal accounting. See U. L. Leonhauser, "A National Fund for Accounting and Reporting," *Annals* 41 (May 1912): 304–6.

38. Duncas MacInness, "Uniformity in Municipal Accounting," *Proceedings of the National Tax Association*, 3 (1909): 271. For the origins, ideology, and activity of the National Tax Association see Yearley, *Money Machines*, pp. 187–91.

39. LeGrand Powers, "Governmental Accounting for Efficiency and Economy of Administration," *Government Accountant* 3 (May 1909): 26; Allen, "How to Overtake the Grafter by Municipal Accounting," *Proceedings of the Buffalo Conference . . . Sixteenth Annual Meeting . . . November 1910*, p. 501.

40. *The Finance Commission of the City of Boston* (1908–12), 1: 3–10; Harvey N. Shepard, "The Boston Finance Commission," *Proceedings of the Cincinnati Conference . . . Fifteenth Annual Meeting . . . November 1909*, pp. 207–8.

41. *Finance Commission of . . . Boston*, 1: 340–45.

42. Ibid., 1: 267, 270–72; 2: 202–5; also 3: 1083–88.

43. Ibid., 1: 480–82; 2: 205–6.

44. Ibid., 2: 211, 278–80.

45. Ibid., 2: 278–81.

46. Ibid., 2: 231; 7: 228–30.

47. Ibid., 2: 196–200; "Plan Two—A Hope," *City Affairs* (Boston) 3 (October 1909): 1–2. *City Affairs* was the organ of the Good Government Association of Boston.

48. John F. Moors, "The Boston Plan—Appointments of the Mayor Subject to Approval by a Civil Service Commission," *Proceedings of NCSRL*, 1910, pp. 176–78; Reed and Webbink, *Municipal Government*, pp. 186–89.

49. Reed and Webbink, pp. 189–91, 305–6.

50. "The 1910 Budget," *City Club Bulletin* (Chicago) 3 (December 15, 1909): 80–81, 83–84; Merriam, "The Work and Accomplishments of the

Chicago Commission on City Expenditures," ibid., 4 (August 16, 1911): 197–98. Merriam was chairman of the commission.

51. Quoted in "The 1910 Budget," p. 80; Merriam, "Chicago Commission on City Expenditures," pp. 198–99.

52. "Investigations as a Means of Securing Administrative Efficiency," *Annals* 41 (May 1912): 285.

53. Merriam, "Chicago Commission on City Expenditures," pp. 199–204.

54. *Final Report of Municipal Efficiency Commission, City of Chicago, March 8, 1911*, pp. 14–19.

55. "Investigations as a Means of Securing Administrative Efficiency," p. 300; see also Woodrow Wilson, "Hide and Seek Politics," *NAR* 191 (April 1910): 597.

56. "Problems of Local Administration," *Proceedings of the National Tax Association*, 2 (1908): 529; see also "Report of Committee on Administration of Laws for Taxation of Property," ibid. 5 (1911): 370–71.

57. Yearley, *Money Machines*, pp. 167–250.

58. "Who Pays for Graft and Inefficient Government?" *New York Sunday World*, November 28, 1908, in Cleveland, *Municipal Administration and Accounting*, p. 26.

59. "Municipal Budgets and Expenditures," *Proceedings of the Cincinnati Conference . . . Fifteenth Annual Meeting . . . November 1909*, p. 269; see also "Report of the Committee on Municipal Budgets to the National Association of Comptrollers and Accounting Officers at the Sixth Annual Convention, Buffalo, N.Y., June 7, 1912," in *Proceedings of the National Association of Comptrollers and Accounting Officers* 7 (1912): pp. 67, 74–75.

60. Paine, "The Municipal Situation in Boston," *City Club Bulletin* (Philadelphia) 2 (February 10, 1910): 46; Henry Bruere, "Program vs. Protest in City Economy," *Real Estate Record and Builders Guide*, May 24, 1913, p. 1081.

61. National Municipal League, "Report of the Committee on Municipal Budgets," *NMR* 3 (January 1914): 219–21; Ralph E. George, "Increased Efficiency as a Result of Increased Governmental Functions," *Annals* 54 (March 1916): 81–87.

CHAPTER VI. RESEARCH AND REFORM

1. J. Rogers Hollingsworth, "Perspectives on Industrializing Societies," in *Emerging Theoretical Models in Social and Political History*, ed. Allen G. Bogue (1973), pp. 109–10. His interpretation of political culture in industrial societies applies to American urban politics and reform in the early twentieth century.

2. Allen, "Reminiscences" (Columbia University Oral History Project, 1950), pp. 65, 100; Jane S. Dahlberg, *The New York Bureau of Municipal Research* (1966), pp. 7–8, 11.

3. Davis, *Spearheads for Reform* (chap. 4, n. 34), pp. 185–86; Dahlberg, *New York Bureau of Municipal Research*, pp. 9, 12.

4. Bruere, "Reminiscences" (Columbia University Oral History Project,

1950), pp. 29–32, 35–36; Dahlberg, *New York Bureau of Municipal Research*, pp. 12–16.

5. Bureau of Municipal Research, *Purposes and Methods of the Bureau of Municipal Research* (pamphlet, New York, 1907), pp. 1–4.

6. Ibid., pp. 19–20.

7. Ibid., pp. 26–28.

8. Bruere, "Reminiscences," pp. 29–35, Dahlberg, *New York Bureau of Municipal Research*, pp. 12–13, 17–19.

9. Bureau of Municipal Research, *Purposes and Methods*, p. 13.

10. William H. Allen, "Better Business Methods for Cities," *Review of Reviews* 37 (February 1908): 196–97; Robert Sloss, *The City House Cleaning* (pamphlet, Bureau of Municipal Research, 1908), pp. 5–6.

11. Richard Skolnick, "The Crystallization of Reform in New York City, 1890–1917" (Ph.D. dissertation, Yale University, 1964), p. 331.

12. Frederick A. Cleveland, "The Application of Scientific Management to the Activities of the State," in *Addresses and Discussion at the Conference on Scientific Management held October 12, 13, 14, 15, 1911* (1912, pp. 313–29; Samuel Haber, *Efficiency and Uplift: Scientific Management in the Progressive Era, 1890–1920* (Chicago: University of Chicago Press, 1964), pp. 111–13.

13. Mosher, *Democracy and the Public Service*, pp. 74–75.

14. "Efficiency in City Government," *City Club Bulletin* (Chicago) 2 (April 22, 1908): 127; see also Allen's *Efficient Democracy* (1908), pp. viii–x.

15. Bureau of Municipal Research, *How Should Public Budgets be Made?* (New York: Bureau of Municipal Research, 1909), pp. 3, 6, 11–12.

16. Mary B. Sayles, "The Budget and the Citizen," *Outlook* 92 (August 28, 1909): 1057–59; Dahlberg, *New York Bureau of Municipal Research*, pp. 164–65.

17. Herbert T. Wade, "An Influence for Efficiency in Municipal Government: The New York Budget Exhibit of 1910," *Engineering Magazine* 40 (January 1911): 587–91, 602; J. Harold Braddock, "Efficiency Value of the Budget Exhibit," *Annals* 41 (May 1912): 153–57.

18. Ibid., p. 8; Augustus Cerillo, Jr., "The Reform of Municipal Government in New York City: From Seth Low to John Purroy Mitchell," *New York Historical Society Quarterly* 57 (January 1973): 60–61.

19. Benjamin F. Welton, "The Problem of Securing Efficiency in Municipal Labor," *Annals* 41 (May 1912): 103–5; Bruere, "Efficiency in City Government," ibid., pp. 15–16. Other structural reformers expressed similar criticism. See "Report of the Committee on the Application of the Merit System to the Higher Municipal Offices," *Proceedings of NCSRL*, 1908, pp. 102–7; Guy C. Emerson, "Scientific Management in the Public Works of Cities," *NMR* 2 (October 1913): 577–78.

20. Bruere, "Efficiency in City Government," pp. 16–17.

21. "Reminiscences" (Columbia University Oral History Project, 1956), p. 31.

22. Cohen, *Progressives and Urban School Reform*, pp. 79–80.

23. Bureau of Municipal Research, *Six Years of Municipal Research for*

Greater New York: Record for 1906-1911 (1911), pp. 10-51; "A National Program to Improve Methods of Government," *Municipal Research*, no. 71 (March 1916), pp. 3-5, 11-12, 36-37.

24. Quoted in Skolnick, "Reform in New York City," p. 340.

25. "Reminiscences," p. 154.

26. *Six Years of Municipal Research*, pp. 42-43; George B. Hopkins, "The New York Bureau of Municipal Research," *Annals* 41 (May 1912): 240-43.

27. Allen to Shaw, January 22, 1908, Shaw Papers; Cutting, "The Major Beneficence," *NAR* 194 (September 1911): 382. See also Allen, *Efficient Democracy*, pp. 283-84.

28. *The New City Government: Discussion of Municipal Administration Based on a Survey of Ten Commission Governed Cities* (1912), p. 100.

29. *Six Years of Municipal Research*, pp. 69-71; Allen, *Reminiscences*, p. 154.

30. Quoted in *Six Years of Municipal Research*, pp. 72-73.

31. During the bureau's early years there was occasional debate over the merits of "outside" work. Some members of the agency felt that such work would undermine projects in New York, while others saw the local efforts as being strengthened by a national program of municipal research. See "Memorandum on the Organization of Bureau of Municipal Research," March 2, 1914, Seligman Papers, Box 30-31.

32. *Business Methods in Public Business: Purposes and Program of the Bureau of Municipal Research of Philadelphia* (pamphlet, Bureau of Municipal Research, 1910), pp. 5-6; "Citizen Agencies for Research in Government," *Municipal Research*, no. 77 (September 1916), pp. 8-10.

33. *Business Methods in Public Business*, pp. 2-3.

34. Jesse D. Burks, "The Outlook for Municipal Efficiency in Philadelphia," *Annals* 41 (May 1912): 253-54; George Burnham, Jr., "The Philadelphia Bureau of Municipal Research," *NMR* 5 (July 1916): 467-68. Burks was director of the Bureau and Burnham a member of its board of trustees.

35. "Citizen Agencies for Research in Government," pp. 18-20; Burnham, "Philadelphia Bureau of Municipal Research," p. 468.

36. Burks, "Municipal Efficiency in Philadelphia," p. 252; "Citizen Agencies for Research in Government," pp. 14-15; John M. Walton, "The Application to a Municipality of Modern Methods of Accounting," *Annals* 41 (May 1912): 64-68.

37. Frederick P. Gruenberg, "The Need of a Budget in Philadelphia," *Civic Club Bulletin* (Philadelphia) 10 (May 1916): 10; Jesse D. Burks, "Budget Making," *NMR* 2 (January 1913): 16; "Citizen Agencies for Research in Government," p. 26.

38. Minutes, meeting of the board of trustees, New York Bureau of Municipal Research, March 2, 1908, Shaw Papers.

39. Miller, *Boss Cox's Cincinnati*, p. 157.

40. Rufus H. Miles, "The Cincinnati Bureau of Municipal Research," *Annals* 41 (May 1912): 267-69.

41. Charles E. Merriam, "The Work of the Chicago Bureau of Public Efficiency," an address delivered to the City Club of Philadelphia, October 22, 1910, in *City Club Bulletin* (Philadelphia) 3 (November 2, 1910): 63-66; "The

Chicago Bureau of Public Efficiency," *City Club Bulletin* (Chicago) 3 (June 8, 1910): 325.

42. "Citizen Agencies for Research in Government," pp. 28–29; Merriam, "Chicago Bureau of Public Efficiency," p. 66.

43. Gustavus A. Weber, *Organized Efforts for the Improvement of Methods of Administration in the United States* (1919), pp. 225–27.

44. Ibid., p. 227.

45. Still, *Milwaukee*, pp. 516–19.

46. Stuart Morris, "The Wisconsin Idea and Business Progressivism," *Journal of American Studies* 4 (July 1970): 40–45; Haber, *Efficiency and Uplift*, pp. 106, 147.

47. John R. Commons, *Eighteen Months Work of the Milwaukee Bureau of Economy and Efficiency* (1912), pp. 3–4.

48. Benjamin M. Rastall, *Plan and Methods in Municipal Efficiency* (Milwaukee: C. Kronenberger, 1911), pp. 3–4; Commons, *Milwaukee Bureau of Economy and Efficiency*, p. 9.

49. J.E. Treleven, "The Milwaukee Bureau of Economy and Efficiency," *Annals* 41 (May 1912): 272–78; Commons, *Milwaukee Bureau of Economy and Efficiency*, pp. 10–18.

50. Weber, *Methods of Administration*, p. 205.

51. January 31, 1914, Taylor Collection.

52. To Alyse Gregory, December 1915, Bourne Papers, Box 2.

53. Bureau of Municipal Research, *Six Years of Municipal Research for Greater New York*, p. 68; see also "Citizen Agencies for Research in Government," p. vii.

54. "The Uses of City Government," lecture delivered at Yale University, May 1914, McAneny Papers, pp. 2–3.

55. Lissner to Hiram Johnson, February 14, 1911, Lissner Papers, Box 2; Roosevelt to Willard, November 14, 1912, Willard Papers, Box 7.

56. Albert H. Clodius, "The Quest for Good Government in Los Angeles, 1890–1910" (Ph.D. dissertation, Claremont Graduate School, 1953), p. 495.

57. Edward C. Banfield and James Q. Wilson, *City Politics* (New York: Random House, Vintage Books, 1963), pp. 40–41, 46, 139–40. On the weaknesses of the ethos theory in analyzing contemporary urban politics and government see Raymond E. Wolfinger and John Osgood Field, "Political Ethos and the Structure of City Government," in *Community Structure and Decision-Making: Comparative Analyses*, ed. Terry N. Clark (Scranton, Pa.: Chandler Co., 1968), pp. 159–95.

58. Simon, *Administrative Behavior*, pp. 175–76; see also Waldo, *Administrative State*, p. 202.

59. "Competition for Expert Administrative Positions in City Government," *Proceedings of NCSRL*, 1911, p. 167.

60. "Expert City Management," an address delivered before the league, July 8, 1912, in *NMR* 1 (October 1912): 556–57. See also Roy Lubove, "The Twentieth Century City: The Progressive as Municipal Reformer," *Mid-America* 41 (October 1959): 208–209.

61. "Taking Municipal Contracts out of Politics," *Proceedings of the Cincin-*

nati Conference for Good City Government and 15th Annual Meeting of the National Municipal League, 1909, p. 182.

62. William H. Allen, "Training Men and Women for Public Service," *Annals* 41 (May 1912): 307-9; Skolnick, "Reform in New York City," p. 346.

63. "Report of the Special Committee on the Application of the Merit System to the Higher Municipal Offices," *Proceedings of NCSRL,* 1910, pp. 148-49, 153-54; Clyde Lyndon King, "The Appointment and Selection of Government Experts," *NMR* 3 (April 1914): 304-15.

64. Roy Lubove, *The Urban Community: Housing and Planning in the Progressive Era* (Englewood Cliffs, N.J.: Prentice-Hall, 1967), pp. 6-14; Mel Scott, *American City Planning Since 1890* (Berkeley and Los Angeles: University of California Press, 1971), pp. 1-145.

65. Training School for Public Service, *Announcement* (New York, 1911), p. 2-5.

66. "Application of Scientific Management to the Activities of the State," p. 314.

67. Training School for Public Service, *Annual Report,* 1912, pp. 10, 19-21; Skolnick, "Reform in New York City," p. 347. In 1914, there was some debate over proposals to separate the work of the Bureau of Municipal Research and the Training Schools, with Frederick A. Cleveland as head of the Bureau and William H. Allen as director of the Training School. See "Minutes of Proceedings at the House of Professor Seligman," May 17, Seligman Papers, Box 30-31. Several leading members of both organizations participated in this meeting. Seven years later the Training School and the Bureau were reorganized as the National Institute of Public Administration.

68. "Reminiscences," p. 61.

69. To Frederick Cleveland, December 21, 1911, Lissner Papers, Box 3.

70. "A Survey of Los Angeles City Government," *California Outlook* 14 (April 26, 1913): 10, 17-19; Burton Hunter, *The Evolution of Municipal Organization and Administrative Practice in the City of Los Angeles* (Los Angeles: Parker, Stone and Baird, 1933), pp. 144-45.

71. "A National Program to Improve Methods of Government," *Municipal Research,* no. 71 (March 1916), pp. 27-32.

72. Cohen, *Progressives and Urban School Reform,* chapter 4; Tyack, *One Best System,* pp. 168-76. Roy Lubove, *The Professional Altruist: The Emergence of Social Work as a Career, 1880-1930* (Cambridge, Mass.: Harvard University Press, 1965), pp. 164-71, has an excellent discussion of conflict between the board of directors, volunteer workers, and the professional staff over questions of supervision, specialized expertise, and policy goals in private social-work agencies in the 1920s.

73. Holli, "Urban Reform in the Progressive Era" (chap. 4, n. 29), pp. 145-47.

CHAPTER VII. THE BUSINESSMAN AS ADMINISTRATOR

1. Steffens, *Shame of the Cities,* pp. 3-5, 72-84, 108-10, 117-24, 144-47, 204-8; Frederic C. Howe, *The City: The Hope of Democracy* (1905), pp. 4-5, 70, 86-91.

2. "Principles of Municipal Organization," *Annals* 23 (March 1904): 202.

3. Yearley, *Money Machines*, pp. 123–34; Samuel P. Hays, "The Politics of Reform in Municipal Government in the Progressive Era," *Pacific Northwest Quarterly* 55 (October 1964): 166–67.

4. James Weinstein, *The Corporate Ideal in the Liberal State: 1900-1918* (1968), pp. 94–95; Hays, "Politics of Reform," p. 167.

5. Bradley R. Rice, "The Galveston Plan of City Government by Commission: The Birth of a Progressive Idea," *Southwestern Historical Quarterly* 78 (April 1975): 369–76.

6. George Kibbe Turner, "Galveston: A Business Corporation," *McClure's Magazine* 27 (October 1906): 611–12; Rice, "Galveston Plan of City Government by Commission," pp. 378–402.

7. Turner, "Galveston: A Business Corporation," pp. 613–17.

8. Rice, "Galveston Plan of City Government by Commission," pp. 404–6.

9. Don E. Mowry, "Governing Cities by Commission," *LaFollette's Weekly Magazine* 1 (March 27, 1909): 7; "Spread of the Commission Plan," *Outlook* 89 (July 4, 1908): 495–96.

10. Richard M. Bernard and Bradley R. Rice, "Political Environment and the Adoption of Progressive Municipal Reform," *Journal of Urban History* 2 (February 1975): 149–71.

11. "A Typology for Comparative Local Government" *Midwest Journal of Political Science* 5 (May 1961): 151–52.

12. George Kibbe Turner, "The New American City Government: The Des Moines Plan," *McClure's Magazine* 35 (May 1910): 97–100; Ford H. MacGregor, "Commission Government in the West," *Annals* 38 (November 1911): 734.

13. Quoted in Ernest S. Bradford, *Commission Government in American Cities* (1917), p. 74.

14. John A. Fairlie, "Commission Government in Illinois Cities," *Annals* 38 (November 1911): 750–54.

15. A.M. Fuller, "Commission Government of All Third-Class Cities in Pennsylvania," *American City* 9 (August 1913): 123–24.

16. Frederick W. Donnelly, "Securing Efficient Administration under the Commission Plan," *Annals* 41 (May 1912): 225–26; Woodrow Wilson, *Commission Government* (pamphlet, 1911), quoted in Charles N. Glaab, *The American City: A Documentary History* (Homewood, Ill,: Dorsey Press, 1963), p. 415.

17. MacGregor, "Commission Government in the West," pp. 730–32; Bradford, *Commission Government*, pp. 65–66, 81–82.

18. Bradford, *Commission Government*, pp. 88–89; Irby Roland Hudson, "Nashville's Experience with Commission Government," *NMR* 10 (March 1921): 158; Melvin P. Porter, "The Buffalo Charter," *NMR* 6 (January 1917): 79–80. Some business groups, on the other hand, did not see the commission plan as a dependable alternative to bossism and opposed changing to the new system. See, for instance, J. Paul Mitchell, "Boss Speer and the City Functional: Boosters and Businessmen versus Commission Government in Denver," *Pacific Northwest Quarterly* 63 (October 1972): 156–64.

19. Weinstein, *The Corporate Ideal*, p. 109; Hays, "Politics of Reform," pp. 161–65; see, too, Hays's "Changing Political Structure of the City in Industrial America," pp. 14, 23.

20. Quoted in Hays, "Politics of Reform," p. 160.

21. Quoted in Clinton Rogers Woodruff, ed., *City Government by Commission* (New York: Appleton, 1911), pp. 207–8. Well before the advent of the commission plan some political reformers had argued that the growing complexity of city life necessitated more businessmen in local government. See, for instance, Storey, "Government of Cities," pp. 62–63; MacVeagh, "Business Man in Municipal Politics," pp. 133–39.

22. Kenneth Prewitt, *The Recruitment of Political Leaders: A Study of Citizen-Politicians* (Indianapolis: Bobbs-Merrill, 1970), p. 162.

23. Turner, "Galveston: A Business Corporation," p. 615; Weinstein, *The Corporate Ideal*, pp. 103–4; Fairlie, "Commission Government in Illinois Cities," p. 755.

24. Quoted in Bruere, *New City Government*, pp. 380–81.

25. Bradford, *Commission Government*, pp. 28–29, 46–48, 66–67, 84.

26. "Financial Results under the Commission Form of City Government," *NMR* 1 (1912): 373, 375, 377.

27. Munro, "The Galveston Plan of City Government," *Proceedings of the Providence Conference for Good City Government and the Thirteenth Annual Meeting of the National Municipal League, November 1907*, pp. 147, 149; Allen, "The Des Moines Plan," ibid., pp. 161–63. Woodrow Wilson had expressed similar views before a Johns Hopkins audience in 1896, See *Papers of Woodrow Wilson*, 9:451–54.

28. Sydney Brooks, "The Failure of American Democracy," *Fortnightly Review* 92 (December 1909): 1078; John E. Semonche, *Ray Stannard Baker: A Quest for Democracy, 1870–1918* (Chapel Hill: University of North Carolina Press, 1969), p. 235.

29. *Progressive Democracy* (1914), p. 287.

30. Beverly L. Hodghead, "The Progress of Commission Government," *Pacific Municipalities* 23 (December 1910): 209.

31. Bradford, *Commission Government*, p. 165; also see Robert L. Owen, "Commission Government," *Proceedings of the New York State Conference of Mayors and other Municipal Officials, 1911*, pp. 110–11.

32. *Executive Reorganization and Reform in the New Deal: The Genesis of Administrative Management, 1900–1939* (1963), p. 95.

33. Eliot, *An Address*, January 11, 1907, p. 25; Woodruff, ed., *City Government by Commission*, p. 139.

34. *American City Government: A Survey of Newer Tendencies* (1912), p. 96.

35. "Three Great Experiments," *Independent* 64 (June 18, 1908): 1409–10.

36. To Richard S. Douglas, May 11, 1909, in *The Letters and Journals of Brand Whitlock*, ed. Allan Nevins (New York: Appleton-Century, 1936), 1: 114.

37. Johnson to M.G. Thraves, November 17, 1910, Johnson Papers; Walter A. Webster, "Commission Is an Oligarchy," in E.C. Robbins, ed., *Selected Ar-*

ticles on the Commission Plan of Municipal Government (Minneapolis: H.W. Wilson Co., 1910), p. 126.

38. *Proceedings of the New York State Conference of Mayors and other Municipal Officials,* 1911, p. 186.

39. Adrian and Press, *Governing Urban America,* pp. 222–23.

40. J.R. Palda, "Commission Plan," in Robbins, ed., *Commission Plan of Government,* p. 137; "Experts Discuss the Des Moines Plan," *Bulletin of the League of American Municipalities* 10 (June 1909): 413.

41. "Commission Government Luncheon," *Proceedings of the Buffalo Conference . . . Sixteenth Annual Meeting . . . November 1910,* p. 557.

42. H.S. Gilbertson, "Some Serious Weaknesses of the Commission Plan," *American City* 9 (September 1910): 237; "Report of the Committee of Norfolk Chamber of Commerce," *Municipal Engineering* 49 (August 1915): 52.

43. Bradford, *Commission Government,* p. 295.

44. Elliott H. Goodwin, "Civil Service Provisions in Commission Charters," *Annals* 38 (November 1911): 808–9; Ford H. MacGregor, *City Government by Commission,* Bulletin of the University of Wisconsin, no. 423 (Madison, 1911), pp. 73–74.

45. "Some Defects of Commission Government," *Annals* 38 (November 1911): 869.

46. "Expert Administrators and Popular Government," *APSR* 7 (February 1913): 61; see also Benjamin Parke Dewitt, *The Progressive Movement* (1915), pp. 308–9.

47. Clinton Rogers Woodruff, "Simplicity, Publicity, and Efficiency in Municipal Affairs," *NMR* (January 1913): 3, 5; Thomas H. Reed, "The Value of Experts to a City Government," *Pacific Municipalities* 28 (December 1914): 609–10.

48. "City Not a Business Corporation," in Robbins, ed., *Commission Plan of Government,* p. 120.

49. "Objections to Commission Government," *Annals* 38 (November 1911): 860.

50. Alexander B. Callow, Jr., ed., *American Urban History: An Interpretative Reader with Commentaries,* 2d ed. (New York: Oxford University Press, 1973), p. 217. The statement is by Callow.

51. Bruere, *New City Government,* p. 6.

52. Ibid., p. 87.

53. Ibid., pp. 88–89, 96.

CHAPTER VIII. THE POLITICS OF BUREAUCRATIZATION

1. G. Edward White, "The Social Values of the Progressives: Some New Perspectives," *South Atlantic Quarterly* 70 (Winter 1971): 72–73. See also Morris, "The Wisconsin Idea and Business Progressivism," *Journal of American Studies* 4 (July 1970) 43–46.

2. Lippman, *Drift and Mastery* (1914), pp. 143; Croly, *Progressive Democracy* (1914), pp. 213, 359.

3. "Administrative Experts in Municipal Governments," *NMR* 4 (January 1915): 27.

4. "A Comparison of the Methods and Efficiency of Modern European and American City Government," *Pacific Municipalities* 4 (October 1912): 490–91; see also Foulke, "Expert City Management," *551, 557–58.*

5. "Where the Business Men Rule," *Outlook* 103 (January 25, 1913): 209.

6. Croly, *Progressive Democracy,* p. 360; Lippmann, *A Preface to Politics* (1913), pp. 9, 32, 59–60, 98, 221–22.

7. "Bureaucratic Politics in Comparative Perspective," in *Frontiers of Development Administration,* ed. Fred W. Riggs (1971), pp. 406–10; see also Victor A. Thompson, "Bureaucracy in a Democratic Society," in *Public Administration and Democracy,* ed. Roscoe C. Martin (1967), pp. 211–12.

8. Theodore J. Lowi, *At the Pleasure of the Mayor: Patronage and Power in New York City, 1898–1958* (1964), pp. 61–64.

9. Lately Thomas, *The Mayor Who Mastered New York: The Life and Opinions of William J. Gaynor* (1969), pp. 162–99.

10. William J. Gaynor, "The Problem of Efficient City Government," *Century* 80 (September 1910): 668.

11. James Creelman, "Municipal Non-Partisanship in Operation," *Century* 80 (September 1910): 668. In Gaynor's administration, In Gaynor's administration, 41 percent of all appointees were professional leaders. Theodore Lowi sees this pattern of representation as part of an upward trend toward job orientation in New York's government down to the present day. *Pleasure of the Mayor,* pp. 59–62, 204–5, 212n.

12. Raymond B. Fosdick, *Chronicle of a Generation* (1958), pp. 93–100; Creelman, "Municipal Non-Partisanship in Operation," p. 671.

13. Creelman, pp. 669–72; Thomas, *William J. Gaynor,* pp. 212–21, 254–67.

14. Cohen, *Progressives and Urban School Reform,* pp. 80–86.

15. Address, July 14, 1910, Prendergast Papers.

16. William A. Prendergast, "Efficiency through Accounting," *Annals* 41 (May 1912): 44–56; idem, "Accounting and the Budget," Prendergast Papers, pp. 4–5.

17. "The Work of the Bureau of Municipal Research in Relation to the Administration of the City's Finances," *Real Estate Magazine,* November 1915, pp. 22–23.

18. Miller, *Boss Cox's Cincinnati,* pp. 206–12.

19. Ibid., pp. 214–15.

20. L.D. Upson, "Cincinnati's First Municipal Exhibit," *American City* 7 (December 1912): 530–31.

21. Ibid., p. 532.

22. Miller, *Boss Cox's Cincinnati,* pp. 217–18, 220.

23. Holli, *Reform in Detroit,* pp. 161–71, and his "Urban Reform in the Progressive Era" (chap. 4, n. 29), pp. 139–41.

24. Martin J. Schiesl, "Progressive Reform in Los Angeles under Mayor Alexander, 1909–1913," *California Historical Quarterly* 54 (Spring 1975): 42–44.

25. Ibid., pp. 45–47, 50.

26. T.G. Goos, "Sketches of American Mayors: James M. Curley of Boston," *NMR* 15 (May 1926): 253–54; Francis Russell, "The Last of the Bosses," *American Heritage* 10 (June 1959): 21–25.

27. *I'd Do It Again* (1957), p. 114.

28. Ibid., pp. 116–17, 122; Russell, "Last of the Bosses," p. 85.

29. Russell, "Last of the Bosses," p. 85; Goos, "James M. Curley," pp. 255–56.

30. *I'd Do It Again*, p. 124.

31. "Twelfth Annual Report of the Good Government Association," *City Affairs* (Boston) 9 (March 1915): 5.

32. William B. Munro, "Peters of Boston: A Reform Mayor who did not Fail," *NMR* 11 (March 1922): 85–88; Goos, "James M. Curley," p. 256.

33. Quoted in Clarence H. Cramer, *Newton D. Baker: A Biography* (Cleveland: World, 1961), p. 60; C.C. Arbuthnot, "Mayor Baker's Administration in Cleveland," *NMR* 5 (April 1916): pp. 234–35, 237–38.

34. E.C. Hopwood, "Newton D. Baker's Administration as Mayor of Cleveland and Its Accomplishments," *NMR* 2 (1913): 463–65; Arbuthnot, "Mayor Baker's Administration," pp. 232–37.

35. *Organized Democracy: An Introduction to the Study of Politics* (New York: Longmans, Green, 1913), p. 364.

36. *Proceedings of the New York State Conference of Mayors and other Municipal Officials, June 1914*, p. 190.

37. William D. Miller, *Mr. Crump of Memphis* (Baton Rouge: Louisiana State University Press, 1964), pp. 79–113; Mark Foster, "Frank Hague of Jersey City: The Boss as Reformer," *New Jersey History* 86 (Summer 1968): 111–15.

38. Quoted in Nancy Joan Weiss, *Charles Francis Murphy: Respectability and Responsibility in Tammany Politics* (Northampton, Mass.: Smith College, 1968), p. 75.

39. Samuel P. Hays, "Political Parties and the Community-Society Continuum," in William N. Chambers and Walter Dean Burnham, eds., *The American Party Systems: Stages of Political Development* (1967), pp. 178–80; see, too, Hays's "Changing Political Structure of the City," pp. 16–17, 24–25, and Wiebe, *Search for Order*, pp. 172–74.

40. Michael Paul Rogin and John L. Shover, *Political Change in California: Critical Elections and Social Movements, 1890–1966* (Westport, Conn.: Greenwood, 1970) pp. 35–89; Roger E. Wyman, "Middle-Class Voters and Progressive Reform: The Conflict of Class and Culture," *APSR* 68 (June 1974): 488–504; John D. Buenker, *Urban Liberalism and Progressive Reform* (1973), especially chap. 2–3.

41. Otis A. Pease, "Urban Reformers in the Progressive Era: A Reassessment," *Pacific Northwest Quarterly* 62 (April 1971): 57. See also Lyle W. Dorsett, "The City Boss and the Reformer: A Reappraisal," ibid., 63 (October 1972): 152–54.

42. Roosevelt to C.D. Willard, October 28, 1911, Willard Papers, Box 6; Lissner to J.K. Moffitt, March 14, 1912, Lissner Papers, Box 3.

43. Haber, *Efficiency and Uplift* (chap. 6, n. 12), p. 108n.

44. Donald L. Disbrow, "Reform in Philadelphia under Mayor Blankenburg, 1912-1916," *Pennsylvania History* 28 (October 1960): 379-81.

45. Letter, November 27, 1911, Taylor Collection; see also Cooke Papers, Box 170.

46. Letters, December 1 and 9, 1911, Taylor Collection.

47. "Report of the Joint Special Committee of the Select Common Councils of the City of Philadelphia to Make an Investigation of Appointments, Dismissals, Demotions, and Resignations of City Employees from December, 1911 to December, 1915," Cooke Papers, Box 170.

48. Disbrow, "Reform in Philadelphia," pp. 383-84.

49. Morris L. Cooke, *Our Cities Awake: Notes on Municipal Activities and Administration* (1918), pp. 124-25, 146-49; idem, "The Spirit and Social Significance of Scientific Management," *Journal of Political Economy* 21 (June 1913): 489-91.

50. Charles F. Jenkins, "The Blankenburg Administration: A Symposium," *NMR* 5 (April 1916): 216-17, 220-21; Disbrow, "Reform in Philadelphia," pp. 385-86.

51. Jenkins, "The Blankenburg Administration," pp. 219-20, 223-24; Disbrow, "Reform in Philadelphia," pp. 393-95.

52. Edwin A. Lewinson, *John Purroy Mitchel* (1965), pp. 82-87, 95-96.

53. Cerillo, "Reform of Municipal Government in New York City," p. 68.

54. Lewinson, *John Purroy Mitchel*, p. 100.

55. Henry Bruere, "Mayor Mitchel's Administration of the City of New York," *NMR* 5 (January 1916): 26-28, 31; Lowi, *Pleasure of the Mayor*, pp. 62-65, 204, 212n.

56. "New York City's New Administration," *City Club Bulletin* (Chicago) 7 (June 25, 1914): 216.

57. Bruere, "Mayor Mitchel's Administration," p. 32; John Purroy Mitchel, "The Office of Mayor," *Proceedings of the Academy of Political Science* 5 (April 1915): 483-84.

58. Henry Bruere, "The Budget as an Administrative Program," *Annals* 62 (November 1915): 176-86; Bruere, "Development of Standards in Municipal Government," ibid., pp. 204-5.

59. Wallstein, "Reminiscences" (Columbia University Oral Research Project, 1949), pp. 29-30; Lewinson, *John Purroy Mitchel*, pp. 124-25. Wallstein recalled that Bruere was "valuable in matters relating to the pure science of government as opposed to the practice of politics and the pursuit of expediencies" ("Reminiscences"), pp. 28-29.

60. Michael B. Katz, *Class, Bureaucracy, and Schools: The Illusion of Educational Change in America* (New York: Praeger, 1971), p. 57.

61. *The Bureaucratic Phenomenon* (Chicago: University of Chicago Press, 1964), p. 201. See also Peter M. Blau and Marshall W. Meyer, *Bureaucracy in Modern Society* (1971), pp. 103-6.

62. *A History of American City Government: The Progressive Years and their Aftermath, 1900-1920* (1974), p. 195.

63. Bruere, "Mayor Mitchel's Administration," pp. 28-32; H.S. Gilbertson,

"Municipal Revolution under Mayor Mitchel," *American Review of Reviews* 56 (September 1917): 301.

64. Gilbertson, pp. 302-3; "John Purroy Mitchel: His Chief Contribution to City Government," *Survey* 40 (August 3, 1918): 505-7, 516. The latter piece is a collection of brief articles by the commissioners who headed the social welfare departments in Mitchel's administration.

65. Lewinson, *John Purroy Mitchel,* pp. 245-47; Cohen, *Progressives and Urban School Reform,* pp. 87-99.

66. Lowi, *Pleasure of the Mayor,* pp. 183-85.

67. Holli, *Reform in Detroit,* p. 163; William E. Leuchtenburg, Preface to Lewinson, *John Purroy Mitchel,* p. 11.

68. Griffith, *American City Government,* pp. 171-75.

69. To Guy C. Earl, December 24, 1914, Dickson Papers, Box 9.

70. Munro, *Principles and Methods of Municipal Administration* (1916), p. 14; "The Expert and American Society," *New Republic* 15 (May 4, 1918): 6. See also Charles A. Beard, "Training for Efficient Public Service," *Annals* 64 (March 1916): 217.

71. *Administrative Behavior,* p. 186.

CHAPTER IX. A NEW PROFESSION

1. Schiesl, "Progressive Reform in Los Angeles," p. 49; Schnepp to John R. Haynes, June 19, 1912, Haynes Papers.

2. Charles M. Fassett, "The Weakness of Commission Government," *NMR* 9 (October 1920): 645-46.

3. Ethel Huston, "New Orleans Experience under Commission Government," *NMR* 6 (January 1917): 74-75; Hudson, "Nashville's Experience with Commission Government," p. 157.

4. Letter, April 18, 1912, Haynes Papers.

5. John Porter East, *Council-Manager Government: The Political Thought of Its Founder, Richard S. Childs* (1965), pp. 43-55.

6. "The Lockport Proposal: A City That Wants to Improve the 'Commission Plan,'" *American City* 4 (June 1911): 286; idem, "The Theory of the New Controlled—Executive Plan," *NMR* 2 (January 1913): 77.

7. "The Short Ballot and the Commission Plan," *Annals* 38 (November 1911): 149; see also East, *Council-Manager Government,* pp. 18-20, 31-34.

8. "New Controlled—Executive Plan," pp. 80-81; also Childs's "How to Work for Charter Reform," *American City* 8 (February 1913): 149-50.

9. In 1908 Staunton, Virginia, had already appointed a "general manager," but because of charter restrictions under the state constitution the experiment did not include a commission and was not seen by local reformers as a refinement of the commission form. Henry Oyen, "A City with a General Manager," *World's Work* 23 (December 1911): 223.

10. Quoted in Childs, "The Lockport Proposal," p. 286.

11. Ibid., p. 287; see also F.D. Silvernail, "The Lockport Proposal," *Annals* 38 (November 1911): 884-87.

12. "The City Manager Adopted by Sumter, South Carolina," _American City_ 7 (July 1912): 38; "The Coming of the City Manager Plan," _NMR 3_ (January 1914): 45.

13. Chester E. Rightor, _City Manager in Dayton_ (1919), pp. 2–5; Arch Mandel and Wilbur H. Cotton, "Dayton's Sixteen Years of City Manager Government: An Appraisal of a Pioneer Venture," _NMR_ 19 (July 1930): 497–98.

14. Quoted in Rightor, p. 2.

15. Mandel and Cotton, "City Manager Government," pp. 499–501; Rightor, pp. 9–10.

16. Fred W. Francher, "Two Epoch-Making Campaigns in Dayton, Ohio," _American City_ 9 (June 1913): 47–49; Rightor, pp. 11–15.

17. "From Commission to Commission-Manager?," _Short Ballot Bulletin_ 3 (October 1916): 3–5; Harrison Gray Otis, "The City Manager Movement," _NMR_ 9 (March 1920): 195–98.

18. "Report to the Charter Commission," April, 1912, Haynes Papers. To the dismay of political progressives in Los Angeles, the electorate rejected the new charter in December 1912. Schiesl, "Progressive Reform in Los Angeles," p. 49.

19. James, "The City Manager Plan, the Latest in American City Government," _APSR_ 8 (November 1914), 611–12; "The City Manager Plan," _Outlook_ 104 (August 23, 1913): 888–89.

20. Bernard and Rice, "Political Environment and the Adoption of Progressive Municipal Reform," pp. 155–70. An investigation of 300 suburban governments has found that the manager form was predominant in cities where the inhabitants had above-average incomes. See Leo F. Schnore and Robert R. Alford, "Forms of Government and Socioeconomic Characteristics of Suburbs," _Administrative Science Quarterly_ 8 (June 1963): 1–17.

21. Williams, "Typology for Comparative Local Government," pp. 152–53.

22. "The City Manager Adopted by Sumter, South Carolina," p. 38.

23. Donald H. Thompson, "La Grande under the Commission-Manager Form of Government," _Pacific Municipalities_ 29 (April 1915): 175.

24. Frederick C. Mosher et al., _City Manager Government in Seven Cities_ (1940), pp. 240–41; Harold A. Stone, Don K. Price, and Kathryn H. Stone, _City Manager Government in Nine Cities_ (1940), pp. 8–11, 371–72.

25. Harry Aubrey Toulmin, Jr., _The City Manager: A New Profession_ (1917), p. 42.

26. Carl D. Thompson, "The Vital Points in Charter Making from a Socialist Point of View," _NMR_ 2 (1913): 421–22; Weinstein, _The Corporate Ideal_, pp. 107–13.

27. Richard S. Childs, "How the Commission-Manager Plan Is Getting Along," _NMR_ 4 (July 1915): 379; Stone, Price, and Stone, _City Manager Government_, pp. 11, 223.

28. Thompson, "La Grande under the Commission-Manager Form of Government," p. 177; Reed and Webbink, _Municipal Government_, p. 390.

29. Childs, "How the Commission-Manager Plan Is Getting Along," p. 373.

30. Gladys M. Kammerer et al., *City Managers in Politics: An Analysis of Manager Tenure and Termination* (1962), p. 21.

31. Karl, *Executive Reorganization and Reform*, p. 100.

32. Quoted in Toulmin, *City Manager*, p. 80.

33. H.M. Waite, "The Commission-Manager Plan—Its Advantages," *Proceedings of the New York State Conference of Mayors and other Municipal Officials, June 1914*, pp. 10-11.

34. Mandel and Cotton, "City Manager Government," p. 505; Rightor, *City Manager in Dayton*, p. 49.

35. Henry M. Waite, "The Commission-Manager Plan," *NMR* 4 (January 1915): 43-45.

36. Leonard D. White, *The City Manager* (1927), pp. 74-76; Rightor, *City Manager in Dayton*, pp. 58-59; Mandel and Cotton, "City Manager Government," pp. 506-9.

37. Looking back on Waite's tenure in Dayton, Childs recalled that he "made a national reputation for the city managership idea because he was one big man by anybody's count" "Reminiscences" (Columbia University Oral History Project, 1950), p. 14.

38. Oyen, "City with a General Manager," pp. 220-23; John Crosby, "Municipal Government Administered by a General Manager—The Staunton Plan," *Annals* 38 (November 1911): 880-82.

39. Lindsay Rogers, "Government by City Managers," *World's Work* 44 (September 1922): 522-23; White, *The City Manager, p. 94.*

40. National Municipal League, *The Commission Plan and the Commission-Manager Plan* (New York: National Municipal League, 1914), pp. 17-18; Clinton Rogers Woodruff, ed., *A New Municipal Program* (1919), pp. 120-22, 126, 129-30, 334-35.

41. Adrian and Press, *Governing Urban America*, pp. 229-30; see also Kammerer et al., *City Managers in Politics*, p. 12.

42. Richard Childs et al., "Professional Standards and Professional Ethics in the New Profession of City Managers: A Discussion," *NMR* 5 (April 1916): 200.

43. James, "Some Reflections on the City Manager Plan of Government," *APSR* 9 (August 1915): 505; *Third Annual Report of the City Managers' Association*, 1916, p. 14.

44. Gilbertson, "The City Manager Plan—Its Contribution to the Growth of a Non-Political and Efficient Personnel in Municipal Administration," *Proceedings of NCSRL*, 1913, p. 136; Otis, as quoted in Childs et al., "New Profession of City Managers," p. 206. See also Don K. Price, "The Promotion of the City Manager Plan," *Public Opinion Quarterly* 5 (Winter 1941): 574.

45. *Proceedings of the City Managers Association*, 1915, p. 117.

46. Childs, "How the Commission-Manager Plan Is Getting Along," p. 378; "What City Managers Can Do to Further Advance Good Government," in *Third Annual Report of the City Managers' Association*, 1916, p. 46.

47. Clinton Rogers Woodruff, "The Model City Charter," *Fifth Year Book of the City Managers' Association*, 1919, p. 65.

48. Stone, Price, and Stone, *City Manager Government*, p. 224.

49. G.C. Cummin, "Budget Making," *Proceedings of the City Managers' Association*, 1915, pp. 94–102; Stone, Price, and Stone, *City Manager Government*, pp. 224, 242–43.

50. Stone, Price, and Stone, pp. 238–39. 251.

51. Ibid., pp. 254–55.

52. Rogers, "Government by City Managers," p. 523; Harrison Gray Otis, "City Manager Movement," *NMR* 10 (March 1921): 183–84.

53. Karl, *Executive Reorganization and Reform*, pp. 83–84, 102–4.

54. Louis Brownlow, *A Passion for Anonymity: The Autobiography of Louis Brownlow, Second Half* (1958), pp. 116–21; Karl, *Executive Reorganization and Reform*, pp. 104–5.

55. Brownlow, pp. 121–22, 133–35.

56. Holli, "Urban Reform in the Progressive Era" (chap. 4, n. 29), pp. 148–49.

57. Childs, "How the Commission-Manager Plan Is Getting Along," p. 376; Kenyon Riddle, "Who Benefits from City Government and How?" *Proceedings of the City Managers' Association*, 1914, pp. 32–33. Riddle was manager of Abilene.

58. "Has City Manager Plan Come to Stay?" *Modern City* 5 (July 1920): 9.

59. Thomas H. Reed, "Synopsis of the Achievement Report Recently Submitted to the City Council of San Jose," *Pacific Municipalities* 32 (April 1918): 179–80. Other manager cities in the state experienced similar improvement and expansion of public services between 1915 and 1920. See Timothy Kaun, "City Manager Government in California, 1915–1920," seminar paper, History Department, California State University, Los Angeles, 1975.

60. Harrison Gray Otis, "City Manager Movement," *NMR* 10 (January 1921): 51.

61. *Fourth Year Book of the City Managers' Association*, 1918, p. 48; Childs, "Now That We Have the Commission Manager Plan—What Are We Going to Do with It?" ibid., p. 87.

62. Ossian E. Carr, "Progress, Prospects and Pitfalls of the New Profession," *Fifth Year Book of the City Managers' Association*, 1919, p. 104.

63. *Fifth Year Book*, p. 123.

64. Ibid., p. 128.

65. *Seventh Year Book of the City Managers' Association*, 1921, pp. 207–8. Recent studies of council-manager goverment indicate that many managers see themselves as policy innovators who often take public positions on questions of controversy, while others prefer to limit their political involvement to "safe" administrative areas and avoid more controversial matters. See Deil S. Wright, "The City Manager as a Development Administrator," in Robert T. Daland, ed., *Comparative Urban Research: The Administration and Politics of Cities* (1969), pp. 235–41; Ronald O. Loveridge, *City Managers in Legislative Politics* (Indianapolis: Bobbs-Merrill, 1971), esp. chap. 7.

66. Here I have drawn on Wright, pp. 241–42, and Loveridge, pp. 150–52. See also East, *Council-Manager Government*, pp. 133–37.

67. "The Manager—The Greatest Problem of City Manager Government," *Seventh Year Book of the City Managers' Association*, 1921, p. 201.

68. White, *The City Manager*, p. 316.

CHAPTER X. EPILOGUE: THE MODEL AND POLITICAL REALITY

1. Bryce, as quoted in Clinton Rogers Woodruff, "American Municipal Tendencies," *NMR* 1 (January 1912): 18; Baker, Foreword to Cooke, *Our Cities Awake*, p. ix.

2. "Scientific Criteria for Efficient Democratic Institutions," *Scientific Monthly* 6 (March 1918): 241.

3. *The Semisovereign People: A Realist's View of Democracy in America* (New York: Holt, Rinehart and Winston, 1960), pp. 30–31; see also Arnold M. Rose, *The Power Structure: Political Process in American Society* (New York: Oxford University Press, 1967), pp. 79–80, 86.

4. See, for example, Robert H. Salisbury and Gordon Black, "Class and Party in Partisan and Non-Partisan Elections," in *Political Behavior in America: New Directions*, ed. Heinz Eulau (New York: Random House, 1966), pp. 158–75; Prewitt, *Recruitment of Political Leaders* (chap. 7, n. 23), pp. 142–47.

5. Here I have drawn on Thompson, "Bureaucracy in a Democratic Society," pp. 214–15; Herbert A. Simon, *The Sciences of the Artificial* (Cambridge, Mass.: MIT Press, 1969), pp. 84–87, 94–95, 98–99.

6. Theodore J. Lowi, "Machine Politics—Old and New," *The Public Interest*, no. 9 (Fall 1967), pp. 86–87.

7. Holli, *Reform in Detroit*, pp. 163, 180; Haber, *Efficiency and Uplift* (chap. 6, n. 12), pp. xi–xii, 116; Loren P. Beth, *The Development of the American Constitution, 1877–1917* (New York: Harper, 1971), p. 128.

8. Samuel P. Hays, "The New Organizational Society," Introduction to *Building the Organizational Society: Associational Tendencies in Early-Twentieth Century America*, ed. Jerry Israel (New York: The Free Press, 1972), p. 9; see, too, Hays, "Political Parties and the Community-Society Continuum," pp. 167–69.

9. *Bureaucracy in Modern Society*, p. 157. See also Anthony Downs, *Inside Bureaucracy* (Boston: Little, Brown, 1967), p. 259.

10. On various aspects of governmental efficiency in the years from 1920 to 1940 see Charles N. Glaab, "Metropolis and Suburb: The Changing American City," in *Change and Continuity in Twentieth Century America*, eds., John Braeman et al. (Columbus: Ohio State University Press, 1968), pp. 418–36; Blake McKelvey, *The Emergence of Metropolitan America, 1915–1966* (New Brunswick, N.J.: Rutgers University Press, 1968), pp. 48–63; Carl A. McCandless, *Urban Government and Politics* (New York: McGraw-Hill, 1970), pp. 259–82; Scott, *American City Planning* (chap. 6, n. 64), pp. 192–98, 213–21, 245–55, 300–311, 342–48.

11. Eugene Lewis, *The Urban Political System* (1973), pp. 168, 173, 185.

12. Banfield and Wilson, *City Politics*, pp. 210–16; David Rogers, *The Management of Big Cities: Interest Groups and Social Change Strategies* (Beverly Hills: Sage Publications, 1971), pp. 36–39, 81–83.

13. Rogers, pp. 32–33, 156–57; Lewis, *Urban Political System*, pp. 184–85; John C. Bollens and Henry J. Schmandt, *The Metropolis: Its People, Politics, and Economic Life* (1975), pp. 115–16.

14. Banfield and Wilson, *City Politics*, p. 149; Lewis, *Urban Political System*, p. 164.

15. Lowi, "Machine Politics—Old and New," pp. 88–90; Rogers, *Management of Big Cities*, pp. 42–43, 94–97.

16. "Perspectives on Industrializing Socieites," p. 111.

17. *The Intellectual Crisis in American Public Administration*, rev. ed. (Montgomery: University of Alabama Press, 1974), p. 131.

18. Bollens and Schmandt, *Metropolis*, pp. 214–24.

19. Adrian and Press, *Governing Urban America*, pp. 322–24, 330–34, 386–89; Bollens and Schmandt, pp. 224–27.

20. Bollens and Schmandt, pp. 317–22; Adrian and Press, *Governing Urban America*, pp. 313–315.

21. Bollens and Schmandt, p. 330.

Selected Bibliography

The materials listed as primary sources include works written during the historical period covered by the book and the published memoirs and autobiographies of leading reformers. Hence, books such as Beard's *American City Government* and Bryce's *American Commonwealth* are original sources. Both are studies of politics and government at that time. The "Reminiscences" of the Columbia Oral History Project are unpublished volumes of autobiographical material on municipal government between 1900 and 1920. The secondary works, on the other hand, include the writings of present-day scholars on the subject.

The abbreviations for certain periodicals are explained at the beginning of the Notes section.

PRIMARY SOURCES

Manuscripts

Randolph Bourne Papers. Columbia University Library, New York.

City Reform Club, New York. "Minute Book." New York Public Library.

Morris L. Cooke Papers. Franklin D. Roosevelt Library, Hyde Park.

Thomas McIntyre Cooley Papers. Michigan Historical Collections, University of Michigan, Ann Arbor.

Edward A. Dickson Papers. Research Library, University of California at Los Angeles.

Grosvenor Collection. Buffalo and Erie County Public Library, Buffalo.

John Randolph Haynes Papers. Research Library, University of California, Los Angeles.

Tom L. Johnson Papers. City Hall, Cleveland.

Meyer Lissner Papers. Borel Collection, Stanford University Library, Stanford, California.

George McAneny Papers. Columbia University Library, New York.

William A. Prendergast Papers. Columbia University Library, New York.

Edwin R.A. Seligman Papers. Columbia University Library, New York.

Albert Shaw Papers. New York Public Library.

Lincoln Steffens Papers. Columbia University Library, New York.

Frederick W. Taylor Collection. Stevens Institute of Technology, Hoboken, N.J.

Richard W.G. Welling Papers. New York Public Library.

Everett P. Wheeler Papers. New York Public Library.

Charles Dwight Willard Papers. Henry E. Huntington Library, San Marino, California.

Oral History Project, Columbia University
William H. Allen, "Reminiscences," 1950.
Henry Bruere, "Reminiscences," 1949.
Richard S. Childs, "Reminiscences," 1950.
Luther Gulick, "Reminiscences," 1956.
Leonard M. Wallstein, "Reminiscences," 1949.

Reports and Proceedings
Chicago Municipal Efficiency Commission. *Final Report of the Efficiency Commission.* Chicago, 1911.
City Managers' Year Book, 1914–20.
The Finance Commission of the City of Boston. 7 vol. Boston: Municipal Printing Office, 1908–12.
First Annual Report of the Civil Service Commissioners of Massachusetts Together with the Civil Service Law and the Rules and Regulations Relating Thereto. Boston, 1885.
First Report of the Civil Service Commission of the City of Brooklyn, Presented to Seth Low, Mayor, December 26, 1884. Brooklyn, 1884.
Proceedings of the Conferences for Good City Government and the Annual Meetings of the National Municipal League. Philadelphia, National Municipal League, 1894–1910.
Proceedings of the National Civil Service Reform League. New York, 1882–1920.
Proceedings of the New York State Conference of Mayors and Other Municipal Officials, 1910–20.
Report of the Commissioners to Devise a Plan for the Government of the Cities of New York, New York State Assembly, Document no. 68, *March 6, 1877.* Albany: The Argus Company, 1877.
Training School for Public Service. *Annual Report.* New York, 1912.
U.S. Civil Service Commission. *Fifteenth Report, July 1, 1897 to June 30, 1898.* Washington, 1899.
U.S. Congress, 47 Cong., 1st Sess., Senate, Committee on Civil Service and Retrenchment. *Report of the Committee of the Senate to Regulate and Improve the Civil Service of the United States, No. 576, May 15, 1882.* Washington, 1882.
U.S. Department of Commerce and Labor, Bureau of the Census. *Bulletin 20, Statistics of Cities Having a Population of over 25,000: 1902 and 1903.* Washington, 1905.
———. *Special Reports, Statistics of Cities Having a Population of over 30,000: 1907.* Washington, 1910.

Articles, Books, and Pamphlets
Adams, Charles Francis. "Municipal Government: Lessons from the Experience of Quincy, Massachusetts." *Forum* 14 (November 1892): 282–92.
Allen, William H. *Efficient Democracy.* New York: Dodd, Mead, 1908.
———. "How to Overtake the Grafter by Municipal Accounting."

Proceedings of the Buffalo Conference, 18th Annual Meeting, National Municipal League, 1910, pp. 497–504.

———. "The Budget as an Instrument of Financial Control." *Government Accountant* 2 (September 1908): 192–200.

Allinson, Edward P., and Boies Penrose. *The City Government of Philadelphia.* Studies in Historical and Political Science, ser. 5, no. 1–2. Baltimore: Johns Hopkins University Press, 1887.

Arbuthnot, C.C. "Mayor Baker's Administration in Cleveland." *NMR* 5 (April 1916): 226–41.

Beard, Charles A. *American City Government: A Survey of Newer Tendencies.* New York: Century, 1912.

———. "Training for Efficient Public Service." *Annals* 64 (March 1916): 215–26.

Bradford, Ernest S. *Commission Government in American Cities.* New York: Macmillan, 1917.

———. "Financial Results under the Commission Form of City Government." *NMR,* 1 (1912): 373–77.

Bradford, Gamaliel. "Municipal Government." *Scribner's Magazine* 2 (July–December 1887): 485–92.

Breen, Matthew P. *Thirty Years of New York Politics.* New York: John Polhemus Co., 1899.

Brooks, Robert C. "Bibliography of Municipal Problems." *Municipal Affairs* 5 (March 1901): 1–346.

———. "Business Men in Civic Service: The Merchants' Municipal Committee of Boston." *Municipal Affairs* 1 (September 1897): 499–508.

Browne, George Morgan. "Municipal Reform." *New Englander* 45 (February 1886): 152–60.

Brownlow, Louis. *A Passion for Anonymity: The Autobiography of Louis Brownlow, Second Half.* Chicago: University of Chicago Press, 1958.

Bruere, Henry. "The Budget as an Administrative Program." *Annals* 62 (November 1915): 176–91.

———. "Efficiency in City Government." *Annals* 41 (May 1916): 3–22.

———. "Mayor Mitchel's Administration of the City of New York." *NMR* 5 (January 1916): 24–37.

. *The New City Government: Discussion of Municipal Administration Based on a Survey of Ten Commission Governed Cities.* New York: Appleton, 1912.

Bryce, James. *The American Commonwealth.* 2 vols. New York: Macmillan, 1888.

Bugbee, James. *City Government of Boston.* Studies in Historical and Political Science, ser. 5, no. 3. Baltimore: Johns Hopkins University Press, 1887.

Bureau of Municipal Research [New York]. *How Should Public Budgets be Made?* New York, 1909.

———. *Purposes and Methods of the Bureau of Municipal Research.* New York, 1907.

————. *Six Years of Municipal Research for Greater New York: Record for 1906–1911.* New York, 1912.

Burks, Jesse D. "Efficiency Standards in Municipal Management." *NMR* 1 (July 1912): 364–71.

————. "The Outlook for Municipal Efficiency in Philadelphia." *Annals* 41 (May 1912): 245–61.

Burnham, George Jr. "The Philadelphia Bureau of Municipal Research." *NMR* 5 (July 1916): 465–69.

Business Methods in Public Business: Purposes and Program of the Bureau of Municipal Research of Philadelphia. Philadelphia, 1910.

Capen, Samuel B. "The Boston Municipal League." *American Journal of Politics* 5 (July 1894): 1–13.

Carpenter, Dunbar F. "Some Defects of Commission Government." *Annals* 38 (November 1911): 862–76.

Chase, Harvey S. "Uniform Accounting Applied to Boston, Baltimore, and Other Municipalities." *Proceedings of the Boston Conference, 8th Annual Meeting. National Municipal League*, 1902, pp. 307–21.

Cheesborough, E.R. "Galveston's Commission Plan of City Government." *Annals* 38 (November 1911): 891–900.

Childs, Richard S. "How the Commission-Manager Plan is Getting Along." *NMR* 4 (July 1915): 371–82.

————. "The Lockport Proposal: A City That Wants to Improve the 'Commission Plan.'" *American City* 4 (June 1911): 285–87.

————. "Now That We Have the Commission Manager Plan—What Are We Going to Do With It?" In *Fourth Year Book of the City Managers' Association*, 1918, pp. 82–87.

————. "The Theory of the New Controlled-Executive Plan." *NMR* 2 (January 1913): 76–81.

Childs, Richard S., et al. "Professional Standards and Professional Ethics in the New Profession of City Manager." *NMR* 5 (April 1916): 195–208.

"Citizen Agencies for Research in Government." *Municipal Research*, no. 77 (September 1916).

Cleveland, Frederick A. *Chapters on Municipal Administration and Accounting.* New York: Longmans, Green, 1909.

————. "Evolution of the Budget Idea in the United States." *Annals* 62 (November 1915): 15–35.

————. "The Application of Scientific Management to the Activities of State and Municipal Government." In *Addresses and Discussion at the Conference on Scientific Management Held October 12, 13, 14, 1911.* Hanover, N.H.: Dartmouth College, 1912, pp. 313–35.

Clow, Frederick R. *A Comparative Study of the Administration of City Finances in the United States, with Special Reference to the Budget.* Publication of the American Economic Association, 3d ser., no. 4. New York: Macmillan, 1901.

————. "Suggestions for the Study of Municipal Finance." *Quarterly Journal of Economics* 10 (July 1896): 455–66.

Coler, Bird S. "The Government of Greater New York." *NAR* 159 (July 1899): 90–100.

————. "Mistakes of Professional Reformers." *Independent* 53 (June 20, 1901): 1405-7.

Commons, John R. *Eighteen Months Work of the Milwaukee Bureau of Economy and Efficiency.* Milwaukee: Bureau of Economy and Efficiency, 1912.

Cooke, Morris L. *Our Cities Awake: Notes on Municipal Activities and Administration.* Garden City, N.Y.: Doubleday, Page, 1918.

————. "The Spirit and Social Significance of Scientific Management." *Journal of Political Economy* 21 (June 1913): 481-93.

Cooper, Walter G. "Objections to Commission Government." *Annals* 38 (November 1911): 853-61.

Crandon, Frank P. "Misgovernment of Great Cities." *Popular Science Monthly* 30 (1886-87): 296-310; 520-29.

Creelman, James. "Municipal Non-Partisanship in Operation: What Has Been Saved and Gained in New York in the First Six Months of Mayor Gaynor's Administration." *Century* 80 (September 1910): 667-74.

Croly, Herbert. *Progressive Democracy.* New York: Macmillan, 1914.

Curley, James M. *I'd Do It Again: A Record of All My Uproarious Years.* Englewood Cliffs, N.J.: Prentice-Hall, 1957.

Dana, Richard Henry, Jr. "Taking Municipal Contracts out of Politics." *Proceedings of the Cincinnati Conference, 15th Annual Meeting of the National Municipal League,* 1909 pp. 179-96.

Donnelly, Frederick W. "Securing Efficient Administration under the Commission Plan." *Annals* 41 (May 1912): 218-32.

Durand, Edward Dana. *The Finances of New York City.* New York: Macmillan, 1898.

Eaton, Dorman B. *Civil Service in Great Britain: A History of Abuses and Reforms and Their Bearing upon American Politics.* New York: Harper, 1880.

————. "The Public Service and the Public." *Atlantic Monthly* 41 (February 1878): 241-52.

————. "Tenure of Office." *Lippincott's Magazine* 27 (June 1881): 582-90.

Eliot, Charles W. "One Remedy for Municipal Misgovernment." *Forum* 12 (September 1891): 153-68.

Ely, Richard T. *The Coming City.* New York: Crowell, 1902.

"Experts Discuss the Des Moines Plan." *Bulletin of the League of American Municipalities* 10 (June 1909): 408-13.

Fairlie, John A. "Commission Government in Illinois Cities." *Annals* 38 (November 1911): 748-56.

————. *Essays in Municipal Administration.* New York: Macmillan, 1908.

————. "The Problems of City Government from the Administative Point of View." *Annals* 28 (1906): 132-54.

Fassett, Charles M. "The Weaknesses of Commission Government." *NMR* 9 (October 1920): 642-47.

Fassett, J. Sloat. "Why Cities Are Badly Governed." *NAR* 150 (May 1890): 631-37.

Ford, Henry Jones. "Principles of Municipal Organization." *Annals* 23 (March 1904): 195-22.

_____. *The Rise and Growth of American Politics: A Sketch of Constitutional Development.* New York: Macmillan, 1898.

Fosdick, Raymond B. *Chronicle of a Generation: An Autobiography.* New York: Harper, 1958.

Foulke, William Dudley. "Expert City Management." *NMR* 1 (October 1912): 549–61.

Gaynor, William J. "The Problem of Efficient City Government." *Century* 80 (September 1910): 663–67.

George, Ralph E. "Increased Efficiency as a Result of Increased Governmental Functions." *Annals* 64 (March 1916): 77–88.

Gilbertson, H.S. "Some Serious Weaknesses of the Commission Plan." *American City* 9 (September 1913): 236–37.

_____. "The City Manager Plan—Its Contribution to the Growth of a Non-Political and Efficient Personnel in Municipal Administration." *Proceedings of the National Civil Service Reform League,* 1913, pp. 127–38.

Godkin, E.L. "A Key to Municipal Reform." *NAR* 151 (October 1890): 422–31.

_____. "The Problems of Municipal Government." *Annals* 4 (May 1894): 857–82.

_____. "Why the City Government Is Bad." *Nation* 38 (January 10, 1884): 26–27.

Goodnow, Frank J. *Comparative Administrative Law.* 2 vols. New York: Putnam, 1893.

_____. *Politics and Administration.* New York: Macmillan, 1900.

Goos, T.G. "Sketches of American Mayors: James M. Curley of Boston." *NMR* 15 (May 1926): 253–59.

Greenlaw, Edwin A. "Office of Mayor in the United States." *Municipal Affairs* 3 (March 1899): 33–60.

Gruenberg, Frederick P. "The Need of a Budget in Philadelphia." *Civic Club Bulletin* (Philadelphia) 10 (May 1916): 9–10.

Harrison, Carter H., Jr. *Stormy Years: The Autobiography of Carter H. Harrison, Jr.* Indianapolis: Bobbs-Merrill, 1935.

Hartwell, Edward M. "Report of the Committee on Uniform Municipal Accounting and Statistics." *Proceedings of the Boston Conference, 8th Annual Meeting, National Municipal League,* 1902, pp. 292–305.

_____. "Report of Committee on Uniform Accounting and Statistics." *Proceedings of the New York Conference, 11th Annual Meeting, National Municipal League,* 1905, pp. 206–34.

"Has City Manager Plan Come to Stay?" *Modern City* 5 (July 1920): 8–10.

Haskins, Charles Waldo. "The Municipal Accounts of Chicago." *Proceedings of the Rochester Conference, 17th Annual Meeting, National Municipal League,* 1901, pp. 302–14.

Hatton, Augustus R. "The Manager—The Greatest Problem of City Manager Government." *Seventh Year Book of the City Managers' Association,* 1921, pp. 197–205.

_____, comp. *Digest of City Charters Together with Other Statutory and*

Constitutional Provisions Relating to Cities. Chicago: Chicago Charter Convention, 1906.

Hodghead, Beverly L. "A Comparison of the Methods of Efficiency of Modern European and American City Government." *Pacific Municipalities* 4 (October 1912): 489–99.

Hollander, Jacob H. *The Financial History of Baltimore.* Baltimore: Johns Hopkins University Press, 1899.

Hooker, George E. "Mayor Quincy of Boston." *Review of Reviews* 19 (May 1899): 575–78.

Hopkins, George B. "The New York Bureau of Municipal Research." *Annals* 41 (May 1912): 235–44.

Hopwood, E.C. "Newton D. Baker's Administration as Mayor of Cleveland and Its Accomplishments." *NMR* 2 (July 1913): 461–66.

"How to Improve Municipal Government." *NAR* 153 (November 1891): 580–95.

Howe, Frederic C. *The City: The Hope of Democracy.* New York: Scribner's, 1905.

———. *The Confessions of a Reformer.* New York: Scribner's, 1925.

Hudson, Irby Roland. "Nashville's Experience with Commission Government." *NMR* 10 (March 1921): 156–60.

Ivins, William M. "Municipal Government." *PSQ* 2 (June 1887): 291–312.

James, Herman G. "Some Reflections on the City Manager Plan of Government." *APSR* 9 (August 1915): 504–6.

Jenkins, Charles F. "The Blankenburg Administration in Philadelphia: A Symposium." *NMR* 5 (April 1916): 211–25.

Johnson, Tom L. *My Story.* New York: Huebsch, 1913.

Kasson, John A. "Municipal Reform." *NAR* 137 (July 1883): 218–30.

Keller, John W. "Municipal Reformers in Party Politics." *Municipal Affairs* 4 (June 1900): 343–46.

Lambert, Henry. *The Progress of Civil Service Reform in the United States.* Boston, 1885. Pamphlet.

Leser, Oscar. "Problems of Local Administration." *Proceedings of the National Tax Association* 2 (1908): 527–35.

Letters Addressed by the Civil Service Reform Association to the Various Candidates for the Governorship, and for Congress, the Assembly, and City Offices during the Campaign of 1882 with Replies to the Same. New York, 1882.

Lippman, Walter. *Drift and Mastery: An Attempt to Diagnose the Current Unrest.* New York: Mitchell Kennerley, 1914.

———. *A Preface to Politics.* New York: Mitchell Kennerley, 1913.

Low, Seth. "The Government of Cities in the United States." *Century* 42 (September 1891): 730–36.

———. "Obstacles to Good City Government." *Forum* 5 (May 1888): 260–66.

Lowell, A. Lawrence. "Administrative Experts in Municipal Governments." *NMR* 4 (January 1915): 26–31.

Lowell, Francis G. "The Municipal Service of Boston." *Atlantic Monthly* 81 (March 1898): 311–22.

MacGregor, Ford H. "Commission Government in the West." *Annals* 38 (November 1911): 726–47.

MacIness, Duncan. "Uniformity in Municipal Accounting." *Proceedings of the National Tax Association,* 1909, pp. 267–74.

MacVeagh, Franklin. "The Business Man in Municipal Politics." *Proceedings of the Louisville Conference, 3rd Annual Meeting, National Municipal League, May 1897,* pp. 133–44.

————. "A Programme of Municipal Reform." *American Journal of Sociology* 1 (March 1896): 551–62.

Merriam, Charles E. "Investigations as a Means of Securing Administrative Efficiency." *Annals* 41 (May 1912): 281–303.

————. "The Work and Accomplishments of the Chicago Commission on City Expenditures." *City Club Bulletin* (Chicago) 4 (August 16, 1911): 195–208.

————. "The Work of the Chicago Bureau of Public Efficiency." *City Club Bulletin* (Philadelphia) 3 (November 2, 1910): 62–71.

Metz, Herman A. "The Reorganization of Accounts and Methods of Transacting Municipal Business in New York City." *Government Accountant* 3 (May 1909): 1–13.

Miles, Rufus E. "The Cincinnati Bureau of Municipal Research." *Annals* 41 (May 1912): 262–69.

Mitchel, John Purroy. "The Office of Mayor." *Proceedings of the Academy of Political Science,* 1915, pp. 479–94.

Morison, Frank. "Municipal Government, A Corporate Not a Political Problem." *Forum* 13 (August 1892): 788–94.

A Municipal Program: Report of the Committee of the National Municipal League, Adopted by the League, November 17, 1899. New York: Macmillan, 1900.

Munro, William B. *A Bibliography of Municipal Government in the United States.* Cambridge, Mass.: Harvard University Press, 1913.

————. "The Galveston Plan of City Government." *Proceedings of the Providence Conference, 13th Annual Meeting, National Municipal League,* 1907, pp. 142–55.

————. *Principles and Methods of Municipal Administration.* New York: Macmillan, 1916.

Myers, Gustavus. "The Results of Reform in New York City." *Independent* 55 (October 22, 1903): 2491–96.

"A National Program to Improve Methods of Government." *Municipal Research,* no. 71 (March 1916).

"New Civil Service Regulations for New York City." *Civil Service Record* 4 (September 1884): 29–32.

New York Civil Service Reform Association. *Purposes of the Civil Service Reform Association.* New York, 1881.

Otis, Harrison Gray. "City Manager Movement." *NMR* 10 (January 1921): 50–53.

Owen, Robert L. "Commission Government." *Proceedings of the New York State Conference of Mayors and Other Municipal Officials,* 1911, pp. 107–22.

Paine, Robert Treat, Jr. "The Municipal Situation in Boston." *City Club Bulletin* (Philadelphia) 2 (February 10, 1910): 45–46.

Parton, James. "Outgrown City Government." *Forum* 2 (February 1887): 537–48.

Patten, Simon. "The Decay of State and Local Governments." *Annals* 1 (July 1890): 26–42.

Patterson, C. Stuart. "Municipal Reform and Civil Service Reform." *Penn Monthly* 13 (April 1882): 295–302.

Pavey, Frank P. "Mayor Strong's Experiment in New York City." *Forum* 23 (June 1897): 539–53.

Powers, LeGrand. "The Bureau of Census as an Agent of Municipal Reform." *Proceedings of the Pittsburgh Conference, 14th Annual Meeting, National Municipal League*, 1908, pp. 328–36.

———. "Municipal Budgets and Expenditures." *Proceedings of the Cincinnati Conference, 15th Annual Meeting, National Municipal League*, 1909, pp. 258–72.

Prendergast, William A. "Efficiency through Accounting." *Annals* 41 (May 1912): 43–56.

Prentiss, George L. *The National Bane, or The Dry Rot in American Politics.* New York, 1877.

Prichard, Frank P. "The Study of the Science of Municipal Government." *Annals* 2 (January 1892): 458–70.

Quincy, Josiah. "Municipal Progress in Boston." *Independent* 62 (February 15, 1900): 424–26.

Rastall, Benjamin McKee. *Plan and Method in Municipal Efficiency.* Milwaukee: C. Kronenberger, 1911.

Reed, Thomas H. "The Value of Experts to a City Government." *Pacific Municipalities* 28 (December 1914): 607–12.

Reed, Thomas H., and Paul Webbink, eds. *Documents Illustrative of American Municipal Government.* New York: Century, 1926.

Reemelin, Charles. *A Critical Review of American Politics.* Cincinnati: Robert Clark and Co., 1881.

"Report of the Committee on Administration of Laws for Taxation of Property." *Proceedings of the National Tax Assocation*, 1911, pp. 363–76.

"Report of the Special Committee on the Application of the Merit System to the Higher Municipal Offices." *Proceedings of the National Civil Service Reform League*, 1910, pp. 145–54.

Rightor, Chester E. *City Manager in Dayton: Four Years of Commission-Manager Government, 1914–1917; and Comparisons with Four Preceding Years under the Mayor-Council Plan, 1910–1913.* New York: Macmillan, 1919.

Rogers, Lindsay. "Government by City Managers." *World's Work* 44 (September 1922): 519–24.

Roosevelt, Theodore. *An Autobiography.* New York: Macmillan, 1916.

———. *The Letters of Theodore Roosevelt.* Edited by Elting E. Morison. 8 vols. Cambridge, Mass.: Harvard University Press, 1951–54. Vols. 1–3.

———. "The Merit System versus the Patronage System." *Century* 39 (February 1890): 628–33.

Rowe, Leo S. "American Political Ideas and Institutions in Their Relation to the Problem of City Government." *Proceedings of the Louisville Conference, 3rd Annual Meeting, National Municipal League,* 1897, pp. 75–88.

Schurz, Carl. "The Relation of Civil Service Reform to Municipal Reform." *Proceedings of the National Conference for Good City Government,* 1894, pp. 123–33.

Shaw, Albert. "Civil Service Reform in Municipal Government." *Proceedings of the National Civil Service Reform League,* 1897, pp. 120–32.

––––––. *Municipal Government in Continental Europe.* New York: Century, 1895.

Shepard, Edward M. "The Brooklyn Idea in City Government." *Forum* 16 (September 1893): 38–47.

Steffens, Lincoln. *The Autobiography of Lincoln Steffens.* 2 vols. New York: Harcourt, Brace, 1931.

––––––. *The Shame of the Cities.* 1904. Reprint. New York: Hill and Wang, 1957.

Sterne, Simon. "Administration of American Cities." *International Review* 4 (September 1877): 631–46.

Stickney, Albert. *The Political Problem.* New York: Harper, 1890.

Storey, Moorfield. "The Government of Cities: The Need of a Divorce of Municipal Business from Politics." *Proceedings of the National Civil Service Reform League,* 1891, pp. 47–67.

––––––. *Politics as a Duty and as a Career.* New York: Putnam, 1889.

Thompson, Carl D. "The Vital Points in Charter Making from a Socialist Point of View." *NMR* 2 (1913): 416–26.

Tolman, William H. *Municipal Reform Movements in the United States.* New York: Revell, 1895.

Toulmin, Harry Aubrey, Jr. *The City Manager: A New Profession.* New York: Appleton, 1916.

Training School for Public Service. *Announcement.* New York, 1911.

Trevelen, J.E. "The Milwaukee Bureau of Economy and Efficiency." *Annals* 41 (May 1912): 270–78.

Turner, George Kibbe. "Galveston: A Business Corporation." *McClure's Magazine* 27 (October 1906): 610–20.

––––––. "The New American City Government." *McClure's Magazine* 35 (May 1910): 97–108.

Upson, Lent D. "Cincinnati's First Municipal Exhibit." *American City* 7 (December 12): 530–32.

Wade, Herbert T. "An Influence for Efficiency in Administration: The New York Budget Exhibit of 1910." *Engineering Magazine* (January 1911): 585–604.

Waite, Henry M. "The Commission-Manager Plan—Its Advantages." *Proceedings of the New York State Conference of Mayors and Other Municipal Officials,* 1914, pp. 9–15.

Walton, John M. "The Application to a Municipality of Modern Methods of Accounting and Reporting." *Annals* 41 (May 1912): 64–68.

Weber, Gustavus A. *Organized Efforts for the Improvement of Methods of Ad-*

ministration in the United States. New York: Appleton, 1919.

Welton, Benjamin F. "The Problem of Securing Efficiency in Municipal Labor." *Annals* 41 (May 1912): 103–14.

Welsh, Herbert. "The Influence of the Spoils Idea upon the Government of American Cities." *Proceedings of the National Civil Service Reform League,* 1894, pp. 57–67.

"What City Managers Can Do to Further Advance Good Government." *Third Annual Report of the City Managers' Association,* 1916, pp. 44–51.

Wheeler, Everett P. "Civil Service Reform." *Civil Service Record* 4 (January 1885): 65–68.

————. *Sixty Years of American Life: Taylor to Roosevelt, 1830–1910.* New York: Dutton, 1917.

White, Andrew D. "The Government of American Cities." *Forum* 10 (December 1890): 357–72.

White, Leonard D. *The City Manager.* Chicago: University of Chicago Press, 1927.

White, Thomas Raeburn. "The Revolution in Philadelphia." *Proceedings of the Atlantic Conference, 12th Annual Meeting, National Municipal League,* 1906, pp. 135–55.

Whitlock, Brand. *Forty Years of It.* New York: Appleton, 1914.

"Why the City Is Not Well Governed." *Nation* 50 (March 12, 1890): 216.

Wilby, Charles B. "Municipal Reform Impossible under the Spoils System." *Proceedings of the National Civil Service Reform League,* 1894, pp. 79–96.

Wilcox, Delos F. *The American City.* New York: Macmillan, 1904.

Williamson, Charles C. *The Finances of Cleveland.* Studies in History, Economics, and Public Law, vol. 25, no. 3. New York: Columbia University Press, 1907.

Wilson, Woodrow. "Democracy and Efficiency." *Atlantic Monthly* 87 (March 1901): 289–99.

————. *The Papers of Woodrow Wilson.* Edited by Arthur S. Link and Associates. 12 vols. to date. Princeton: Princeton University Press, 1966–). Vols. 5–9.

————. "The Study of Administration." *PSQ* 2 (June 1887): 197–222.

Woodruff, Clinton Rogers. "American Municipal Tendencies." *NMR* 1 (January 1912): 3–19.

————. "The Overthrow of the Spoils System in Philadelphia." *Proceedings of the National Civil Service Reform League,* 1905, pp. 152–59.

————. ed. *City Government by Commission.* New York: Appleton, 1911.

————. *A New Municipal Program.* New York: Appleton, 1919.

Wright, Albert H. "Scientific Criteria for Efficient Democratic Institutions." *Scientific Monthly* 6 (March 1918): 237–41.

Young, James T. "The Basis of Present Reform Movements." *Annals* 21 (March 1903): 238–51.

SECONDARY SOURCES

Adrian, Charles R., and Charles Press. *Governing Urban America.* 4th ed. New York: McGraw-Hill, 1972.

Banfield, Edward C., and James Q. Wilson. *City Politics.* New York: Random House, Vintage Books, 1963.

Benjamin, Philip S. "Gentlemen Reformers in the Quaker City, 1870–1912." *PSQ 85* (March 1970): 67–79.

Bernard, Richard M., and Bradley R. Rice. "Political Environment and the Adoption of Progressive Municipal Reform." *Journal of Urban History* 2 (February 1975): 149–74.

Blassingame, Lurton W. "Frank J. Goodnow: Progressive Urban Reformer." *North Dakota Quarterly* 40 (Summer 1972): 22–30.

Blau, Peter M., and Marshall W. Meyer. *Bureaucracy in Modern Society.* 2d ed. New York: Random House, 1971.

Blodgett, Geoffrey. *The Gentle Reformers: Massachusetts Democrats in the Cleveland Era.* Cambridge, Mass.: Harvard University Press, 1966.

Bollens, John C., and Henry J. Schmandt. *The Metropolis: Its People, Politics, and Economic Life.* 3d ed. New York: Harper & Row, 1975.

Buenker, John D. *Urban Liberalism and Progressive Reform.* New York: Scribner's, 1973.

Clodius, Albert H. "The Quest for Good Government in Los Angeles, 1890–1910." Ph.D. dissertation, Claremont Graduate School, 1953.

Cerillo, Augustus, Jr. "The Reform of Municipal Government in New York City: From Seth Low to John Purroy Mitchel." *New York Historical Society Quarterly* 57 (January 1973): 51–71.

Cohen, Sol. *Progressives and Urban School Reform: The Public Education Association of New York City, 1895–1954.* New York: Bureau of Publications, Teachers College, Columbia University, 1964.

Crooks, James B. *Politics and Progress: The Rise of Urban Progressivism in Baltimore, 1895–1911.* Baton Rouge: Louisiana State University Press, 1968.

Dahl, Robert A. *Who Governs? Democracy and Power in an American City.* New Haven: Yale University Press, 1961.

Dahlberg, Jane S. *The New York Bureau of Municipal Research: Pioneer in Government Administration.* New York: New York University Press, 1966.

Disbrow, Donald W. "Reform in Philadelphia under Mayor Blankenburg, 1912–1916." *Pennsylvania History* 27 (October 1960): 379–96.

Dobson, John M. *Politics in the Gilded Age: A New Perspective on Reform.* New York: Praeger, 1972.

Dorsett, Lyle W. "The City Boss and the Reformer: A Reappraisal." *Pacific Northwest Quarterly* 63 (October 1972): 150–54.

East, John Porter. *Council-Manager Government: The Political Thought of Its Founder, Richard S. Childs.* Chapel Hill: University of North Carolina Press, 1965.

Graybar, Lloyd J. *Albert Shaw of the "Review of Reviews": An Intellectual Biography.* Lexington: University Press of Kentucky, 1974.

Greer, Scott. *Metropolitics: A Study of Political Culture.* New York: Wiley, 1963.

Griffith, Ernest S. *A History of American City Government: The Progressive*

Years and Their Aftermath, 1900–1920. Published for the National Municipal League. New York: Praeger, 1974.

Hays, Samuel P. "The Changing Political Structure of the City in Industrial America." *Journal of Urban History* 1 (November 1974): 6–38.

———. "Political Parties and the Community-Society Continuum." In *American Party Systems: Stages of Political Development,* edited by William N. Chambers and Walter Dean Burnham, pp. 152–81. New York: Oxford University Press, 1967.

———. "The Politics of Reform in Municipal Government in the Progressive Era." *Pacific Northwest Quarterly* 55 (October 1964): 157–69.

Holli, Melvin G. *Reform in Detroit: Hazen S. Pingree and Urban Politics.* New York: Oxford University Press, 1969.

Hollingsworth, J. Rogers. "Perspectives on Industrializing Societies." In *Emerging Theoretical Models in Social and Political History,* edited by Allan G. Bogue, pp. 97–121. Beverly Hills: Sage Publications, 1973.

Hoogenboom, Ari. *Outlawing the Spoils: A History of the Civil Service Reform Movement.* Urbana: University of Illinois Press, 1961.

Jackson, Joy J. *New Orleans in the Gilded Age: Politics and Urban Progress, 1880–1896.* Baton Rouge: Louisiana State University Press, 1969.

Johnson, Claudius O. *Carter Henry Harrison I: Political Leader.* Chicago: University of Chicago Press, 1928.

Kammerer, Gladys M., et al. *City Managers in Politics: An Analysis of Manager Tenure and Termination.* University of Florida Monographs, Social Sciences, no. 13. Gainesville, University of Florida Press, 1962.

Karl, Barry Dean. *Executive Reorganization and Reform in the New Deal: The Genesis of Administrative Management, 1900–1939.* Cambridge, Mass.: Harvard University Press, 1963.

Kingsbury, Joseph Bush. "The Merit System in Chicago from 1895 to 1915. The Administration of the Civil Service Law under Various Mayors." *Public Personnel Studies* 4 (May 1926): 154–65.

Klebanow, Diana. "E.L. Godkin, the City, and Civic Responsibility." *New York Historical Society Quarterly* 55 (January 1971): 52–75.

Knerr, George F. "The Mayoral Administration of William L. Strong, New York City, 1895–1897." Ph.D. dissertation, New York University, 1958.

Komons, Nick A. "Chicago, 1893–1907: The Politics of Reform." Ph.D. dissertation, George Washington University, 1961.

Kurland, Gerald. *Seth Low: The Reformer in an Urban and Industrial Age.* New York: Twayne, 1971.

Lewinson, Edwin R. *John Purroy Mitchel: The Boy Mayor of New York.* New York: Astra, 1965.

Lewis, Eugene. *The Urban Political System.* Hinsdale, Ill.: Dryden Press, 1973.

Lowi, Theodore J. *At the Pleasure of the Mayor: Patronage and Power in New York City, 1898–1958.* New York: The Free Press of Glencoe, 1964.

———. "Machine Politics—Old and New." *The Public Interest,* no. 9 (Fall 1967), pp. 83–92.

Lubove, Roy. "The Twentieth Century City: The Progressive as Municipal Reformer." *Mid-America* 41 (October 1959): 195–207.

McFarland, Gerald F. "Partisan of Nonpartisanship: Dorman B. Eaton and the Genteel Reform Tradition." *Journal of American History* 64 (March 1968): 806–22.

McKelvey, Blake. *The Urbanization of America, 1860–1915.* New Brunswick, N.J.: Rutgers University Press, 1963.

Miller, Zane L. *Boss Cox's Cincinnati: Urban Politics in the Progressive Era.* New York: Oxford University Press, 1968.

Mosher, Frederick C. *Democracy and the Public Service.* New York: Oxford University Press, 1968.

Mosher, Frederick C., et al. *City Manager Government in Seven Cities.* Chicago: Public Administration Service, 1940.

Murdock, Eugene C. "Cleveland's Johnson: The Cabinet." *Ohio Historical Quarterly* 66 (October 1957): 374–90.

Nevins, Allan. *Abram S. Hewitt: With Some Account of Peter Cooper.* 1935. Reprint. New York: Octagon Books, 1967.

Pease, Otis A. "Urban Reformers in the Progressive Era: A Reassessment." *Pacific Northwest Quarterly* 62 (April 1971): 49–58.

Rice, Bradley R. "The Galveston Plan of City Government by Commission: The Birth of a Progressive Idea." *Southwestern Historical Quarterly* 78 (April 1975): 365–408.

Riggs, Fred W. "Bureaucratic Politics in Comparative Perspective." In *Frontiers of Development Administration,* edited by Fred W. Riggs, pp. 375–414. Durham, N.C.: Duke University Press, 1971.

———. *The Ecology of Public Administration.* Bombay: Asia Publishing House, 1961.

Rogers, David. *The Management of Big Cities: Interest Groups and Social Change Strategies.* Beverly Hills: Sage Publications, 1971.

Russell, Francis. "The Last of the Bosses." *American Heritage* 10 (June 1959): 21–25, 85–91.

Schiesl, Martin J. "Progressive Reform in Los Angeles under Mayor Alexander, 1909–1913." *California Historical Quarterly* 54 (Spring 1975): 37–56.

Simon, Herbert A. *Administrative Behavior: A Study of Decision-Making Processes in Administrative Organization.* New York: Free Press Paperback, 1965.

Skolnick, Richard. "The Crystallization of Reform in New York City, 1890–1917." Ph.D. dissertation, Yale University, 1964.

———. "George Edwin Waring, Jr.: A Model for Reformers." *New York Historical Society Quarterly* 52 (October 1968): 354–78.

Sproat, John G. *"The Best Men": Liberal Reformers in the Gilded Age.* New York: Oxford University Press, 1968.

Stewart, Frank Mann. *A Half Century of Municipal Reform: The History of the National Municipal League.* Berkeley and Los Angeles: University of California Press, 1950.

Still, Bayrd. *Milwaukee: The History of a City.* Rev. ed. Madison: State Historical Society of Wisconsin, 1965.

Stone, Harold A., Don K. Price, and Kathryn M. Stone. *City Manager Government in Nine Cities.* Chicago: Public Administration Service, 1940.

Syrett, Harold C. *The City of Brooklyn, 1865–1898: A Political History.* New York: Columbia University Press, 1944.

Tager, Jack. *The Intellectual as Urban Reformer: Brand Whitlock and the Progressive Movement.* Cleveland: Case Western Reserve University Press, 1968.

Thelen, David P. *The New Citizenship: Origins of Progressivism in Wisconsin, 1885–1900.* Columbia: University of Missouri Press, 1972.

Thomas, Lately. *The Mayor Who Mastered New York: The Life and Times of William J. Gaynor.* New York: Morrow 1969.

Thompson, Victor A. "Bureaucracy in a Democratic Society." In *Public Administration and Democracy: Essays in Honor of Paul H. Appleby,* edited by Roscoe C. Martin, pp. 205–26. Syracuse: Syracuse University Press, 1967.

Tobin, Eugene M. "The Progressive as Politician: Jersey City, 1896–1907." *New Jersey History* 91 (Spring 1973): 5–23.

Tyack, David B. *The One Best System: A History of American Urban Education.* Cambridge, Mass.: Harvard University Press, 1974.

Waldo, Dwight. *The Administrative State: A Study of the Political Theory of American Public Administration.* New York: Ronald Press, 1948.

————. "Development of Theory of Democratic Administration." *American Political Science Review* 46 (March 1952): 81–103.

Warner, Sam Bass, Jr. *The Private City: Philadelphia in Three Periods of Its Growth.* Philadelphia: University of Pennsylvania Press, 1968.

Weinstein, James. *The Corporate Ideal in the Liberal State: 1900–1918.* Boston: Beacon Press, 1968.

Weiss, Nancy Joan. *Charles Francis Murphy, 1858–1924: Respectability and Responsibility in Tammany Politics.* Northampton, Mass.: Smith College, 1968.

White, G. Edward. "The Social Values of the Progressives: Some New Perspectives." *South Atlantic Quarterly* 70 (Winter 1971): 62–76.

Wiebe, Robert H. *The Search for Order, 1877–1920.* New York: Hill and Wang, 1967.

Williams, Oliver P. "A Typology for Comparative Local Government." *Midwest Journal of Political Science* 5 (May 1961): 150–64.

Wilson, James Q. "The Economy of Patronage." *Journal of Political Economy* 69 (August 1961): 369–80.

Wright, Deil S. "The City Manager as a Development Administrator." In *Comparative Urban Research: The Administration and Politics of Cities,* edited by Robert T. Daland, pp. 203–48. Beverly Hills: Sage Publications, 1969.

Yearley, C.K. *The Money Machines: The Breakdown and Reform of Governmental and Party Finance in the North, 1860–1920.* New York: State University of New York Press, 1970.

Index